BLACK AMERICAN PROSE WRITERS
OF THE HARLEM RENAISSANCE

Writers of English: Lives and Works

BLACK AMERICAN
PROSE WRITERS

OF THE HARLEM RENAISSANCE

Edited and with an Introduction by

Harold Bloom

CHELSEA HOUSE PUBLISHERS
New York   Philadelphia

03644272

Jacket illustration: Romare Bearden (1914–1988), *The Blues* (courtesy of the Honolulu Academy of Arts).

CHELSEA HOUSE PUBLISHERS

Editorial Director Richard Rennert
Executive Managing Editor Karyn Gullen Browne
Picture Editor Adrian G. Allen
Copy Chief Robin James
Art Director Robert Mitchell
Manufacturing Director Gerald Levine
Production Coordinator Marie Claire Cebrián-Ume

Writers of English: Lives and Works

Senior Editor S. T. Joshi
Series Design Rae Grant

Staff for BLACK AMERICAN PROSE WRITERS OF THE HARLEM RENAISSANCE

Research Richard Fumosa, Robert Green
Editorial Assistant Mary B. Sisson
Picture Researcher Villette Harris

First Printing

1 3 5 7 9 8 6 4 2

Library of Congress Cataloging-in-Publication Data

Black American prose writers of the Harlem renaissance / edited and with an introduction by Harold Bloom.
    p. cm.—(Writers of English)
    Includes bibliographical references.
    ISBN 0-7910-2203-X.—ISBN 0-7910-2228-5 (pbk.)
    1. American prose literature—Afro-American authors—Bio-bibliography. 2. American prose literature—Afro-American authors—Dictionaries. 3. American prose literature—20th century—Bio-bibliography. 4. American prose literature—20th century—Dictionaries. 5. Afro-Americans—Intellectual life—Dictionaries. 6. Afro-Americans in literature—Dictionaries. 7. Harlem Renaissance—Dictionaries. I. Bloom, Harold. II. Series.
PS366.A35B58 1994   93-17979
818'.520809896073—dc20   CIP

◼ Contents

▩ User's Guide

THIS VOLUME PROVIDES biographical, critical, and bibliographical information on the thirteen most significant black American prose writers of the Harlem Renaissance. Each chapter consists of three parts: a biography of the author; a selection of brief critical extracts about the author; and a bibliography of the author's published books.

The biography supplies a detailed outline of the important events in the author's life, including his or her major writings. The critical extracts are taken from a wide array of books and periodicals, from the author's lifetime to the present, and range in content from biographical to critical to historical. The extracts are arranged in chronological order by date of writing or publication, and a full bibliographical citation is provided at the end of each extract. Editorial additions or deletions are indicated within carets.

The author bibliographies list every separate publication—including books, pamphlets, broadsides, collaborations, and works edited or translated by the author—for works published in the author's lifetime; selected important posthumous publications are also listed. Titles are those of the first edition; if a work has subsequently come to be known under a variant title, this title is supplied within carets. In selected instances dates of revised editions are given where these are significant. Pseudonymous works are listed but not the pseudonyms under which these works were published. Periodicals edited by the author are listed only when the author has written most or all of the contents. For plays we have listed date of publication, not date of production; unpublished plays are not listed. Titles enclosed in square brackets are of doubtful authenticity. All works by the author, whether in English or in other languages, have been listed; English translations of foreign-language works are not listed unless the author has done the translation.

▧ The Life of the Author

Harold Bloom

NIETZSCHE, WITH EXULTANT ANGUISH, famously proclaimed that God was dead. Whatever the consequences of this for the ethical life, its ultimate literary effect certainly would have surprised the author Nietzsche. His French disciples, Foucault most prominent among them, developed the Nietzschean proclamation into the dogma that all authors, God included, were dead. The death of the author, which is no more than a Parisian trope, another metaphor for fashion's setting of skirt-lengths, is now accepted as literal truth by most of our current apostles of what should be called French Nietzsche, to distinguish it from the merely original Nietzsche. We also have French Freud or Lacan, which has little to do with the actual thought of Sigmund Freud, and even French Joyce, which interprets *Finnegans Wake* as the major work of Jacques Derrida. But all this is as nothing compared to the final triumph of the doctrine of the death of the author: French Shakespeare. That delicious absurdity is given us by the New Historicism, which blends Foucault and California fruit juice to give us the Word that Renaissance "social energies," and not William Shakespeare, composed *Hamlet* and *King Lear*. It seems a proper moment to murmur "enough" and to return to a study of the life of the author.

Sometimes it troubles me that there are so few masterpieces in the vast ocean of literary biography that stretches between James Boswell's great *Life* of Dr. Samuel Johnson and the late Richard Ellmann's wonderful *Oscar Wilde*. Literary biography is a crucial genre, and clearly a difficult one in which to excel. The actual nature of the lives of the poets seems to have little effect upon the quality of their biographies. Everything happened to Lord Byron and nothing at all to Wallace Stevens, and yet their biographers seem equally daunted by them. But even inadequate biographies of strong writers, or of weak ones, are of immense use. I have never read a literary biography from which I have not profited, a statement I cannot make about any other genre whatsoever. And when it comes to figures who are central to us—Dante, Shakespeare, Cervantes, Montaigne, Goethe, Whitman, Tolstoi, Freud, Joyce, Kafka among them—we reach out eagerly for every scrap that the biographers have gleaned. Concerning Dante and Shakespeare we know much too little, yet when we come to Goethe and Freud, where we seem to know more than everything, we still want to know more. The death of the author, despite our current resentniks, clearly was only a momentary fad. Something vital in every authentic lover of literature responds to Emerson's battle-cry sentence: "There is no history, only biography." Beyond that there is a deeper truth, difficult to come at and requiring a lifetime to understand, which is that there is no literature, only autobiography, however mediated, however veiled, however transformed. The events of Shakespeare's life included the composition of *Hamlet,* and that act of writing was itself a crucial act of living, though we do not yet know altogether how to read so doubled an act. When an author takes up a more overtly autobiographical stance, as so many do in their youth, again we still do not know precisely how to accommodate the vexed relation between life and work. T. S. Eliot, meditating upon James Joyce, made a classic statement as to such accommodation:

> We want to know who are the originals of his characters, and what
> were the origins of his episodes, so that we may unravel the web of memory
> and invention and discover how far and in what ways the crude material
> has been transformed.

When a writer is not even covertly autobiographical, the web of memory and invention is still there, but so subtly woven that we may never unravel it. And yet we want deeply never to stop trying, and not merely because we are curious, but because each of us is caught in her own network of memory and invention. We do not always recall our inventions, and long before we age we cease to be certain of the extent to which we have invented our memories. Perhaps one motive for reading is our need to unravel our own webs. If our masters could make, from their lives, what we read, then we can be moved by them to ask: What have we made or lived in relation to what we have read? The answers may be sad, or confused, but the question is likely, implicitly, to go on being asked as long as we read. In Freudian terms, we are asking: What is it that we have repressed? What have we forgotten, unconsciously but purposively: What is it that we flee? Art, literature necessarily included, is regression in the service of the ego, according to a famous Freudian formula. I doubt the Freudian wisdom here, but indubitably it is profoundly suggestive. When we read, something in us keeps asking the equivalent of the Freudian questions: From what or whom is the author in flight, and to what earlier stages in her life is she returning, and why?

Reading, whether as an art or a pastime, has been damaged by the visual media, television in particular, and might be in some danger of extinction in the age of the computer, except that the psychic need for it continues to endure, presumably because it alone can assuage a central loneliness in elitist society. Despite all sophisticated or resentful denials, the reading of imaginative literature remains a quest to overcome the isolation of the individual consciousness. We can read for information, or entertainment, or for love of the language, but in the end we seek, in the author, the person whom we have not found, whether in ourselves or in others. In that quest, there always are elements at once aggressive and defensive, so that reading, even in childhood, is rarely free of hidden anxieties. And yet it remains one of the few activities not contaminated by an entropy of spirit. We read in hope, because we lack companionship, and the author can become the object of the most idealistic elements in our search for the wit and inventiveness we so desperately require. We read biography, not as a supplement to reading the author, but as a second, fresh attempt to understand what always seems to evade us in the work, our drive towards a kind of identity with the author.

This will-to-identity, though recently much deprecated, is a prime basis for the experience of sublimity in reading. *Hamlet* retains its unique position in the Western canon not because most readers and playgoers identify themselves with the prince, who clearly is beyond them, but rather because they find themselves again in the power of the language that represents him with such immediacy and force. Yet we know that neither language nor social energy created Hamlet. Our curiosity about Shakespeare is endless, and never will be appeased. That curiosity itself is a value, and cannot be separated from the value of *Hamlet* the tragedy, or Hamlet the literary character. It provokes us that Shakespeare the man seems so unknowable, at once everyone and no one as Borges shrewdly observes. Critics keep telling us otherwise, yet something valid in us keeps believing that we would know Hamlet better if Shakespeare's life were as fully known as the lives of Goethe and Freud, Byron and Oscar Wilde, or best of all, Dr. Samuel Johnson. Shakespeare never will have his Boswell, and Dante never will have his Richard Ellmann. How much one would give for a detailed and candid *Life of Dante* by Petrarch, or an outspoken memoir of Shakespeare by Ben Jonson! Or, in the age just past, how superb would be rival studies of one another by Hemingway and Scott Fitzgerald! But the list is endless: think of *Oscar Wilde* by Lord Alfred Douglas, or a joint biography of Shelley by Mary Godwin, Emilia Viviani, and Jane Williams. More than our insatiable desire for scandal would be satisfied. The literary rivals and the lovers of the great writers possessed perspectives we will never enjoy, and without those perspectives we dwell in some poverty in regard to the writers with whom we ourselves never can be done.

There is a sense in which imaginative literature *is* perspectivism, so that the reader is likely to be overwhelmed by the work's difficulty unless its multiple perspectives are mastered. Literary biography matters most because it is a storehouse of perspectives, frequently far surpassing any that are grasped by the particular biographer. There are relations between authors' lives and their works of kinds we have yet to discover, because our analytical instruments are not yet advanced enough to perform the necessary labor. Perhaps a novel, poem, or play is not so much a regression in the service of the ego, as it is an amalgam of *all* the Freudian mechanisms of defense, all working together for the apotheosis of the ego. Freud valued art highly, but thought that the aesthetic enterprise was no rival for psycho-analysis, unlike religion and philosophy. Clearly Freud was mistaken; his own anxieties about his indebtedness to Shakespeare helped produce the weirdness of his joining in the lunacy that argued for the Earl of Oxford as the author of

Shakespeare's plays. It was Shakespeare, and not "the poets," who was there before Freud arrived at his depth psychology, and it is Shakespeare who is there still, well out ahead of psychoanalysis. We see what Freud would not see, that psychoanalysis is Shakespeare prosified and systematized. Freud is part of literature, not of "science," and the biography of Freud has the same relations to psychoanalysis as the biography of Shakespeare has to *Hamlet* and *King Lear*, if only we knew more of the life of Shakespeare.

Western literature, particularly since Shakespeare, is marked by the representation of internalized change in its characters. A literature of the ever-growing inner self is in itself a large form of biography, even though this is the biography of imaginary beings, from Hamlet to the sometimes nameless protagonists of Kafka and Beckett. Skeptics might want to argue that all literary biography concerns imaginary beings, since authors make themselves up, and every biographer gives us a creation curiously different from the same author as seen by the writer of a rival *Life*. Boswell's Johnson is not quite anyone else's Johnson, though it is now very difficult for us to disentangle the great Doctor from his gifted Scottish friend and follower. The life of the author is not merely a metaphor or a fiction, as is "the Death of the Author," but it always does contain metaphorical or fictive elements. Those elements are a part of the value of literary biography, but not the largest or the crucial part, which is the separation of the mask from the man or woman who hid behind it. James Joyce and Samuel Beckett, master and sometime disciple, were both of them enigmatic personalities, and their biographers have not, as yet, fully expounded the mystery of these contrasting natures. Beckett seems very nearly to have been a secular saint: personally disinterested, heroic in the French Resistance, as humane a person ever to have composed major fictions and dramas. Joyce, self-obsessed even as Beckett was preternaturally selfless, was the Milton of the twentieth century. Beckett was perhaps the least egoistic post-Joycean, post-Proustian, post-Kafkan of writers. Does that illuminate the problematical nature of his work, or does it simply constitute another problem? Whatever the cause, the question matters. The only death of the author that is other than literal, and that matters, is the fate only of weak writers. The strong, who become canonical, never die, which is what the canon truly is about. To be read forever is the Life of the Author.

◼ Introduction

THAT BIOGRAPHICAL CRITICISM should be of particular value in the study of African-American authors does not mean that their differences from other American writers necessarily are thereby enhanced. Both Richard Wright and Zora Neale Hurston were remarkable personalities, fierce individualities by any standard, quite aside from the societal and historical contexts in which they had to live out their lives and literary careers. But it matters that Wright was a Seventh-Day Adventist in his youth, that later he was very active in the Communist party, and that he lived in France from 1947 onward. A man of powerful will, his force of being impelled him beyond compromises into a life of opposition and exile. *Black Boy*, which seems to me his best book, cannot be understood without an even fuller biographical criticism than we presently possess. African-American autobiography, already widely read and deeply studied, achieves an intensity, partly indebted to Wright, that is equaled by few other American genres.

Like all writers who work to found or refound a tradition, Wright had to suffer the tribulations of breaking a new road. But the inner torments seem to have been exorbitant as well. His sense of his mother's suffering never left him, and may have overdetermined his relation to his principal literary precursor, Theodore Dreiser, who excelled in representing the travail of women. This is an Oedipal blindness in Wright's life and work that again makes biographical criticism quite crucial if he is to be read with sympathy, particularly by women.

Wright's reaction to Zora Neale Hurston's poignant triumph, *Their Eyes Were Watching God*, was both ideological and defensive. He found in it a lack of thought, a judgment peculiar even from his Marxist perspective. Barbara Johnson shrewdly observed of Wright that "the figure of the black woman as *reader* in his work is fundamental." Hurston, a freer spirit, involves us in far subtler relations between biography and creativity. She rebelled against all overdeterminations, including those that would confine her writing to societal protest. Her life, like her writing, is a series of catastrophe creations, heroic in its vigor, but increasingly overcome by the ways in which neither the white nor the black worlds could accept her nonconformist temperament. Something of the pattern of Hurston's difficult literary career continues now in her critical fate, particularly when she is subjected to ideological condemnation by certain African-American critics. She never did submit to any authority except her own, and her writing still fights back against politicized opponents. More even than Wright, she requires and deserves the fullest possible biographical criticism if she is to receive the disinterested aesthetic judgments that she always sought.

—H. B.

Arna Bontemps
1902–1973

ARNAUD WENDELL BONTEMPS was born on October 13, 1902, in Alexandria, Louisiana, to Paul Bismark and Maria Carolina Pembroke Bontemps. When Arna was three, the Bontemps moved to Los Angeles after encountering racist incidents. Mrs. Bontemps was a schoolteacher and appears to have greatly encouraged Arna's love for books and learning until her death in 1915. To the disappointment of his father, Arna's literary interests led him away from the traditional family trade of brick masonry. Between 1917 and 1920 he attended San Fernando Academy, a white boarding school, and, upon graduation, entered Pacific Union College in Angwin, California, from which he graduated in 1923.

Bontemps, who resented much of his formal education as devoid of recognition of the achievements of fellow blacks, guarded against losing contact with black society and the rich cadences of creole and black dialects. Bontemps's literary career began in 1924 with the publication of one of his poems in the *Crisis*. In the same year he moved to New York to take a teaching position at the Harlem Academy. Bontemps's poetry won him the *Opportunity* magazine's Alexander Pushkin Poetry Prize in 1926 and 1927. During his short stay in Harlem, Bontemps married Alberta Johnson (in 1926) and found friends among the Harlem Renaissance writers and white literati from other parts of New York. Bontemps shared with the Harlem writers an atavistic longing for African traditions and was greatly influenced by Langston Hughes, who also became a great friend of his, and Countee Cullen, among others.

Bontemps's first novel, *God Sends Sunday*, was published in 1931. The book is set within the black sporting world and is highly praised for Bontemps's economical and poetic use of language as well as his ability to capture the rhythmic cadences of black dialect. In 1939 Bontemps collaborated with Countee Cullen on adapting the novel for the stage.

Bontemps resigned from the Harlem Academy in 1931 and moved to Huntsville, Alabama, to teach at Oakwood Junior College. *Opportunity* awarded him the 1932 literary prize for his short story "A Summer Tragedy." In Alabama Bontemps began writing juvenile literature, partly in the hope of presenting a positive image of blacks in America. His first children's book, *Popo and Fifina* (1932), was written in collaboration with Langston Hughes, and tells of the adventures of two children in rural Haiti. In 1934 *You Can't Pet a Possum* appeared. Bontemps wrote many other works for children, including *We Have Tomorrow* (1945), *Slappy Hooper, the Wonderful Sign Painter* (1946), and *Mr. Kelso's Lion* (1970). He also wrote two biographical works for young adults on the abolitionist Frederick Douglass—*Frederick Douglass: Slave, Fighter, Freeman* (1959) and *Free at Last: The Life of Frederick Douglass* (1971)—as well as a young adult biography of Booker T. Washington, *Young Booker: Booker T. Washington's Early Days* (1972).

In 1934 Bontemps resigned his position at Oakwood Junior College. The next year he accepted a teaching position at Shiloh Academy and moved to Chicago. In 1937 he resigned from Shiloh Academy to add his talents to the Illinois Writers' Project. In 1936 Bontemps published *Black Thunder*, which proved to be his most celebrated work. The novel draws much from early slave narratives and is set in the historical context of a slave insurrection in 1800 in Henrico County, Virginia. *Black Thunder* was praised for its uninhibited retelling of the black revolutionary sentiment brewing in the slave states of early America, but it was Bontemps's powerful use of language, especially dialect, that brought the novel its critical acclaim.

In 1938 Bontemps gave up teaching in order to write full-time. He accepted the Rosenwald Fellowship and set out for the Caribbean. *Drums at Dusk* (1939) was the result of his travels—a depiction of a Haitian slave revolt around the time of the French Revolution. The book was disparaged by some reviewers for its romantic landscape painting and weak narrative structure. In 1943 Bontemps completed his masters of library science at the University of Chicago and became librarian at Fisk University in Nashville, Tennessee, a position that he held until 1965. He devoted his energies to enlarging the library's collection of black American literature and anthologizing black American writings and folklore in such volumes as *Golden Slippers: An Anthology of Negro Poetry for Young Readers* (1941), *American Negro Poetry* (1963; rev. 1974), *Great Slave Narratives* (1969), and *The Harlem Renaissance Remembered* (1972), which contributed much to the history of black American literary achievement. Arna Bontemps died on June 4, 1973, in Nashville, Tennessee.

◈ Critical Extracts

W. E. B. DU BOIS   Arna Bontemps' first venture in fiction ⟨*Gods Sends Sunday*⟩ is to me a profound disappointment. It is of the school of *Nigger Heaven* and *Home to Harlem*. There is a certain pathetic touch to the painting of his poor little jockey hero, but nearly all else is sordid crime, drinking, gambling, whore-mongering, and murder. There is not a decent intelligent woman; not a single man with the slightest ambition or real education, scarcely more than one human child in the whole book. Even the horses are drab. In the "Blues" alone Bontemps sees beauty. But in brown skins, frizzled hair and full contoured faces, there are to him nothing but ugly, tawdry, hateful things, which he describes with evident caricature.

One reads hurriedly on, waiting for a gleam of light, waiting for the Sunday that some poor ugly black God may send; but somehow it never comes; and if God appears at all it is in the form of a little drunken murderer riding South to Tia Juana on his back.

I suppose I am not tuned right to judge this book and am a prey to hopeless prejudices. Somehow, I cannot fail to see the open, fine, brown face of Bontemps himself. I know of his comely wife and I can imagine a mother and father for each of these, who were at least striving and ambitious. I read with ever recurring wonder Bontemps' noble "Nocturne at Bethesda;" but here in this, nothing of that other side is even hinted.

Well,—as I know I have said several times before,—if you like this sort of thing, then this will be exactly the sort of thing you will especially like, and in that case you ought to run and read it.

> W. E. B. Du Bois, [Review of *Gods Sends Sunday*], *Crisis* 38, No. 9 (September 1931): 304

RICHARD WRIGHT   In that limited and almost barren field known as the Negro novel, Arna Bontemps's *Black Thunder* fills a yawning gap and fills it competently. Covering all those skimpy reaches of Negro letters I know, this is the only novel dealing forthrightly with the historical and revolutionary traditions of the Negro people.

Black Thunder is the true story of a slave insurrection that failed. But in his telling of the story of that failure Bontemps manages to reveal and dramatize through the character of his protagonist, Gabriel, a quality of folk courage unparalleled in the proletarian literature of this country. ⟨. . .⟩

The plan for the uprising is so simple and daring that when it is disclosed and tracked to its source, the fear-ridden whites can scarcely believe it. But Gabriel believes, he believes even when he is caught; even when the black cowl is capped about his head, even when the ax swings, he believes. Why?

For me the cardinal value of Bontemps's book, besides the fact that it is a thumping story well told, lies in the answer to that question. Perhaps I am straying further afield than the author did in search for an answer. If I do, it is because I believe we have in *Black Thunder* a revelation of the very origin and source of folk values in literature.

Even though Gabriel's character is revealed in terms of personal action and dialogue, I feel there is in him much more than mere personal dignity and personal courage. There is in his attitude something which transcends the limits of immediate consciousness. He is buoyed in his hope and courage by an optimism which takes no account of the appalling difficulties confronting him. He hopes when there are no objective reasons or grounds for hope; he fights when his fellow-slaves scamper for their lives. In doing so, he takes his place in that gallery of fictitious characters who exist on the plane of the ridiculous and the sublime. Bontemps endows Gabriel with a myth-like and deathless quality. And it is in this sense, I believe, that *Black Thunder* sounds a new note in Negro fiction, thereby definitely extending the boundaries and ideology of the Negro novel.

Richard Wright, "A Tale of Folk Courage," *Partisan Review & Anvil* 3, No. 3 (April 1936): 31

IONE MORRISON RIDER   In 1935 the young author brought his wife and three young children to visit in Los Angeles. We of a small branch of the Los Angeles Public Library remember a man of quiet aspect and sensitive features applying for a borrower's card. His backhand signature had an almost feminine spidery grace. Where had we seen that name before? One of the staff suddenly realized that it was on a book on our shelves— on two of them. *God Sends Sunday* happened to be in. We asked the quiet reader, was it his? It was, he answered with a slight smile.

Thereafter he came almost daily to read. We looked forward to learning his opinions on this or that new book, in brief intervals between desk and reference demands. He kept in touch with the best current writing, and although reticent shared his views generously when asked.

During this interval he watched over his children's reading, and continued his study of the simplification of dialect. He read and analyzed children's books suggested by our children's librarian, and showed keen interest in teaching methods in neighborhood schools. He came to talk to children at the library story hour—a weekly event held, because of the lack of a separate room, right in the children's room with the hubbub of the charging desk just beyond. The gentle artist must have been shocked within himself to find waiting, not the usual fifty, but about two hundred urchins of different races, including Mexican, Negro, Japanese. They surged in waves around him on the clean linoleum floor. He had to pick his way between grimy hands and bare feet to the corner from which he told the story of Toussaint L'Ouverture and read aloud several of Langston Hughes's poems.

Then came the evening when Mr. Bontemps brought in Langston Hughes, en route from Mexico. Mr. Hughes is a charming citizen of the world; sophisticated, poised. He looked with interest over our collection of books, spoke of liking Helen Sewell's drawings for *The Dream Keeper*, was amused to learn that his adult books are stolen here as they are in other libraries. He's happiest, he mentioned, among people of the theater. Among artists there is no such thing as race-consciousness; there is only art-consciousness. Nevertheless, it is evident that he is dedicated to conscious expression as a Negro. ⟨. . .⟩

For some time Mr. Bontemps has been working on an adventure story for older boys, with a Caribbean background. He also has under way another historical novel, which is concerned with Haiti. Twice recently he has revisited that fascinating island. "No one," he wrote recently from there, "has yet done this island justice. It is too heavy with color. One must *see* the flamboyant tree in flower, or he will never know."

True, beyond a doubt. Yet we venture to hope that through the seeing of such artists as Arna Bontemps we also may feel its magic, gain some measure of understanding of its proud people. Whatever is yet to come from his pen we await with anticipation, confident that it will be poetically conceived, and written with distinction.

Ione Morrison Rider, "Arna Bontemps," *Horn Book* 15, No. 1 (January–February 1939): 17, 19

HUGH M. GLOSTER   Also a record of the Negro's quest for freedom is Bontemps' second historical novel, *Dreams at Dusk*, an account of the black insurrection which resulted in the independence of Haiti and the emergence of Toussaint L'Ouverture. Making but few revisions in the generally accepted versions of the early stages of the revolution, Bontemps builds the historical narrative around the romance of Celeste Juvet, a girl of French parentage, and Diron de Sautels, a young French aristocrat who is a member of Les Amis des Noirs, an antislavery worker, and an ardent reader of such thinkers as La Rochefoucauld, Lafayette, Danton, Robespierre, Brissot, Gregoire, and Raynal. Celeste lives with her grandmother on the large Breda plantation superintended by M. Bayou de Libertas, a benevolent overseer employed by a French nobleman whose profligate cousin, Count Armand de Sacy, uses the vast colonial estate as a dumping ground for discarded mistresses. De Sacy's inhuman treatment of sick bondmen and the subsequent mass suicide of twenty-four Gold Coast slaves serve to hasten the peasant uprising which results in the overthrow of the aristocracy and the ascendance of Toussaint L'Ouverture. In the bloody holocaust which accompanies the insurrection de Sacy meets a horrible death, and a terrific toll of life is taken on both sides. ⟨. . .⟩

Bontemps paints a vivid picture of social upheaval and class prejudice in tropical San Domingo. Struggling for control are the wealthy elite, the low-class whites, and the free mulattoes. The aristocrats, dominating slaves who outnumber all other inhabitants by nearly ten to one, keep their positions secure by intimidating the blacks and playing them against the mulattoes. The patricians live in luxury, diverting themselves with expensive banquets and dazzling apparel. Miscegenation is rampant, as lecherous aristocrats frequently manifest a preference for "chocolate" and openly flaunt their yellow mistresses. In handling black workers, however, the wealthy class is not so tender. Revolting conditions prevail in slave ships, where diseased natives are packed spoon-fashion, and on many plantations. This cruel treatment accelerates the extension of liberal views and the meteoric rise of such leaders as Brisson, Boukman, and L'Ouverture. In brief, *Drums at Dusk*, a worthy successor to *Black Thunder*, is another vivid illustration of the richness of the Negro's past as a source for historical fiction.

Hugh M. Gloster, *Negro Voices in American Fiction* (Chapel Hill: University of North Carolina Press, 1948), pp. 215–16

SAUNDERS REDDING   Near the end of his new book ⟨*100 Years of Negro Freedom*⟩, Arna Bontemps writes: "The story of the Negro in the United States as seen in the leadership he has recognized since Emancipation does not pull strands together into a single thread as it reaches the present." But pulling the strands together is exactly what Bontemps attempts to do in *100 Years of Negro Freedom*. That he does not completely succeed is due partly to the intractability of historical fact and partly to his choice of those he recognizes as Negro leaders.

Few readers will quarrel with most of his choices. Though the great figures, including Frederick Douglass, W. E. B. Du Bois, and Philip Randolph, are perhaps equally imperative in the demands they make on a historical writer's emotional and intellectual resources, it is Booker Washington who gets the fullest treatment. Many, doubtless, will say that this is as it should be. But Bontemps's treatment of Washington has a certain ambivalence in it: his urge to tell the hard truth is too nicely balanced by a soft desire to preserve the hero image. ⟨. . .⟩ The fact is that Washington was a ruthless infighter, who tried to ruin those he could not control, and who sometimes drank more than was good for him. In much of Bontemps's treatment of the "wizard" of Tuskegee the myth prevails over the man. ⟨. . .⟩

The most fascinating portrait is of P. B. S. Pinchback, first a professional gambler, then businessman and successful politician, and always a *bon vivant*. Whether he was also a Negro "leader" is debatable. His paper, the *Louisianan*, did protest against the rise of Kluxism and the influence of "corruptionists" and "bulldozers" over Negro voters. He did go about the country making speeches to conventions of Negroes. And, heeding what Fred Douglass had to say about the reputation of Negroes being the responsibility of Negroes in the public eye, Pinchback, in his short term as acting Governor of Louisiana, was called "honest." Still, opinion must hold that he was a clever self-seeker. But whatever he was or was not, his story makes an exciting chapter in an expertly written book.

> Saunders Redding, "In the Vanguard of Civil Rights," *Saturday Review*, 12 August 1961, p. 34

JACK CONROY   It has now been more than a year since Arna, my cherished friend and esteemed colleague for such a long period, died. On June 4, 1973, to be exact. I recently looked through the small volume of his verse, *Personals*, published by Paul Breman in London in 1963, and realized that it will soon be half a century since Arna, a wide-eyed young poet fresh out of college, arrived in New York City from California. His first impressions—expressed in more detail in his memoir which introduces *The Harlem Renaissance Remembered* (Dodd, Mead, 1972), a collection of essays he edited—are set down in the preface to *Personals*:

> In some places the autumn of 1924 may have been an
> unremarkable season. In Harlem it was like a foretaste of

paradise. A blue haze descended at night and with it strings of
fairy lights on the broad avenues. From the window of a
small room in an apartment on Fifth and 129th Street I looked
over the rooftops of Negrodom and tried to believe my eyes.
What a city! What a world!

And what a city for a colored boy to be leaving home for the
first time! Twenty-one, sixteen months out of college, full
of golden hopes and romantic dreams, I had come all the way
from Los Angeles to find the job I wanted, to hear the music
of my taste, to see serious plays and, God willing, to become a
writer.

The Negro Renaissance was beginning to build up a full head of steam,
and young Bontemps was soon an active participant. He was able to find
some teaching assignments in private schools while continuing his studies,
and during that first year in Harlem he had his first poem accepted for
publication in *The Crisis,* then edited by W. E. B. Du Bois. It was indeed
a good year for the young poet, as was 1926 when he won his first poetry
prize and took unto himself a wife. Somehow, Harlem remained a pleasant
and exhilarating haven during the twenties, though racial disturbances
erupted in other American cities. "Spared these convulsions," Bontemps
notes, "New York became a locus for what I would regard as a more exciting
and perhaps more telling assault on oppression than the dreary blood-in-
the-streets strategy of preceding years."

This statement, it seems to me, provides a clue to Arna's creative method,
which often evoked a more poignant emotional response by quiet eloquence
than a more violent and hortatory approach might have accomplished. 〈. . .〉

Looking through the copy of *Personals* Arna inscribed for me ("to Jack,
these vestiges of the Twenties"), I thought as I read such selections as
"Southern Mansion," "To a Young Girl Leaving the Hill Country," and
"A Black Man Talks of Reaping" that Arna had never lost that precious
sense of wonder and discovery that flooded him when he first beheld Harlem.
There is the elegiac and nostalgic note that pervades much of his later
work, both in prose and verse, and makes it so appealing and heart-warming.

Jack Conroy, "Memories of Arna Bontemps: Friend and Collaborator," *American
Libraries* 5, No. 11 (December 1974): 605–6

ROBERT BONE   In a little-noticed but important essay which
appeared in 1950, Arna Bontemps discusses the demise of the Harlem
Renaissance. "The Depression," he asserts, "put an end to the dream world
of renaissance Harlem . . ." 〈"Famous WPA Authors," *Negro Digest,* June

1950⟩. Yet even as he laments the passing of those exciting years, he cele-brates the advent of a second literary awakening, "less gaudy but closer to realities" than the first. He associates this new development with the Federal Writers Projects of the 1930's, and more precisely with the Illinois Project, whose headquarters were located in the city of Chicago.

Bontemps was himself a firsthand witness of these events. Having left Alabama in the fall of 1933, he spent almost two years with his relatives in Watts before moving on to Chicago. There he enrolled at the university as a graduate student of English in the fall of 1935. Before many months had passed, he made the acquaintance of Richard Wright, and through him, the South Side Writers Group, whose membership included such aspiring authors as poet Margaret Walker and playwright Theodore Ward. Founded by Wright in April of 1936, this group offered mutual criticism and moral support to young black writers within the framework of a Marxist ideology. ⟨. . .⟩

Under the influence of these associations, Bontemps' writing took a turn to the left. If we examine his work prior to 1935—his early verse, his first novel, *God Sends Sunday* (1931), and his Alabama tales—we find a sensibility molded by the themes and forms of the Harlem Renaissance. After 1935, however, Bontemps accommodates to the new revolutionary mood. His second novel, *Black Thunder* (1936), depicts the slave rebellion led by Gabriel Prosser, while his third, *Drums at Dusk* (1939), is concerned with the Haitian insurrection whose leader was Toussaint L'Ouverture. ⟨. . .⟩

This alteration in the mythic content of black writing signals the emer-gence of a new literary generation. From the perspective of 1950, Bontemps tries to define the relationship of the Wright generation to his own: "Obvi-ously the new talents come in schools or waves. Either the writing impulse spreads by a sort of chain reaction or given conditions stimulate all who are exposed to them. One way or the other, Harlem got its renaissance in the middle twenties, centering around the *Opportunity* contests and Fifth Avenue Awards Dinners. Ten years later Chicago reenacted it on WPA without finger bowls but with increased power."

The clear implication is that Chicago, no less than Harlem, was the site of a cultural awakening. If Bontemps is correct, literary historians should be thinking in terms of a Chicago Renaissance. The issues are complex, for variables both of space and time are involved. The torch was passing not only from Harlem to Chicago, but from one generation to the next. Not all of the important work of the Wright generation was accomplished in the city of Chicago, but the new movement clearly had its focus there.

Robert Bone, "Arna Bontemps," *Down Home: A History of Afro-American Short Fiction from Its Beginnings to the End of the Harlem Renaissance* (New York: G. P. Putnam's Sons, 1975), pp. 284–86

VIOLET J. HARRIS   ⟨Bontemps and Jack Conroy⟩ produced three
picture books for children: *Fast Sooner Hound* (1942), *Slappy Hooper, the
Wonderful Sign Painter* (1946), and *Sam Patch, the High, Wide, and Handsome
Jumper* (1951). These books are notable because they are relatively well
written, and because the collaborators adopted many of the elements associated with the oral tradition such as characters with exceptional physical
skills, reminiscent of Pecos Bill. Also, the characters are white. Although
white authors had written books comprised primarily of African-American
characters, few African-American authors wrote books comprised solely
of white characters. One might argue that Bontemps exercised literary
prerogative in doing so, but one might just as well argue that his wide
reading, religious perspective, upbringing in integrated settings, and self-
confidence enabled him to create whatever literary situations he desired.
Or the books might simply have resulted from the acceptance of a contract
from publishers who did not request books that reflected African-American
experiences or that contained African-American characters. ⟨. . .⟩

⟨. . .⟩ Bontemps's fiction ⟨for children⟩ reflected African-American folk
culture, language patterns, and in the case of *Lonesome Boy* (1955), an
adventuresome manipulation of fantasy. In addition to *Lonesome Boy*, Bontemps produced *You Can't Pet a Possum* (1934) and *Sad-Faced Boy* (1937).
Oakwood, Alabama in the 1930s provided Bontemps with the characters,
language, and thematic motifs for those two books. His fondness for African-
American folk culture and the opportunities to observe aspects of the culture
sustained him as he coped with the religious sternness of Oakwood College
(Seventh Day Adventist) and the decidedly anti-intellectual attitudes of
its white head. Despite the parochial environment and the anti-intellectu-
alism, the head of the college ordered Bontemps to burn his books. Bontemps
turned the situation to his advantage and two books resulted.

In contrast to *Sad-Faced Boy* and *You Can't Pet a Possum*, the lyrical and
slightly surreal *Lonesome Boy* presents a portrait of Louisiana and two familiar
motifs, the jazz musician and the supernatural. Arguably, *Lonesome Boy* is
Bontemps's finest piece of children's literature. One indication of its literary
merit rests in the reviews that accompanied its initial publication. Undoubtedly, Bontemps drew on his remembrances of Louisiana, the stories of family
members, and similar kinds of characters he might have encountered in
Harlem and Los Angeles.

Violet J. Harris, "From Little Black Sambo to Popo and Fifina: Arna Bontemps and
the Creation of African-American Children's Literature," *The Lion and the Unicorn*
14, No. 1 (June 1990): 114–15

DANIEL REAGAN   Many recent studies of African-American literature assume that the foundations of black cultural identity rest in vernacular traditions. John F. Callahan states this assumption succinctly when he
claims that the characteristic African-American literary voice is defined by
"the attempt to conjure the spoken word into symbolic existence on the
page." Arna Bontemps' novel *Black Thunder: Gabriel's Revolt: Virginia: 1800*
(1936) makes a crucial contribution to this oxymoronic literary-vernacular
tradition by exploring the significance and limitations of writing the spoken
word. Through a variety of voices and points of view, the novel tells the
story of an actual slave rebellion, led by Gabriel Prosser, which almost
succeeded in capturing Richmond, Virginia. In this work, Bontemps juxta-
poses written and oral cultures by depicting the white community as the
literate producers and consumers of printed texts and the slave community as
illiterate generators of oral discourse. The slaves' orality, Bontemps suggests,
differs from the printed word because it is pneumatological, that is, it
originates in nature and is both alive and life giving. An anonymous refugee
from the San Domingo slave revolt who watches Gabriel's hanging identifies
the pneumatological nature of speech when he mutters, "words like *freedom*
and *liberty* drip blood—always, everywhere there is blood on such words."
This compelling statement suggests that only when spoken aloud do such
words as "freedom" and "liberty" come alive. Bontemps' interest in the
animating power of orality leads him to undertake what Callahan has more
recently defined as the "sacred political purpose involved in many African-
American writers' use of voice: the pursuit of freedom, equality, and diversity
as American principles." ⟨. . .⟩

⟨. . .⟩ critics who have expressed so much recent interest in the oral and
folk sources of Afro-American literature strangely overlook *Black Thunder*,
even though it is one of the first black novels to examine the nature of
orality. In fact, these studies elide the issue that Bontemps would say is critical
in the movement from oral expression to written word, the fundamental
difference between the act of speaking and the printed text as social forces.
Instead of highlighting the differences between writing and orality as racial
and cultural markers, recent commentators have attempted to articulate the
similarities between written texts and spoken words. Callahan, for example,
claims that a residue of orality resides in printed texts. Because readers hear
as well as see words, he argues, writing keeps oral expression alive. Bontemps,
on the other hand, suggests that although orality itself binds speaker and
audience, the written reduplication of orality necessarily distances the reader
from the spoken voice. As a result, his book does not affirm Callahan's
model of Afro-American literary history as a progressive movement toward

the principles of freedom, equality, and diversity. Instead, Bontemps' narrative posits that the black literary tradition is defined by an alternation between the progressive demand for freedom and the suppression of liberty through the very act of writing itself. ⟨. . .⟩

The various tropes Bontemps employs to portray oral folk culture suggest that both the individual and communal identities of slaves are forged in a wordless discourse that excludes outsiders and depends for its vitality on its ephemeral and situational nature. The most provocative and significant statements of African-American cultural identity in *Black Thunder* occur not in writing but in oral discourse. Further, the printed text radically distorts the social and communal nature of oral expression. Bontemps' assertion that the written word fails both rhetorically and sociologically to be a tool for revolutionary change therefore renders paradoxical his effort to write the spoken word. He acknowledges this limit of writing when he observes that "I never felt the kind of change a novel could bring would be instantaneous or explosive; nor did I want it to have an explosive effect." If, as Callahan contends, the African-American literary voice transforms orality into the written word, Bontemps examines the limits and difficulties inherent in that transformation. His attempt to give voice to the silence surrounding orality may only be a shadowed success; nonetheless, the whispered yet powerful voices he evokes reveal the complex dynamics of suppression that shape African-American literary history and suggest that the resulting silence is as meaningful as the song of the thrasher.

Daniel Reagan, "Voices of Silence: The Representation of Orality in Arna Bontemps' *Black Thunder*," *Studies in American Fiction* 19, No. 1 (Spring 1991): 71–72, 81

🏵 *Bibliography*

God Sends Sunday. 1931.

Popo and Fifina, Children of Haiti (with Langston Hughes). 1932.

You Can't Pet a Possum. 1934.

Black Thunder: Gabriel's Revolt: Virginia: 1800. 1936.

Sad-Faced Boy. 1937.

Drums at Dusk. 1939.

Golden Slippers: An Anthology of Negro Poetry for Young Readers (editor). 1941.

Father of the Blues: An Autobiography by W. C. Handy (editor). 1941.

The Fast Sooner Hound (with Jack Conroy). 1942.

We Have Tomorrow. 1945.

They Seek a City (with Jack Conroy). 1945, 1966 (as *Anyplace But Here*).

Slappy Hooper, the Wonderful Sign Painter (with Jack Conroy). 1946.

American Missionary Association Archives in Fisk University. 1947.

Story of the Negro. 1948.

The Poetry of the Negro 1746–1949 (editor; with Langston Hughes). 1949, 1970.

George Washington Carver. 1950.

Sam Patch, the High, Wide, and Handsome Jumper (with Jack Conroy). 1951.

Chariot in the Sky: A Story of the Jubilee Singers. 1951.

The Story of George Washington Carver. 1954.

A List of Manuscripts, Published Works and Related Items in the Charles Waddell Chesnutt Collection of the Erastus Milo Cravath Memorial Library, Fisk University. 1954.

Lonesome Boy. 1955.

The Book of Negro Folklore (editor; with Langston Hughes). 1958.

Frederick Douglass: Slave, Fighter, Freeman. 1959.

100 Years of Negro Freedom. 1961.

American Negro Poetry (editor). 1963, 1974.

Personals. 1963.

I Too Sing America (with Langston Hughes). 1964.

Famous Negro Athletes. 1964.

Negro American Heritage (editor). 1968.

Great Slave Narratives (editor). 1969.

Hold Fast to Dreams: Poems Old and New (editor). 1969.

Mr. Kelso's Lion. 1970.

Free at Last: The Life of Frederick Douglass. 1971.

Young Booker: Booker T. Washington's Early Days. 1972.

The Harlem Renaissance Remembered (editor). 1972.

The Old South: "A Summer Tragedy" and Other Stories of the Thirties. 1973.

Arna Bontemps–Langston Hughes Letters 1925–1967. Ed. Charles H. Nichols. 1980.

Sterling A. Brown
1901–1989

STERLING ALLEN BROWN was born in Washington, D.C., on May 1, 1901. The last of six children, he was the son of a former slave, the Reverend Sterling Nelson Brown, the pastor of the Lincoln Temple Congregational Church and a professor of religion at Howard University. Stanley's mother, Adelaide Allen, was valedictorian at Fisk University and one of the original Jubilee Singers of Fisk, who introduced many spirituals to the general public.

Brown was raised in an atmosphere of literature and poetry, where bookshelves held such works as W. E. B. Du Bois's *The Souls of Black Folk*, the works of Alain Locke, and the histories of black life by Carter C. Woodson and Archibald H. Grimke.

In racially segregated Washington, D.C., Brown attended Lucretia Mott School, named after a well-known abolitionist and feminist. In Dunbar High School (named after the black writer Paul Laurence Dunbar), the young Sterling was a pupil of Haley Douglass, the grandson of Frederick Douglass, and of Neville Thomas, then president of the NAACP branch chapter. At this time, public schools were important in nurturing black pride; they were a source of great inner strength to many students and clearly enabled Brown to enter Williams College, in Williamstown, Massachusetts.

At that time Williams, a small, exclusive liberal arts college, admitted only a handful of black students, and they were kept apart from the white students by school officials. Brown and his friends literally hid when playing jazz, then considered inappropriate listening matter for a member of the student body. However, Brown was most influenced by a literature professor, George Dutton, who introduced him to European literature. Brown was encouraged to read Flaubert, Henry James, and the novels of Sinclair Lewis, and he embraced critical realism, an approach in literature that was in vogue at that time. Modern American poetry, taught by Lewis Untermeyer, was also an influence upon Brown, who upon graduation from Williams began to write poetry. The regionalism of Edwin Arlington Robinson, Robert Frost, Carl Sandburg, and A. E. Housman influenced the young poet.

Brown entered Harvard in 1922. Upon graduation, he immediately pursued his desire to teach and was employed as an English professor at Virginia Seminary in Lynchburg, Virginia, for three years. He subsequently taught at Lincoln University in Missouri (1926–28) and at Fisk University (1928–29). In 1929 he began what would be a forty-year teaching career at Howard University. Retiring in 1969, he resumed teaching in 1973 at the Howard University Institute for the Arts and Humanities, remaining there for two years.

Brown called himself an "amateur folklorist." He became interested in black culture and visited many black establishments in Nashville and other rural communities of the South. He loved the "yarnspinning" or oral tales told by such people as "Slam" in the Jefferson City Hotel and Calvin "Big Boy" Davis. Some of these tales find their way into his poetry.

Although Brown is best known as a poet—his first poetry volume was *Southern Road* (1932)—he wrote and edited several landmark works on black American fiction, poetry, and folklore. He was appointed the Federal Writers' Project's national editor for Negro affairs, serving from 1936 to 1940. His most important prose works were written at this time: *The Negro in American Fiction* and *Negro Poetry and Drama* (both 1937). With Arthur P. Davis and Ulysses Lee, he edited *The Negro Caravan* in 1941.

It is not clear why Brown published so little from 1941 to 1975. A book of poems, *No Hiding Place*, was rejected in 1937, leaving Brown embittered. The resurgence of interest in black literature in the 1960s and 1970s finally encouraged Brown—then regarded as a "living legend"—to issue *The Last Ride of Wild Bill and Eleven Narrative Poems* in 1975. Michael S. Harper edited Brown's *Collected Poems* in 1980. Sterling Brown died in Washington, D.C., on January 17, 1989.

▨ Critical Extracts

STERLING A. BROWN   The treatment of the Negro in American fiction, since it parallels his treatment in American life, has naturally been noted for injustice. Like other oppressed and exploited minorities, the Negro has been interpreted in a way to justify his exploiters.

> I swear their nature is beyond my comprehension. A strange
> people!—merry 'mid their misery—laughing through their
> tears, like the sun shining through the rain. Yet what simple

philosophers they! They tread life's path as if 'twere strewn
with roses devoid of thorns, and make the most of life with
natures of sunshine and song.

Most American readers would take this to refer to the Negro, but it was
spoken of the Irish, in a play dealing with one of the most desperate
periods of Ireland's tragic history. The Jew has been treated similarly by his
persecutors. The African, and especially the South African native, is now
receiving substantially the same treatment as the American Negro. Literature
dealing with the peasant and the working-class has, until recently, conformed
to a similar pattern. ⟨. . .⟩

We shall see in this study how stereotypes—that the Negro is *all* this,
that, or the other—have evolved at the dictates of social policy. When
slavery was being attacked, for instance, southern authors countered with
the contented slave; when cruelties were mentioned, they dragged forward
the comical and happy-hearted Negro. Admittedly wrong for white people,
slavery was represented as a boon for Negroes, on theological, biological,
psychological warrant. Since Negroes were of "peculiar endowment," slavery
could not hurt them, although, inconsistently, it was their punishment,
since they were cursed of God. A corollary was the wretched freedman, a
fish out of water. In Reconstruction, when threatened with such dire fate
as Negroes' voting, going to school, and working for themselves (i.e., Negro
domination), southern authors added the stereotype of the brute Negro.
Even today much social policy demands that slavery be shown as blessed
and fitting, and the Negro as ludicrously ignorant of his own best good.

Many authors who are not hostile to the Negro and some who profess
friendship still stress a "peculiar endowment" at the expense of the Negro's
basic humanity. Some antislavery authors seemed to believe that submissive-
ness was a mystical African quality, and chose mulattoes for their rebellious
heroes, attributing militancy and intelligence to a white heritage. Many
contemporary authors exploit the Negro's quaintness, his "racial qualities."
Whether they do this for an escape from drab, standardized life or out of
genuine artistic interest or, in the case of Negro authors, out of race pride,
their work suffers from the narrowness of allegory. It must be added that
these authors play into the hands of reactionaries, who, once a difference
is established, use it to justify peculiar position and peculiar treatment.

Whether the Negro was human was one of the problems that racked the
brains of the cultured Old South. The finally begrudged admission that
perhaps he was, has remained largely nominal in letters as in life. Complete,
complex humanity has been denied to him. He is too often like characters
in the medieval allegories: now Loyalty, or Mirth, or Servility, or Quaintness,

or Exuberance, or Brutishness, or Lust. Only seldom is he shown as Labor or Persecution, although he was brought here to supply the first, and as payment received the second.

Since there is no stereotype without some basis in actuality, it goes without saying that individuals could be found resembling Page's loyal Uncle Billy or Stark Young's William Veal, or Dixon's brutal Gus, or Scarlet Sister Mary or Van Vechten's Lasca, or even Uncle Tom and Florian Slappey. But when, as is frequent, generalizations are drawn from these about a race or a section, the author oversteps his bounds as novelist, and becomes an amateur social scientist whose guesses are valueless, and even dangerous. Fiction, especially on so controversial a subject as the American Negro, is still subjective, and novelists would do well to recognize that they are recording a few characters in a confined social segment, often from a prejudiced point of view. They cannot, like Bacon, take all for their province. ⟨. . .⟩

In spite of the publishers' dicta that certain authors know *the* Negro better than Negroes themselves; in spite of certain authors who believe that slave-holding ancestry is necessary in order truly to know Negroes (on the theory that only the owner, or his descendants, can know the owned); in spite of the science of Negro mind-reading, flourishing below the Mason-Dixon line, it is likely that Negro authors will, after the apprentice years, write most fully and most deeply about their own people. As we go to the Russians, the Scandinavians, and the French for the truth about their people; as we go to the workers and not to the stockholders, to the tenants and croppers and not to the landlords, for the truth about the lives of tenants and croppers, so it seems that we should expect the truth of Negro life from Negroes. The Negro artist has a fine task ahead of him to render this truth in enduring fiction. So far, much of what seems truthful has been the work of sympathetic white authors. In all probability white authors will continue to write about the Negro. Sometimes similarly conditioned in America's class structure, sometimes extremely sensitive and understanding, they will get at valuable truth. But Negro novelists must accept the responsibility of being the ultimate portrayers of their own.

Sterling A. Brown, "Introduction," *The Negro in American Fiction* (Washington, DC: Associates in Negro Folk Education, 1937), pp. 1–4

CHARLES H. ROWELL   "What motivates a middle-class Black man and a Harvard graduate . . . to devote his life to portraying less well-to-do folks?" queries Genevieve Ekaete. She answers:

Being Black is the key. . . . According to [Sterling Brown], he
was indignant at the corrupted folk speech publicized by "white
comic writers like Octavus Roy Cohen." From his experience,
Brown says, he knew his people didn't talk that way. It
wasn't enough for him to enjoin them to "Stop knowing it all!"
He had to bring some semblance of balance by putting his
people down on black and white to counter the proliferating
distortions from other sources. ⟨"Sterling Brown: A Living
Legend," *New Directions*, Winter 1974.⟩

Then, too, early in his teaching career Brown "read the new realistic poetry
in American life"—that of Frost, Sandburg, Masters, Lindsay and Robinson,
for example. In their "democratic approach to the people," Brown saw much
that reflected his own thoughts about ordinary people. Brown recalls: "when
Carl Sandburg said 'yes' to the American people, I wanted to say 'yes' to
my people." Brown's "yes" was to give us carefully wrought poems portraying
"common" black folk "in a manner constant with them." His "yes" to black
people was also to give us a series of critical works which attempted to
counter "the proliferating distortions" of black folk life and character. As
early as the Twenties, Brown began writing a series of critical studies and
reviews on the portrayal of blacks in American literature. In 1929, he
observed that

From Kennedy's "Swallow Barn," about the first treatment of
the plantation, down to Dixon's rabid Ku Klux Klan propaganda,
the Negro has been shown largely as an animal. Kennedy, doing
a piece of special pleading, showed the Negro as parasitical,
excessively loyal, contented, irresponsible, and so forth. Dixon
showed his Negro characters, not as faithful dogs, but as
mad curs. His brutes are given to rapine, treachery, bestiality,
and gluttony.

Like other New Negro writers, Brown knew that such portrayals were neither
accurate characterizations nor true expressions of the souls of black folk.

After study at Williams and Harvard, Brown prepared himself to counter
distorting images of black people perpetuated in American literature. To
do so, he read widely and critically into the literature by and about black
people, and carefully studied Afro-American history and folk culture. Hence
his *Negro Poetry and Drama, The Negro in American Fiction* (both 1937),
and several important periodical essays and reviews—sources which no
serious student of American literature can ignore. But to counter the distorting images as poet, Brown knew that he had to go beyond books and
his Washington experiences for material: he went directly to black people

in the South. That is, as he taught and traveled in the South, he lived among and carefully observed those peasants who created black folk traditions—traditions which sustained them in their daily lives. Writing in 1934 about Brown as "folk poet," Alain Locke asserted that

> Sterling Brown has listened long and carefully to the folk in
> their intimate hours, when they are talking to themselves, not, so
> to speak, as in Dunbar, but actually as they do when the masks
> of protective mimicry fall. Not only has he dared to give
> quiet but bold expression to this private thought and speech,
> but he has dared to give the Negro peasant credit for
> thinking.

In a word, when Brown taught and traveled in the South, he became an insider to the multifarious traditions and verbal art forms indigenous to black folk, and through his adaptations of their verbal art forms and spirit he, as poet, became an instrument for their myriad voices. Hence *Southern Road*.

Charles H. Rowell, "Sterling A. Brown and the Afro-American Folk Tradition," *Studies in the Literary Imagination* 7, No. 2 (Fall 1974): 133–34

JOANNE V. GABBIN   From 1936 to 1940 Brown focused his attention on the Federal Writers' Project. It was the only period in his career that was not devoted primarily to teaching. Brown brought to his position as editor of Negro affairs a ranging knowledge of literature, criticism, and American folklore with which he tied an enthusiastic interest in American history and culture. In a period in which economic woes had turned ethnic and racial groups against each other and in which the knowledge of the past and present cultural and sociological situation of Blacks was still very much in the dark ages of myth and propaganda, Brown's energy and talents would be sorely tested. ⟨. . .⟩

However, as it happened, Brown made his single most enduring contribution to the Writers' Project in the early days of his association. As an editor on the national staff, Brown was involved in writing the massive guidebook, *Washington: City and Capital*. To this volume, which was published in 1937, Brown contributed the essay, "The Negro in Washington." At once an assessment and indictment of the plight of Blacks in Washington, the essay was Brown's master stroke of social criticism.

In recounting the story of Black life in the nation's capital—the blight of the slave yards ensconced in the seat of justice, the notorious alley system

and the crime, squalor, and disease that laced it, the network of self-help organizations, and the separate and unequal participation of Blacks in the workings of Washingtonian "democracy," Brown was able to suggest the city's duplicity. He began his essay with the subtle statement of irony by the Irish poet Thomas Moore who had visited the capital when it was still young. Moore's lines brought into sharp contrast two societies, one slave and one free, and the medley of "manacles and rights" that characterized them. Continuing this theme, Brown traced the incongruous co-existence of the ideal of freedom and justice and the often disappointing reality of Black life in the District. He wrote about Blacks' zeal for education which was fired by the knowledge of a tradition of overcoming insuperable odds, he cited their political apathy resulting from decades of disenfranchisement, and he noted their seething rage, the result of a heritage of frustration and despair, which threatened to erupt in riots and racial violence. "In this border city, Southern in so many respects, there is a denial of democracy, at times hypocritical and at times flagrant." And more important, Brown, with the controlled, perceptive view of an insider, a Black Washingtonian, presented for the first time the vibrant portrait of a people whose very presence represented a challenge to Washington's democracy.

Brown's essay sent shock waves through the seats of government. In April, 1939, Representative Frank Keefe, a Republican from Wisconsin, charged the central office with allowing "the influence of communistically inspired agitators" to insert "insidious propaganda" into the Washington guide. This was not the first time that a Project publication had been labeled Communist propaganda. Sterling Brown, who had the final responsibility for the essay, found himself the object of FBI scrutiny for the next five years.

The so-called "insidious propaganda" that Brown allowed in the guide was a report that George Washington Parke Custis, foster son of President Washington and father-in-law of Robert E. Lee, had left a tract in Arlington to his Black daughter, Maria Syphax. Though Keefe labeled this material libelous and "stimulating racial intolerance," Brown considered his charges as "badges of honor." Ulysses Lee, who had assisted Brown with much of the original research, was amazed that so much was being made of this issue, especially since the Custis family had not objected to the material mentioned in the essay. He was also surprised to find the files missing when he returned to the public library at which he had done his original research. Unfortunately, in the subsequent edition of the Washington guide, for all its brave facts and revelations, this episode was deleted.

Joanne V. Gabbin, *Sterling A. Brown: Building the Black Aesthetic Tradition* (Westport, CT: Greenwood Press, 1985), pp. 67, 81–82

JOHN S. WRIGHT   In a talk before the Conference on the Character and State of Studies in Folklore in 1946, Brown looked back at his years
with the ⟨Federal Writers'⟩ Project: "I became interested in folklore," he
recalled, "because of my desire to write poetry and prose fiction. I was first
attracted by certain qualities I thought the speech of the people had, and
I wanted to get for my own writing a flavor, a color, a pungency of speech.
Then later I came to something more important—I wanted to get an understanding of people" ⟨"The Approach of the Creative Artist," *Journal of
American Folklore*, October 1946⟩. Respectful of the scientific approaches
to folklore but untroubled by any definitional or procedural obstacles that
might block his access to the "living-people-lore" of, for instance, so fascinating a tribe as urban jazzmen, Sterling Brown had developed a flexible,
functionalist approach to folklore. It was an approach that, as Alan Lomax
advocated in the same session, rejected views of the folk "as ignorant
receptacles for traditions and ideas which they do not themselves understand,
and which make very little sense until they are pieced together and explained
in historical terms by the comparative scholar." Such an approach instead
saw folklore as "equipment for living," saw the folklorist as performing not
only an archaeological role but one of recording a vigorous human tradition,
and it recognized that "the best interpretations of folklore may be obtained
in the end from the folk themselves."

In the early forties, the conviction that the folk may be their own best
interpreters became one of the trademarks of Sterling Brown's series of
articles on black folk expression. His synoptic essay in *The Negro Caravan*
in 1941, on the sources and genres of black oral literature, stands even
today as the single best introduction to the subject because, in threading
its way through all the scholarship and interpretative quandaries of the
previous decades, it maintains its balance by never falling victim to the
disorienting proposition that, as Newman White had myopically insisted,
"the Negro never contemplated his low estate."

"Nigger, your breed ain't metaphysical," one of the voices in Robert Penn
Warren's poeticized fable "Pondy Woods" had proclaimed, confronting New
Negroes with the old stereotype of the crusading New South. "Cracker,
your breed ain't exegetical," Sterling Brown responded dialectically, as he
outlined a critique that treated black forms as distillations of communal
mind and *ethos*. In his essays on the blues in particular, Brown treated the
products of folk imagination as *self-conscious* wisdom—tragic, comic, ironic,
shrewd, emotionally elastic and attitudinally complex, capable of supporting
a variety of stances toward life, and resistant, as such, to ideological straitjack-
eting or implications of naïveté. Worldly and self-aware, the spirit of the

blues, he submitted, is defined by the songs themselves, in lines which assert that "the blues ain't nothin' but a poor man's heart disease" or "the blues ain't nothing but a good man way, way down" or, more obliquely, "Woke up this morning, blues walking round my bed / Went in to eat my breakfast, blues was all in my bread." The blues fused stoicism in a concrete, *metaphoric metaphysic:* It was a frank Chaucerian *attitude* toward sex and love that kept even the bawdiest authentic blues from being prurient and pornographic. It was "elemental *honesty,*" "depth of *insight,*" and *sophistication* about human relations that lay behind their appeal across caste lines. It was *imagination* making the love of life and the love of words memorably articulate which turned the best blues into potent lyric poetry.

John S. Wright, "The New Negro Poet and the Nachal Man: Sterling Brown's Folk Odyssey," *Black American Literature Forum* 23, No. 1 (Spring 1989): 102–3

CHARLES H. ROWELL and STERLING BROWN

ROWELL: In his preface to the 1968 combined edition of your *Negro Poetry and Drama* and *The Negro in American Fiction*, Robert Bone describes your studies as "comprehensive surveys in the field of iconography, tracing through American fiction, poetry, and drama the changing image of the Negro. Their real focus," he says, "is a sociology of literature, the politics of culture. They are concerned with the uses and abuses of the image-making function in society." It seems to me that your studies are more than a sociology of literature.

BROWN: I think Bone is straining there to stay in with the New Critics. It was an ungenerous introduction. He speaks, for instance, of its not being great criticism, but who in the world is writing great criticism today? You keep the phrase "great criticism" for Matthew Arnold. . . . Bone knew that the book was written for a very definite purpose, and he knew that the book had to be confined. You see, I could not write at full in the book. This was part of a series and it had to be a certain length and so I was kept down. But I have just as much literary criticism of many of those novels as he did in his work that was devoted only to Negro novelists. He worked under me. I was his advisor on his thesis, you see. He knew that. I never meant the book as great criticism. I stated what the book was. I had two jobs to do: I had to evaluate the books, and I also had to discuss certain stereotypes. I think I did in the book as a whole. I think I did it better in *The Negro in American Fiction* than in *Negro Poetry and Drama*, because the confined space was just too much to handle poetry and drama. I got in trouble with Alain Locke who edited the series because I ran *The Negro in*

American Fiction a little longer than I was supposed to; I was to keep it to 125 pages, but I just couldn't do it. A lot of stuff I wanted to say I . . . but my criticism of single works is running through *Opportunity*, a magazine. . . . Anybody who ever took a course from me knows that I always paid attention to the craft of fiction. I pay attention to craft, but in this book there was a whole lot to do, to cover the range of American fiction with all of its stupidity and all of its ignorance and to prove it. Most people just dismiss books and say that the white man is stereotyping. Of course, I didn't do that. Most of the white books were stereotyping blacks, but some were not. ⟨. . .⟩

ROWELL: I think Zora Neale Hurston ⟨. . .⟩ accused Locke of not having a real knowledge of black folk tradition. She said he sat and listened to what other people said and then wrote about the tradition.

BROWN: That is not fair. She was angry. She fell out with most men. She was an early women's liberator. She was kicked around. She had much right on her side. She fought with Langston Hughes. She fought with Dick Wright, and she wrote a bad attack on Dick Wright. She fought with me, because of what I said about her novel called *Their Eyes Were Watching God*, which I think is a good novel. It is the best thing she ever did. *Mules and Men* is second. On that novel I stressed the hard lives the people on the farm lived. I stressed this from a viewpoint of social realism. She said I wasn't going to make a communist out of her, and she turned away. But now, see, she was all involved with Fannie Hurst with whom I had a big quarrel. Zora Neale [Hurston] was involved with literary patrons in New York City. I never had any dealings with those people. I don't even know what's in the Van Vechten business at Yale because of my distaste for the man. I have tremendous distaste for Carl Van Vechten. I don't ever say "Harlem Renaissance," because it wasn't Harlem. It was the "Negro Renaissance." What I disliked was black writers' reliance on Van Vechten and their acceptance of his leadership. I felt that he set up an exotic primitive. His heart was not really with us in that he was a voyeur. I'm doing an essay in this book for the Howard University Press called "Carl Van Vechten Voyeur and Robert Penn Warren Informer." Both of them are very false friends. Zora Neale was very friendly to us. She came here, sat on the sofa there [*pointing*] and told us some stories. She was a beautiful storyteller; she was a wonderful actress. She knew a lot of stuff, and I think she's been underestimated. She battled, and she battled men. She had some grouch. I didn't know this little thing you told me about Locke. ⟨. . .⟩ She couldn't get along with people.

Charles H. Rowell and Sterling A. Brown, " 'Let Me Be with Ole Jazzbo': An Interview with Sterling A. Brown," *Callaloo* 14, No. 4 (Fall 1991): 803–5

❖ Bibliography

Outline for the Study of the Poetry of American Negroes. 1931.

Southern Road. 1932.

The Negro in American Fiction. 1937.

Negro Poetry and Drama. 1937.

The Negro Caravan: Writings by American Negroes (editor; with Arthur P.
      Davis and Ulysses Lee). 1941.

The Last Ride of Wild Bill and Eleven Narrative Poems. 1975.

Collected Poems. Ed. Michael S. Harper. 1980.

Countee Cullen
1903–1946

COUNTEE CULLEN was born Countee Leroy Porter on May 30, 1903. He was probably born in Louisville, Kentucky, although both New York City and Baltimore have been cited as his birthplace. Orphaned in childhood, he was raised by a Mrs. Porter, who was probably his grandmother. In his teens he was adopted by African Methodist Episcopal Church minister Frederick Asbury Cullen and his wife Carolyn, who encouraged Countee to write. Cullen's poetry was already seeing regular publication by the time he graduated from New York University in 1925. His first book, *Color*, appeared that same year; Cullen won the Harmon Gold Award and critical praise for his Keatsian verse and his frank depiction of racial prejudice.

Cullen received an M.A. from Harvard in 1926, then became assistant editor of the National Urban League journal *Opportunity*. In 1927 he published the acclaimed *Copper Sun* and *The Ballad of the Brown Girl*, and edited *Caroling Dusk*, a historic anthology of work by black poets. The following year he married Yolande Du Bois, daughter of W. E. B. Du Bois, and traveled to Paris on a Guggenheim Fellowship. Yolande filed for divorce before he returned; their relationship inspired the tortured love poetry of *The Black Christ and Other Poems* (1929).

Back in the United States, Cullen published a novel of life in Harlem, *One Way to Heaven* (1932), and a verse adaptation of Euripides' *Medea* (1935). From 1932 to 1945 Cullen settled into a teaching position at a junior high school in New York City. In 1940 he married Ida Mae Roberson and published a children's book of verse entitled *The Lost Zoo (A Rhyme for the Young, but Not Too Young)*, sharing the bylines with his pet, Christopher Cat. Two years later he published a prose work for children, *My Lives and How I Lost Them* (1942), which purported to be Christopher's autobiography. Cullen authored and coauthored a number of plays, most of which were not published; his own selection of his best poems was published posthumously as *On These I Stand: An Anthology of the Best Poems of Countee Cullen* (1947). Countee Cullen died on January 9, 1946. Gerald Early has now assembled Cullen's collected writings under the title *My Soul's High Song* (1991).

▨ *Critical Extracts*

RUDOLPH FISHER   The danger of falling below expectations is especially great in the case of the poet who turns novelist. Mr. Cullen, whose poetry is admired by so many, and whose danger therefore is the greater, has nevertheless challenged fate successfully. His first novel ⟨*One Way to Heaven*⟩ goes over. ⟨. . .⟩

Be not misled by the announcement that "this is a mad and witty modern picture of high life in Harlem." That part of it which portrays the "high life" of Harlem is not important and seems even less important than it might, because its effect is completely submerged in the larger and simpler realities of the rest of the book. This is because Mr. Cullen has chosen to change his method and his viewpoint in dealing with the upper level. Here he becomes a caricaturist, suppressing all his sympathies, sketching with a sharp and ungracious pen. But the less pretentious folk he has treated gently and delicately, in color. This juxtaposition of two so different subjects so differently handled is somehow like exhibiting a lovely pastel and a cartoon in the same frame.

But the pastel has in it such clear beauty as has escaped the eye and hand of most other portrayers of darkskinned America. Aunt Mandy, devout Christian and equally devout believer in fortune-telling cards; Mattie, simple child, torn between love for her Sam and love for her Jesus, and Sam, beloved rascal wiping the slate clean with a last splendid lie—these are real people who, for all the author's lightness of touch, live, breathe, and convince. Their creator, however, has achieved more than that. He has given them a beauty which his predecessors have been reluctant to dwell upon— a black beauty. And this beauty emanates so unmistakably from within these characters that it should never again be necessary for anyone to insist that fine souls are really white inside.

Rudolph Fisher, "Revealing a Beauty That Is Black," New York Herald Tribune Books, 28 February 1932, p. 3

MARTHA GRUENING   Countee Cullen's first novel ⟨*One Way to Heaven*⟩ pictures two widely different phases of Negro life. The first tells, competently if not profoundly, the story of the simple servant girl, Mattie, whose conversion to religion is precipitated by the trick of a cheerful rascal Sam Lucas. Sam's racket is playing the revivals by shamming conversion and the renunciation of an evil life for what he can get out of it. Almost simultaneously with her conversion Mattie falls in love with the man to whom she feels she owes her salvation. She never dreams of doubting his good faith. Sam, who also loves her, lacks the courage to disillusion her and is considerably embarrassed after their marriage by finding that she still expects him to behave as though he were saved. While the story is original and amusingly told in a style that is pleasing, direct, and economical, its emotional implications seem somehow to have eluded the writer. It is frequently almost but never wholly touching, retaining throughout a quality of sketchiness and understatement as if he himself never quite realized Sam and Mattie as beings of flesh and blood. But if his treatment of these two is somewhat external it is, at least, firm and consistent. When their lives dovetail with that of Mattie's employer, Constantia ⟨sic⟩ Brandon, and her circle of Harlem sophisticates he becomes curiously wavering and unsure, so that the reader remains uncertain if his detailed and gleeful chronicling of their puerilities is prompted by admiration or derision. They hardly seem interesting enough for the space he gives them and the structure of the book suffers by their inclusion.

Martha Gruening, "Two Ways to Harlem," *Saturday Review of Literature*, 12 March 1932, p. 585

UNSIGNED   The first collaboration of Countee Cullen and his cat turned out to be a blend of verse and prose, *The Lost Zoo*, not quite like anything in the extensive special literature of cat fancy. The present work ⟨My *Lives and How I Lost Them*⟩, which does away with poetry and speaks altogether from cat experience from early kittenhood on, is quite as hard to classify. It cannot be called a children's book, for adults will read it— but children will read it too: all that is needed to let a person into its audience is a capacity for being interested in cats. This involves a capacity for respect: Mr. Cullen respects Christopher, and does not feel it beneath his dignity to become his interpreter through life.

Through eight-and-a-fraction lives, in fact; the prime contribution of the work to natural history is that cats themselves reckon their ages not by years but by the numbers of lives they have already lost or have yet to go. Christopher's went fast at first: his earliest action was to plump out of the opera hat in which he was born—along with a family as many as the Muses— and practically knock his breath out. Each of his adventures culminates in some such narrow escape: it is like a polite, graceful comic-strip series in which the hero squeezes out of some tight squeak in every instalment. The tales may be fabulous, but they are not fables: the cats may and do speak a charming English among themselves, but they act and think according to their kind—and any one who enjoys their kind will chuckle his way through picture-strewn pages that leave their hero still going strong.

Unsigned, "Mancat Tales," New York Herald Tribune Books, 19 April 1942, p. 13

ROBERT BONE   Countee Cullen has often been described as one of the more "respectable" Renaissance novelists, with the implication that he avoided the "sordid" subject matter of the Harlem School. Nothing could be farther from the truth. Cullen neither exploited low-life material for its own sake nor avoided it when it served his artistic ends. Though distinctly not of a Bohemian temperament, neither did he value respectability above art. His mischievous sense of humor and his penchant for satire differentiated him from those Renaissance novelists who were forever defending the race before the bar of white opinion. Countee Cullen had a lighter and truer touch, which speaks for itself in *One Way to Heaven*. ⟨. . .⟩

The aesthetic design of the novel consists of variations on a theme. The moral ambiguity of Sam's life and death is echoed in the lives of the other characters. Both the evangelist and the Reverend Drummond are sincere men of God, but neither is above a little showmanship for the Lord's sake. The devout but worldly wise Aunt Mandy takes a practical view of Mattie's marital difficulties: "Sometimes when the angels is too busy to help you, you have to fight the devil with his own tools." Even Mattie, "the gentle servitor of the gentlest of all the gods," abandons her Jesus for a conjure-woman and nearly murders her husband's mistress. The author's point is clear: he that is without sin among you, let him cast the first stone at Sam Lucas.

Sam's cards and razor provide an appropriate symbol for Cullen's theme. Like people, the cards and razor contain potentialities for either good or evil. In Sam's hands, they are the tools of deceit, yet they are no less the instruments of Mattie's salvation. In Mattie's possession, they are the sacred tokens of her conversion, but in her extremity she uses them as a voodoo charm. When Sam asks Aunt Mandy, "Don't you think that cards is evil?" she replies, "It all depends on the kind of cards you have and what you do with them." In Cullen's view the moral universe is infinitely complex. Form is unimportant; there is more than one way to heaven.

Robert Bone, The Negro Novel in America (New Haven: Yale University Press, 1958),
pp. 78–79

STEPHEN H. BRONZ   Cullen's satire ⟨of middle-class black Americans in *One Way to Heaven*⟩ is friendly; Mrs. Brandon is never malicious and is a most likeable character. But it was satire directed towards Negroes, and doubtless some of Cullen's own patrons, and such satire stands practically alone in the Harlem Renaissance. Perhaps most important is the relationship of the satire to Cullen's own career. From Harlem newspapers and from the portrayal of Mrs. Brandon and her friends, we can infer that the middle class Harlem reading public often bought Harlem Renaissance books without reading them, and were more concerned with the fact of a Negro literary renaissance than with the quality of the writings. Much of Cullen's own poetry, with its chauvinism and cloistered romanticism, seems to have been directed towards this group. And Cullen himself indulged almost as much as Mrs. Brandon in using high-sounding language where simple Anglo-Saxon words would suffice.

By 1932, judging from *One Way to Heaven*, Cullen was disillusioned, detached, and a little quizzical towards the Harlem Renaissance. Here he was breaking his own dictum that Negro writers should present only the appealing sides of Negro life to the white public. And he was ridiculing a main source of his own reputation, along with the excesses of chauvinism the Harlem Renaissance produced. The same year *One Way to Heaven* was published, Cullen, to the surprise of many, announced that he was joining the Foster and Ford Committee, a group of prominent writers, including Lincoln Steffens, Sherwood Anderson, Edmund Wilson, and Langston Hughes, pledged to support the Communist ticket in the 1932 elections. Cullen seems to have backed the Communists without great passion; there is scant indication of socialist leanings in his writings and, in 1939, he remarked that he had "never been interested in politics."

Stephen H. Bronz, *Roots of Negro Racial Consciousness: The 1920's: Three Harlem Renaissance Authors* (New York: Libra Publishers, 1964), pp. 63–64

DARWIN T. TURNER   Cullen had given credit for coauthorship of *The Lost Zoo* to Christopher, a cat who recited stories which he had heard from his father. In his final book ⟨*My Lives and How I Lost Them*⟩, Cullen, identified merely as the amanuensis of Christopher, created a work possibly superior stylistically and structurally to his earlier novel. In Chris, Countee Cullen found a *persona* he could enjoy. Confident of the innate superiority of his species, as he informs the reader in his first words, Christopher suffers neither the frustration nor the inhibitions of his human scribe;

consequently, he is relaxed and self-assured as he explains to his dull-witted human amanuensis how he lost his first eight lives.

Comparison of the two individuals emphasizes the fact that Cullen escaped into a character free from the restrictions which had limited his own life. Christopher's father was a distinguished aristocrat: he traced his lineage to Noah's ark. His mother, though a commoner, provided all the love a growing kitten needs. With two brothers, three sisters, and a patient father determined to educate his kittens in proper "cateristics," Christopher, even during his first life, enjoyed family security which the human Cullen lacked until he was in his teens. Furthermore, not harassed by fellow cats urging him to be realistic or imagistic or chauvinistic or atavistic, or to write about this or that (Cullen did not dare to prescribe Chris's subjects), Chris was free to tell his story as he wished—sentimentally, suspensefully, digressively.

Reared with his brothers, and sisters—intellectual Claude, vain Claudia, lazy Carlos and Carole, and his twin Christobelle, young Chris learns the lessons essential to an educated cat: how to lap milk, how to wash, how to purr, and how to arch. He also learns that fathers sometimes err. Having been warned to avoid Rat, who is not a respectable companion for a cat, Chris meets Rufus the Ritten (if a young cat is a "kitten," then surely a young rat is a "ritten"; so Chris reasons with Humpty-Dumpty's logic). Similarly, Rufus's father has warned him against cats. Despite their prejudiced parents, Chris and Rufus become friends when they discover that they have identical habits and interests. ⟨. . .⟩

Even in these books for children, however, Cullen never persuades a reader that he has evaded consciousness of the discriminations against blacks. Christopher is a "catitarian" (and perhaps more sensitive than a "humanitarian"); consequently, in *The Lost Zoo*, he expresses chagrin that his ancestor had signed the petition against Sammie Skunk. Sammie's only fault was that, at times, he smelled bad; as Cullen reminded readers in *One Way to Heaven*, the allegedly offensive odor of blacks is a reason which bigots have used to justify the segregation of blacks and whites. Furthermore, in *My Lives and How I Lost Them*, Christopher Senior's explanation of why Chris must avoid rittens directly echoes bigots' pronouncements of the inferiority of black people.

Darwin T. Turner, "Countee Cullen: The Lost Ariel," *In a Minor Chord: Three Afro-American Writers and Their Search for Identity* (Carbondale: Southern Illinois University Press, 1971), pp. 85–87

JAMES O. YOUNG   In his novel, *One Way to Heaven* (1932),
Countee Cullen consciously satirized much of the black middle class which
Jessie Fauset had satirized unconsciously. Cullen was particularly interested
in the professional class which was a part of the Renaissance in Harlem.
The novel is ostensibly about Sam Lucas, a one-armed itinerant panhandler
who makes his living as a professional convert at revival meetings. ⟨. . .⟩
Cullen contrasted Sam's charlatanry with that of Reverend Johnson, who
was really as much a faker as Sam and a bit more hypocritical. These themes
of doubt and salvation were common in Cullen's poetry and were well
developed in this novel even if the lives and character portraits of Sam and
Mattie were not. But Cullen was more interested in Sam's spiritual salvation
than in the reality of his life.

Although the story of Sam and Mattie was supposed to be the central
theme of *One Way to Heaven*, Cullen devoted at least half of the novel to
Constancia Brandon, a Harlem socialite whose soirees were a "must" for
the fashionable crowd. Constancia's only relationship to the main plot of
the story resided in the fact that Mattie was her maid. On this flimsy pretext
Cullen was able to satirize the Negro middle class and much of the Harlem
Renaissance. Although Constancia is shamelessly frivolous, she undoubtedly
reflects Cullen's viewpoint. ⟨. . .⟩

⟨. . .⟩ Constancia chimes in with what was a typical Renaissance attitude.
"I could go white if I wanted to," she explains, "but I am too much of a
hedonist; I enjoy life too much, and enjoyment isn't across the line. Money
is there, and privilege, and the sort of power that comes with numbers; but
as for enjoyment, they don't know what it is. . . ." For Constancia, blackness
means a hedonistic style of life; it does not mean grinding poverty and
ignorance. Her attitude is the same as that romantically expressed by Cullen
in some of his Renaissance poetry.

It is significant that a novel in which the plot is concerned with the
salvation of "low-life" figures, the most carefully delineated character is
a middle-class socialite. Had Cullen attempted to contrast the world of
Constancia with that of Sam and Mattie, there would have been sufficient
rationale for his emphasis on her. But Cullen did not do this. Unlike the
young realists who appear later in the thirties, he did not take a close look
at the substance of "low-life" existence to give it the reality which he gave
to Constancia's parties.

James O. Young, *Black Writers of the Thirties* (Baton Rouge: Louisiana State University
Press, 1973), pp. 207–9

ARTHUR P. DAVIS   Countee Cullen's single novel, *One Way to Heaven* (1932), belongs to that group of Harlem novels—among them *Nigger Heaven*, by Van Vechten, and *Home to Harlem*, by McKay—which sprang up during the Renaissance. The works of McKay and Van Vechten played up the more sensational aspects of the black ghetto and were obviously written to cater to the new taste in America for the exotic and primitive. Cullen's novel is more of an "inside" book than McKay's. It was designed to appeal primarily to a Negro audience. As a result, Cullen's picture of Harlem, covering not just the lower-class but the middle-class "intellectuals" as well, is closer to the *real* Harlem than McKay's, though certainly not as colorful. Some critics have blamed Cullen for his twofold approach, claiming that he wrote *two* novellas rather than *one* novel. The charge is not wholly warranted because the two plots do touch *naturally*—that is, they are not forced beyond plausibility.

Cullen was trying to tell a story about the religious life of the ordinary Harlemites, a story of their church life and what it meant to them. Knowing that this would be a one-sided account, he used contrapuntally the activities of the class to which he belonged to sharpen the focus on both groups. One must remember that Cullen was a part of both the worlds he delineated. Reared in the parsonage of one of Harlem's largest churches, Cullen, even though he was an intellectual, learned to respect the function of the church in Negro life. On the other hand, he was one of the First Fruits of the Harlem Renaissance, but he was never too close to the movement not to see that it too had its charlatans who were just as phony as Sam Lucas the "religious" hustler. Cullen is satirizing both groups, but it is not a strong attack; it is rather the gentle "ribbing" of one who sees the foibles but appreciates the essential worth of both segments of Harlem life.

Arthur P. Davis, *From the Dark Tower: Afro-American Writers 1900–1960* (Washington, DC: Howard University Press, 1974), pp. 81–82

ALAN R. SHUCARD   The fact is that Cullen does get closer to the folk in *One Way to Heaven* than in any of his other published works, but he could never, even in his novel, quite put aside all of his innate reserve. In his poetry he could never draw convincingly from the music or speech of the Afro-American folk tradition as Langston Hughes did, nor, as a rule, did it interest him to try to do so. In the novel, however, Cullen brings to life certain folk types—Sam, the fake-convert trickster, with his tools of the devil, playing cards and an "evil shining" razor; old reliable matriarchal Aunt Mandy; the preachers, the Reverend Clarence Johnson and the Reverend Drummond. The dialogue is always carefully in character, and Cullen introduces bits of black folklore, notably when Sam lies dying. As Sam rests in his deathbed, he hears Aunt Mandy explain to Mattie, "If you're going to be lost, you still has visions, but of another kind. It gets dark and you can't see with your eyes open, and sometimes the devil himself comes for you like a big black bat or a snake." The life that the folk tradition breathes into the novel, plus the poetic precision and power that Cullen was able to bring to its best passages—Sam's initial sham conversion, Constancia's circuses, Sam's death scene—raise *One Way to Heaven* a notch above many other Harlem Renaissance novels, including Hughes's *Not Without Laughter*, a book close to it in texture, theme, and publication date.

Part of Cullen's success in delineating the broadly comic character of Constancia Brandon resides in the contrast between the common black folk speech of Aunt Mandy and the love-plot people and the highfalutin self-parody of Constancia. Part of his limitation, however, resides in her speeches sounding perilously close to Cullen's own high-flown observations as omniscient narration, as a remark of Constancia serves to illustrate:

> When at one of her parties it was suggested to her in fiery language by a spirited young Negro, who could neither forget nor forgive, that a celebrated white writer present was out to exploit and ridicule her, she had replied:
> "Ridicule me? If he contrives to depict me as I am, he shall have achieved his first artistic creation. If he does less, he shall have ridiculed himself. And besides, don't be so damnably self-conscious or you will be miserable all your life. Now vouchsafe me your attendance and let me introduce you to the ogre who has come to devour us all."

Constancia Brandon may abuse the language by drowning it in champagne; she may, at times, be overbearing and a silly romantic, but she is no empty-headed Mrs. Malaprop. She could doubtless find things to do with her time that would better profit humankind, but what she does, she does well, even with a certain sensitivity. Her aim, like that of Countee Cullen himself, is to provide a formal, civilized, artistic forum in which the two races can meet, exchange ideas—even wrongheaded ones—and ultimately gain sufficient respect for each other to live together in a nation free of barbarism.

Alan R. Shucard, *Countee Cullen* (Boston: Twayne, 1984), pp. 76–77

GERALD EARLY   Perhaps Countee Cullen was never fully understood as a poet or a writer because he has never been understood fully as
a man. There is, and always has been, a quality of unknowableness, sheer
inscrutability, that surrounds Cullen and is no more better symbolized, in
a small yet telling way, than by the official, but varied accounts of his
height. His passport of both 1934 and 1938 gives his height as 5' 3", his
selective service registration card of 1942 lists him as 5' 10" and his war
ration book number 3, issued when Cullen was forty years old, gives his
height as 5' 7".

We still do not know where Cullen was born. In James W. Tuttleton's
extremely useful essay "Countee Cullen at 'The Heights,' " which provides
a detailed account of Cullen's undergraduate years at New York University,
we learn that Cullen's college transcript, for which he himself provided the
information, lists his place of birth as Louisville, Kentucky. This transcript
was dated 1922. In the biographical headnote which Cullen wrote for his
selections of poetry—contained in his own anthology of black poetry, *Caroling Dusk*—Cullen says he was born in New York City. ⟨. . .⟩ Whatever the
reasons for Cullen changing the place of his birth, one inescapable fact is
that in 1922 he was a relatively obscure but well-regarded black student
with some poetic inclination and ability. By 1927 only Edna St. Vincent
Millay surpassed him in American poetry circles in critical and press attention. Here with the whole business of birthplaces, we have the difference
between the public and private Cullen. ⟨. . .⟩ Around the time of Cullen's
death, stories began to circulate that he was born in Baltimore (one writer
even says that Mrs. ⟨Ida⟩ Cullen confirms this). But there is little evidence
for this ⟨. . .⟩ Oddly Beulah Reimherr, who had done the most extensive
research into Cullen's childhood and young life, finds no record of anything
about him in either the Louisville or Baltimore Bureau of Vital Statistics.
There is, moreover, no birth record for Cullen in New York City. The
mystery remains unsolved. ⟨. . .⟩

⟨. . .⟩ Cullen was very taken with the art of lying or why else did he have
his cat tell tall tales in *The Lost Zoo* and in *My Lives and How I Lost Them*,
or why else did he translate *The Medea*, which is all about the lying of two
lovers, or why write a novel where the central character lies about his
conversion? The entire scope of Cullen's 1930s career seems a long philosophical and aesthetic examination of the many creative and nefarious
dimensions of lying, deception, and hypocrisy. Also the interest in lying as
art explains the character Sam Lucas in *One Way to Heaven*. Many critics
have felt that Cullen named the character Lucas because his own real name
may have been Lucas. What makes a great deal more sense is that the con

man character of Cullen's novel is named after the great black stage minstrel of the same name who was very popular in the early 1900s. As the novel turns on Lucas's ability to act, to play out a conversion that he does not feel convincingly, both in the beginning of the novel and at the novel's end, we see instantly that the book centers on the art of lying, and what black person was a better professional liar than a minstrel with his degrading, low, stereotypical comedy? In fact, the connection between the novel's character and the minstrel is made even more explicit by the symbols of the playing cards and razor, which Sam tosses away at every conversion. These are of course the props of the stereotypical black minstrel.

> Gerald Early, "Introduction," *My Soul's High Song: The Collected Writings of Countee Cullen, Voice of the Harlem Renaissance*, ed. Gerald Early (New York: Doubleday, 1991), pp. 6–8, 59

▨ Bibliography

Color. 1925.

The Ballad of the Brown Girl: An Old Ballad Retold. 1927.

Copper Sun. 1927.

Caroling Dusk: An Anthology of Verse by Negro Poets (editor). 1927.

The Black Christ and Other Poems. 1929.

One Way to Heaven. 1932.

The Medea and Some Poems. 1935.

The Lost Zoo (A Rhyme for the Young, but Not Too Young). 1940.

My Lives and How I Lost Them. 1942.

On These I Stand: An Anthology of the Best Poems of Countee Cullen. 1947.

My Soul's High Song: The Collected Writings of Countee Cullen, Voice of the Harlem Renaissance. Ed. Gerald Early. 1991.

Jessie Redmon Fauset
1882–1961

JESSIE REDMON FAUSET was born on April 26, 1882, in Fredericksville, New Jersey, the seventh child of the Reverend Redmond Fauset and Anna Seamon Fauset. Fauset's mother died when she was very young, and her father married Belle Huff shortly thereafter. Fauset graduated from the Philadelphia Girls' School in 1900 but was then denied admission to a local teacher's college; she applied to Bryn Mawr, but the school put off a decision about accepting her and urged her to accept a scholarship that she received from Cornell University. In 1905 Fauset became the first black woman to graduate from Cornell.

Wishing to become a teacher, Fauset was denied a position in the Philadelphia school system. She went to Baltimore, where she taught for a year before going to Washington, D.C., where she taught French for fourteen years at the M. Street High School (later named Dunbar High). In 1912 she began contributing articles to the *Crisis*, and in 1919 was urged by its editor, W. E. B. Du Bois, to move to New York to become the literary editor of the journal. In that same year she received a master's degree in French from the University of Pennsylvania.

All four of Fauset's novels deal with racial prejudice. In *There Is Confusion* (1924), the protagonist, Joanna Marshall, battles against discrimination against her and her lover. In *Plum Bun* (1929), a black woman attempts to "pass" as white but in doing so becomes ostracized from her darker-skinned sister. *The Chinaberry Tree* (1931) tells of a love affair between a freed slave woman and her white master. *Comedy, American Style* (1933) is a bitter novel in which the alienating effects of "passing" are again emphasized.

Fauset's later life was uneventful. In 1927 she began teaching at the De Witt Clinton High School in New York City. Having married Herbert E. Harris in 1929, she moved with him to Montclair, New Jersey, in 1939. Fauset retired from teaching in 1944, by which time she had abandoned writing and ceased to be involved in black intellectual circles. She died on May 2, 1961.

Although her novels received mixed reviews upon publication and were dismissed after her death, Fauset is now gaining praise for her "novels of manners," which attempt to depict the role of the black middle class in white society. She is also attaining recognition as an early black feminist for her sharp portrayals of black women.

▨ Critical Extracts

MONTGOMERY GREGORY ⟨*There Is Confusion*⟩ is a sincere effort to view the life of the race artistically—objectively. Heretofore we have either imbibed the depreciatory estimates of our enemies or gulped down the uncritical praise of our friends. We have not dared to see ourselves as we really are nor have our artists treated our life as material to be objectively moulded into creations of beauty. Our writers of the younger school have been the first to catch this sound point of view and upon their strict adherence to it in the future depends the successful development of Negro art and literature. Even Miss Fauset occasionally errs in this respect and diverts the reader's interest from her story into bypaths of special pleading against race prejudice.

Technically *There Is Confusion* more than reaches the level of the better class of contemporary American fiction. The romance of Peter Bye and Joanna Marshall, etched on the interesting background of the family life of the cultured Negroes of Philadelphia and New York, is well conceived and skillfully executed. The plot holds the interest of the reader unflaggingly to the end. There are fewer faults of construction than might be expected in a "first" novel. It may be said, however, that the latter part of the story is the least convincing. ⟨. . .⟩ The characters are cleverly drawn, especially that of Maggie Ellersley who, like Brutus, although not intended to be the leading figure in the story, certainly appeals to the reviewer as the finest achievement of the author. On the other hand, the white Byes, young Meriweather Bye and his grandfather seem to make their entrance on the stage as supernumeraries and to add little to the value of the novel.

Montgomery Gregory, "The Spirit of Phyllis Wheatley," *Opportunity* 2, No. 6 (June 1924): 181–82

GWENDOLYN BENNETT   Many there will be who will quibble
over Miss Fauset's fortunate choice of incident by which all her characters
and happenings are brought together ⟨in *Plum Bun*⟩. This will not be altogether fair since "Truth is stranger than Fiction." I'll wager that Miss Fauset
could match every incident in her book with one from real life. I imagine
this book will be even less convincing to members of the white race. They
still conjecture over the possibility of a Negro's completely submerging
himself in their group without a shadow of detection. But here again Miss
Fauset can smile benignly up her writing sleeve and know whereof she
speaks.

The author of this story does not seem concerned to a great extent with
the inner workings of her characters. In this day of over-emphasis on the
mental musings of people and things this may be called a fault but I feel
that the author was wise in not delving into the mental recesses of people
to whom so much was happening. This is a task for a master psychologist.
Who can tell how the minds of white Negroes work? Is it not a problem
to stump the best of us that they who are so obviously white should feel a
"something" that eventually draws them from the luxury and ease of a life
as a white person back to the burden of being a Negro? Miss Fauset tells
her story, packed as it is with the drama and happenings of a life of passing
for white. It is better for the story that Miss Fauset avoided too much of a
metaphysical turn.

Gwendolyn Bennett, [Review of *Plum Bun*], *Opportunity* 7, No. 9 (September 1929):
287

RUDOLPH FISHER   In *The Chinaberry Tree* it is the author's stated
intention to "depict something of the home life of the colored American
who is not being pressed too hard by the Furies of Prejudice, Ignorance and
Economic Injustice." What are Negroes like, she asks, when they are not
thinking of the race problem? ⟨. . .⟩

The pace of the book is leisurely, the writing simple and unaffected, the
descriptions clear-cut with occasional touches of poetry, and the depictions
of home life unexciting enough to be entirely credible. Characterizations
are lightly drawn. The primary interest is situational. It is plain that anybody,
whatever his degree of pigmentation, would have done just about what
these people did in this situation. It is plain, as Miss Fauset intended it to
be, that these Americans are not essentially different from other Americans.

The inclusion of the restaurant scene, in which Laurentine and Denleigh are embarrassed by a white waiter, is unfortunate, because it is so much more dramatic than most of the other episodes, yet has no place in either the story or the author's voluntary exclusion of the race problem. Otherwise the chronicle travels smoothly toward its climax.

Rudolph Fisher, "Where Negroes Are People," *New York Herald Tribune Books*, 17 January 1932, p. 6

GERALD SYKES   The greater portion of *The Chinaberry Tree* is devoted to the love affair of two colored high-school students who do not know that they are brother and sister. This dramatic theme, singularly enough, is the least exciting part of the story. We learn most about Miss Fauset's book as a whole not through Melissa and Malory, or their narrowly averted incestuous marriage; but through Laurentine, the beautiful apricot-colored dressmaker who is the book's real heroine and symbol of the world it depicts; Laurentine, who sat as a child under the Chinaberry Tree and wondered why other children, either white or black, wouldn't play with her. ⟨. . .⟩

⟨Laurentine⟩ is brought up in comparative luxury, but is a double outcast. And the passion which animates her is closely allied to the passion which animates the book. What does the illegitimate mulatto grow up to want? Respectability. Once she cries: "Oh God, you know all I want is a chance to show them how decent I am." This might serve as the motto for *The Chinaberry Tree*. It is so much the book's real theme that once recognized it helps to explain the striking gentility of certain passages, as well as the exceptional importance attached to small material comforts that most white people would take for granted. ⟨. . .⟩ The book attempts to idealize this polite colored world in terms of the white standards that it has adopted. And here lies the root of Miss Fauset's artistic errors. When she parades the possessions of her upper classes and when she puts her lovers through their Fauntleroy courtesies, she is not only stressing the white standards that they have adopted; she is definitely minimizing the colored blood in them. This is a decided weakness, for it steals truth and life from the book. Is not the most precious part of a Negro work of art that which is specifically Negroid, which none but a Negro could contribute?

We need not look far for the reason for Miss Fauset's idealization. It is pride, the pride of a genuine aristocrat. And it is pride also that makes her such a remarkable psychologist. However many her artistic errors, Miss

Fauset has a rare understanding of people and their motives. ⟨. . .⟩ Every great psychologist has been a thin-skinned aristocrat. Considering the position of a sensitive, educated Negro in America, it is no wonder then that an aristocrat like Miss Fauset has idealized her little world, has made it over-elegant! Inspired by the religious motive which so many Negro writers seem to feel, she has simply been trying to justify her world to the world at large. Her mistake has consisted in trying to do this in terms of the white standard.

Gerald Sykes, "Amber-Tinted Elegance," *Nation*, 27 July 1932, p. 88

MARY ROSS   As in her earlier stories, Miss Fauset writes ⟨in *Comedy: American Style*⟩ with dignity and force about a group of Americans whose lives are little known because they are lived quietly in their own comfortable homes and by preference within intellectual and cultivated circles of their own kind. The tragedy of the book—the title is ironic—is not primarily the limitations imposed by white people but the consequences of those restrictions and prejudices in the interrelationships of these people of mixed blood. ⟨. . .⟩

The lights and shades of the story are harsh, occasionally so violent as to lessen their effectiveness. So strong is the conflict that moves in and about these people that at times situation rather than character becomes the fulcrum of the narrative, and type rather than individuality crops up even in details. The flowers at Theresa's party were "of the aster variety." Her partner was "the type that holds his partner lightly but firmly." . . . If Miss Fauset, however, does at times insist on the situation of her characters so strongly as a little to overwhelm their personalities, that defect is one aspect of the book's virtues: its vigor, honesty and warmth.

Mary Ross, "The Tragedy of Mixed Blood," *New York Herald Tribune Books*, 10 December 1933, p. 6

WILLIAM STANLEY BRAITHWAITE   I daresay, as a novelist Miss Fauset would be credited with many a virtue by certain eminent critics, if she were but obliging enough to ignore the *conventional* ideals and triumphs of the emerged group of the Race. She has been infinitely more honest with her characters than her critics have cared to acknowledge, indeed, to have even suspected. After all, her purpose, whether conscious or unconscious, has been to create in the pages of fiction a society which outside the Race simply did not and preferably, in accordance with granted assumption, could not be allowed to exist. The spirit, the consciousness of pride, dignity, a new quality of moral idealism, was breathed into this darker body of human nature by her passionate sympathy and understanding of its ironic position in the flimsy web of American civilization. Only recently a review of Miss Fauset's latest novel, *Comedy: American Style,* in one of the leading Negro papers, resented what the reviewer charged was a lack of climax and philosophy in the recital of Olivia Cary's color obsession and the pain it brought her family. The philosophy in this latest novel, as in the three earlier ones, is not, and never was intended to be, an imposed thesis upon the surface of the story. Miss Fauset is too good an artist to argue the point; to engrave a doctrine upon so intangible an element as Truth, or to array with a misfitting apparel of rhetoric the logic which like a pagan grace or a Christian virtue should run naked as the wind through the implications that color and shape the lives of her characters and their destinies. I am afraid that Negro critical eyes as well as white critical eyes have quite often failed to discern these implications in which are contained the philosophy of a tremendous conflict; the magnificent Shakespearean conflict of *will* and *passion* in the great tragedies from *Titus Andronicus* to *Coriolanus;* for in this Negro society which Miss Fauset has created imaginatively from the realities, there is the *will,* the confused but burning *will,* to master the *passion* of the organized body of lusty American prejudice.

    William Stanley Braithwaite, "The Novels of Jessie Fauset," *Opportunity* 12, No. 1 (January 1934): 26–27

ABBY ARTHUR JOHNSON   In all ⟨Fauset's⟩ stories, she portrayed black professionals, as she would in her novels. Her main characters were industrious physicians, teachers, engineers and business men and women. With the fiction published in *Crisis* and with the novels which followed, Fauset seemed preoccupied with matters far different from the concerns of her essays. She wrote of people who lived on the borderline of two races and who flirted with the idea of passing. She pictured structured and elite black communities, modeled after old Philadelphia. At times, she showed distinctions among Negro socialites living in Philadelphia, Washington and Baltimore. With such interests, she wrote to a small segment of the black population. Her essays, however, appealed to a wider audience. She discussed issues and events germane to the black community, such as

Pan-Africanism. She applauded novels and poems written about ghetto life and Afro-Americans who were not formally educated. She used a rhetoric which modulated from enthusiasm to anger and which attracted the more militant young Negroes.

Robert Bone thought Fauset a "paradox" because he could not see a connecting link between her work as editor and as novelist. Fauset's work does, nevertheless, mesh into a comprehensible unit. As an educated woman, open to many interests, she could appreciate the changes and new expressions in the Negro community. She tried, while on the staff of *Crisis*, to encourage diversified interests and to attract a large number of readers. When composing fiction, however, she could only write from herself, of the life she knew best.

Abby Arthur Johnson, "Literary Midwife: Jessie Redmon Fauset and the Harlem Renaissance," *Phylon* 39, No. 2 (June 1978): 149

CAROLYN SYLVANDER   If the promotion of the Black middle class, the displaying to whites the virtues of socially and economically select Blacks, is not Fauset's central concern in *There Is Confusion*, it is necessary to look at the book carefully, without preconceptions, to discover the themes which do emerge. There *is* exploration of the kind of racial discrimination and inheritance a Northern urban Black faces. Beyond this exposure, Fauset looks at a wide range of characters and actions possible given American slave history, racially mixed heredity, and various environments. In quiet, subtle ways, she tiptoes across "acceptable" topics and conclusion to explore alternatives to her society's sometimes limiting norms. ⟨. . .⟩ Black folk material as the basis for possible uniqueness in Black artistry is a nicely underplayed but repeated idea present in Joanna's use of a Black children's dance-game as her entree into the theatrical world. The entire book explores the limited alternatives available to women, especially Black women, and also show women breaking out of these limits without being excessively punished. If it is desirable to select "a" theme in *There Is Confusion* to include all the above thematic ideas, probably the best statement of it would be: Life is a corrective, individually and collectively, experientially and historically.

⟨. . .⟩ There is no one "best" way to be Black and to be Black American ⟨in *There Is Confusion*⟩. Such moralizing is foreign to Fauset's interest in individual psychology. There are, however, often "better" ways for each character to deal with his or her life, and the book's plot becomes the story of how each major character makes the discoveries and changes which lead him or her to the best individual perspective. This plot pattern is essentially the same as that of the traditional British *Bildungsroman* where growth of character is depicted in the movement from disordered and confused value distinctions to a revelation of true differences.

> Carolyn Sylvander, *Jessie Redmon Fauset, Black American Writer* (Troy, NY: Whitson, 1981), pp. 152, 155

DEBORAH E. McDOWELL   To be sure, ⟨Fauset⟩ was traditional to some extent, both in form and content, but as Gary de Cordova Wintz rightly observes, "in spite of her conservative, almost Victorian literary habits," Fauset "introduced several subjects into her novels that were hardly typical drawing room conversation topics in the mid-1920s. Promiscuity, exploitative sexual affairs, miscegenation, even incest appear in her novels. In fact prim and proper Jessie Fauset included a far greater range of sexual activity than did most of Du Bois's debauched tenth."

When attention is given Fauset's introduction of these challenging themes, it becomes possible to regard her "novels of manners" less as an indication of her literary "backwardness" and more as a self-conscious artistic stratagem pressed to the service of her central fictional preoccupations. Since many of Fauset's concerns were unpalatable to the average reader of her day and hence unmarketable in the publishing area, the convention of the novel of manners can be seen as protective mimicry, a kind of deflecting mask for her more challenging concerns. ⟨. . .⟩

In addition to the protective coloration which the conventional medium afforded, the novel of manners suited Fauset's works in that the tradition "is primarily concerned with social conventions as they impinge upon character." Both social convention and character—particularly the black female character—jointly form the nucleus of Fauset's literary concerns. The protagonists of all of her novels are black women, and she makes clear in each novel that social conventions have not sided well with them but, rather, have been antagonistic.

Without polemicizing, Fauset examines that antagonism, criticizing the American society which has institutionalized prejudice, safeguarded it by law and public attitude, and in general, denied the freedom of development, the right to well-being, and the pursuit of happiness to the black woman. In short, Fauset explores the black woman's struggle for democratic ideals in a society whose sexist conventions assiduously work to thwart that struggle.

Critics have usually ignored this important theme which even a cursory reading of her novels reveals. This concern with exploring female consciousness is, in a loose sense, feminist in impulse, placing Fauset squarely among the early black feminists in Afro-American literary history. ⟨. . .⟩ A curious problem in Fauset's treatment of feminist issues, however, is her patent ambivalence. She is alternately forthright and cagey, alternately "radical" and conservative on the "woman question." On the one hand, she appeals for women's right to challenge socially sanctioned modes of feminine behavior, but on the other, she frequently retreats to the safety of traditional attitudes about women in traditional roles. At best, then, we can grant that Fauset was a quiet rebel, a pioneer black literary feminist, and that her characters were harbingers of the movement for women's liberation from the constrictions of cultural conditioning.

> Deborah E. McDowell, "The Neglected Dimension of Jessie Redmon Fauset," *Conjuring: Black Women, Fiction, and Literary Tradition*, ed. Marjorie Pryse and Hortense J. Spillers (Bloomington: Indiana University Press, 1985), pp. 87–88

MARY JANE LUPTON   As a woman writer writing *as* a woman, if not *for* women, Fauset was likely to notice the aesthetic relationship between skin and clothing. This kind of thing is important in the daily lives of most middle-class women and, I would guess, of many middle-class men. By including chestnut hair and puff sleeves in her fictional world ⟨of *Comedy: American Style*⟩, Fauset is only being true to the tradition of American realism. But these concerns are not merely gratuitous. ⟨. . .⟩ Fauset uses clothing as a way to articulate not only the racial differences between mother and daughter but also the hierarchy of class/race which she then addresses throughout the novel: the desperate, white-identified mother; the middle-class daughter caught between her mother's notion of "a cruder race" and her own desire to be like her peers; the Black-identified Marise in her "glowing, gay colors"; the naturally gifted, light-skinned Phebe, who is already accumulating capital.

Fauset also captures ⟨. . .⟩ the excitement of adolescent anticipation, the thrill of choosing for oneself what one is to wear and not to wear. Thus Teresa is transformed, through clothing, from "mouse" to warm, young Black woman. As she puts her "nice narrow feet" into "bronze slippers," she becomes reminiscent of Cinderella on her way to the ball—in this case a neighborhood party. It is in fact Teresa's crowning moment. For later she meets a young Black man, falls in love, and is humiliated by her mother, who forces her into a disastrous marriage. The Cinderella Line has reversed itself irrevocably.

Near the end of the novel Olivia visits her daughter: "She found Teresa silent, pale, subdued, the ghost of her former self, still wearing dresses taken from the wardrobe which her mother had chosen and bought for her during her last year of college. The dresses had been turned, darned, cleaned, and made over, combined in new and bizarre fashions. Their only merit was that they were quite large enough. Certainly Teresa had put on no weight." ⟨. . .⟩ Teresa's "former self" has become a "ghost." She is colorless, as are the dresses of unnamed hue. Literally, Teresa has lost her color, her racial identity. As Phebe had once made Teresa the beautiful party dress, so now Teresa makes over and mends the dress of her past. This recreation of identity, however, operates within the closed system of passing or death.

In dismantling the Cinderella Line, Fauset leaves as an alternative a more feminist bourgeois hope in the person of Phebe the dressmaker. Through hard work and through affirmation of her Blackness, Phebe manages to rise from shopgirl to highly paid fashion designer. Her marriage to Teresa's brother, Christopher, is part of the bargain.

Mary Jane Lupton, "Clothes and Closure in Three Novels by Black Women," *Black American Literature Forum* 20, No. 4 (Winter 1986): 412–13

HAZEL V. CARBY   Deborah McDowell, in her introduction to the new edition of Fauset's *Plum Bun*, pleads for a sympathetic consideration for the progressive aspects of Fauset's novels, especially in relation to her implicit critique of the structures of women's romance. However, I would argue that ultimately the conservatism of Fauset's ideology dominates her texts. In *The Chinaberry Tree*, for example, which focused on two women, the movement of the text is away from the figures of isolated unmarried mothers and daughters supporting themselves through their own labor, toward the articulation of a new morality and community in which black women were lifted from the abyss of scandal and gossip, which threatened to overwhelm them, by professional black men who reinserted them into a newly formed and respectable community as dependent wives. The individual and collective pasts of the female characters led them to flounder in the waters of misdirected desires; their history was anarchic and self-destructive. The future, within which the women could survive, was secured when they were grounded, protected, and wrapped around by decent men. In order to represent a new, emergent social group, Fauset by necessity had to sever ties with the past; the characteristics of the new class were those of individual success and triumph over ties to and previous interpretations of history. ⟨. . .⟩ in *The Chinaberry Tree*, Fauset constructed a chaotic and irrelevant history to which the heroes, not the heroines, brought a new order and meaning. The new middle class both emerged from and changed previous history and its interpretations; the forces of previous history alone could not provide a basis for its future. Fauset adapted but did not transcend the form of the romance. It is important that her work did reveal many of the contradictory aspects of romantic conventions of womanhood, but her imaginary resolutions to what were social contradictions confirmed that women ultimately had to be saved from the consequences of their independence and become wives.

> Hazel V. Carby, *Reconstructing Womanhood: The Emergence of the Afro-American Woman Novelist* (New York: Oxford University Press, 1987), pp. 167–68

ELIZABETH AMMONS   The dilemma that Fauset struggles with in *There Is Confusion*, and then throughout her career as a novelist, is basic. In order to survive at all in the art world, an environment both racist and sexist, Joanna must be ruthless and utterly self-centered. In order to be part of the black community, she must think of the group, must be willing to put other people's needs before her own. She must be able to give and to receive love, which involves compromise, sacrifice, and often self-denial. This choice—between making art or being a loving, embraced member of the black community—is unbearable. It translates most directly into having her art or having a relationship with a man. ⟨. . .⟩ The latter choice, which Fauset backs, *is* conservative and *is* disappointing. But given the alternative that she says America constructs, what is the choice? Joanna can center herself in the white world—as a second-class performer, bear in mind—and remain a hard, driven, selfish person who arrogantly sets herself up above Maggie Ellersley and Peter Bye and whose plot spins off individualistically on its own self-absorbed trajectory. Or she can make a choice in favor of staying within the black community, a choice that encourages rather than discourages the giving, feeling parts of her personality and, significantly, keeps her plot line tangled with Maggie's and Peter's.

This theme of art dehumanizing the black woman artist and cutting her off from the black community, especially from sisters and mothers, is so strong and persistent in Fauset's fiction that it very likely articulates her own deepest fears as an African American woman trying both to stay connected to her heritage and community and to succeed as a publishing artist in a commercial and intellectual world dominated and controlled by whites. The protagonist or strongest central character of each of Fauset's four novels is a black woman who physically or emotionally (or both) cuts herself off from her mother—a rupture which, according to Fauset, constitutes becoming "white." ⟨. . .⟩

For Fauset ⟨. . .⟩ this issue of mother-daughter separation was virtually insoluble. The problem was largely political. As an artist, Fauset had to live in the white world, had no choice but to separate herself from her mother's life. The white world ⟨. . .⟩ was where the publishers, editors, and reviewers were. To create—to express herself as an artist—Jessie Fauset had to pass over into that territory, learn its rules, play its games, adopt its values. Her preoccupation with "passing" in her fiction, like that of other turn-of-the-century black women writers, was not simply deference to a conventional theme in African American literature. It was one way of talking about her own impossible situation as a black woman writer in a publishing world controlled by whites. As an artist, the black woman writer constantly had to "pass," to cross over into and negotiate the white world, whether she wanted to or not. She had to leave her mother. What did that mean? What would that do to her as a woman? As a human being?

> Elizabeth Ammons, "Plots: Jessie Fauset and Edith Wharton," *Conflicting Stories: American Women Writers at the Turn into the Twentieth Century* (New York: Oxford University Press, 1991), pp. 151, 154

VASHTI CRUTCHER LEWIS   Fauset does not give Laurentine much racial consciousness ⟨in *The Chinaberry Tree*⟩; however, she is the vehicle through which the reader experiences culture of the Harlem Renaissance. Fauset, a 1920s resident of Harlem, allows Laurentine and the reader to become acquainted with the famed Lafayette Theatre, notable restaurants, and nightclubs of the era. Laurentine's uneasiness with an animated black folk culture in Harlem cabarets indicates Fauset's own rejection of it, as well as that of Du Bois, her mentor. Fauset provides Laurentine with thoughts that mirror some of the reasons why Du Bois was critical of Harlem Renaissance writers who depicted what he considered the exotic in African-American culture. Laurentine is puzzled over reasons why anyone would frequent clubs where a "drunken black woman . . . slapped a handsome yellow girl," and "where a dark, sinuous dancer, singing . . . making movements . . . postured . . ." ⟨. . .⟩

Fauset's portrayals of African-American women who are overly class- and color-conscious must be assessed against the stereotypical images that bordered on the caricature that white writers were using to depict men and women of African descent at the turn of the twentieth century and later. It is not difficult to understand her desire to reverse those images and to write with sympathy and understanding about an educated African-American middle/upper class to which she belonged. The real paradox of so much interest in class-conscious mulattoes is, as suggested earlier, that they depict a select group who have never been representative in number or lifestyle of African-American women. And just as important, the highly class-conscious mulatto has served to perpetuate a divisiveness within African-American culture since the genesis of a mulatto caste in the era of American slavery. Certainly the very images of black female arrogance so often depicted in Fauset's novels are ones that have caused "other Blacks to look at mulattoes as Greeks whose gifts should always bear watching."

Vashti Crutcher Lewis, "Mulatto Hegemony in the Novels of Jessie Redmon Fauset," *CLA Journal* 35, No. 4 (June 1992): 382–83, 385–86

Bibliography

There Is Confusion. 1924.
Plum Bun: A Novel without a Moral. 1929.
The Chinaberry Tree: A Novel of American Life. 1931.
Comedy: American Style. 1933.

Rudolph Fisher
1897–1934

RUDOLPH JOHN CHAUNCEY FISHER was born on May 9, 1897, in Washington, D.C., to John Welsley Fisher and Glendora Williamson Fisher. Shortly after Rudolph's birth the Fishers moved to Providence, Rhode Island. In 1915, after graduating with honors from Classical High School, Fisher began attending Brown University, where he studied English and biology, eventually earning B.A. and M.A. degrees among numerous other honors.

Fisher's aptitude for science and literature made him uncertain what career to pursue, but he determined to give up neither. He entered Howard University Medical School in 1920 and graduated with the highest honors in 1924. During this period he wrote his earliest piece of short fiction, "The City of Refuge," published in the *Atlantic Monthly* in 1925. In this story a poor Southerner flees to Harlem to escape the law. The theme of Southern blacks migrating to Harlem in search of better lives would recur in Fisher's work. His use of realism, irony, and comedy in "The City of Refuge" established him as an influential member of the Harlem Renaissance. In the same year, "South Lingers On," "Ringtail," and "High Yaller" were published in various periodicals, establishing Fisher's reputation as an emerging literary voice.

In 1925, in addition to pursuing his literary interests, Fisher accepted a National Research Council fellowship to attend Columbia University's College of Physicians and Surgeons, where he began writing for medical journals. Fisher incorporated his medical knowledge into some of his works, such as "Blades of Steel" (1927) and *The Conjure-Man Dies* (1932).

In 1927 Fisher established his medical practice in New York and published four short stories: "The Promised Land," "Blades of Steel," "The Backslider," and "Fire by Night," all vividly set in his Harlem surroundings. In the same year, Fisher also published an essay about Harlem in the 1920s called "The Caucasian Storms Harlem," in which he asserts that Harlem has become a popular new playground for white entertainment and exploitation. This proved to be a popular topic throughout the Harlem Renaissance, as many black artists depended on the finances of white patrons.

In 1928 Fisher published his first novel, *The Walls of Jericho*, which presented a realistic portrayal of Harlem without focusing on the seedy aspects. The novel was generally well received by black and white critics— praised for its sound construction, ironic tone, and witty turns of phrase. In 1932 Fisher's second novel appeared, *The Conjure-Man Dies: A Mystery Tale of Dark Harlem*. Fisher incorporated his protagonists from *The Walls of Jericho* into the first all-black detective story. The novel is marked by Fisher's humor and given to philosophical and scientific musings.

From 1932 until his death in 1934 Fisher, aside from holding various positions and offices in the medical community, further expanded his literary achievements with the publication of two children's stories, "Ezekiel" (1932) and "Ezekiel Learns" (1933), which examine a Southern boy's adjustment to life in Harlem. Fisher was also working on a dramatization of *The Conjure-Man Dies*, which was produced posthumously in 1936 at the Lafayette Theatre in Harlem and received mixed reviews. Rudolph Fisher died on December 26, 1934.

◈ *Critical Extracts*

WALTER F. WHITE   ⟨. . .⟩ here ⟨in *The Walls of Jericho*⟩ is the genuine meat of Harlem which needs none of the highly seasoned, largely untrue sensationalism which has given so distorted a picture of Harlem Negroes when some others have attempted to write of that region of Manhattan. More, Dr. Fisher has caught the real humor of the Negro and the result is the first light novel of Negro life. There is none of the black-face Jewishness of Octavus Roy Cohen and none of the cornfield, elephantine funniness of Irvin Cobb. Also Dr. Fisher steers successfully from lugubrious tragedy. There are overtones of the difficulties of the Negro existence, even in Harlem, but one senses more than reads of the perils of a black skin in America. ⟨. . .⟩

In this reviewer's opinion *The Walls of Jericho* is one of the best novels of Harlem yet written. Its language, its humor, its psychology are true to the type it depicts. As a first novel or as any other one it is an excellent achievement. One ventures the bromidic prophecy that its author is one whose future work will profitably be watched with interest and anticipation.

Walter F. White, "A Fine Novel of Negro Life," *New York World*, 5 August 1928, p. 7M

ARTHUR P. DAVIS   Dr. Fisher in *The Conjure-Man Dies* has adhered to ⟨the standard detective novel⟩ formula, and by so doing places his work subject to the standard criticism of detective fiction. In the opinion of the reviewer, the work measures up in every detail to the current works of this type. ⟨. . .⟩

The character of Frimbo, the conjure-man, is a striking creation on the part of Rudolph Fisher. It is in this character that Dr. Fisher makes excellent use of his psychiatric training. The clinical diagnosis of paranoia subtly interwoven with the African sexual ritual as presented in this character is rather unusual in detective fiction. Rudolph Fisher's medical education again stands him in good stead when he allows Dr. Archer to brilliantly interpret a clue based solely on the division of types in the human blood. ⟨. . .⟩

The Conjure-Man Dies is hailed as the first detective story written by a Negro and the first to have all Negro characters. These "firsts," always interesting to us as Negroes at this period, are all very well indeed and should be noted. But far more important is the fact that this first adventure in this new field is a thoroughly standard one. One's final impression at the close of the book is that the author has a subtle, brilliant mind—one peculiarly adapted to this type of fiction. The book is not merely a good Negro detective story. It is a good detective story.

Arthur P. Davis, "Harlem Mysterious," *Opportunity* 10, No. 10 (October 1932): 320

LANGSTON HUGHES   The wittiest of these New Negroes of Harlem, whose tongue was flavored with the sharpest and saltiest humor, was Rudolph Fisher, whose stories appeared in the *Atlantic Monthly*. His novel, *Walls of Jericho*, captures but slightly the raciness of his own conversation. He was a young medical doctor and X-ray specialist, who always frightened me a little, because he could think of the most incisively clever things to say—and I could never think of anything to answer. He and Alain Locke together were great for intellectual wise-cracking. The two would fling big and witty words about with such swift and punning innuendo that

an ordinary mortal just sat and looked wary for fear of being caught in a
net of witticisms beyond his cultural ken. I used to wish I could talk like
Rudolph Fisher. Besides being a good writer, he was an excellent singer,
and had sung with Paul Robeson during their college days. But I guess Fisher
was too brilliant and too talented to stay long on this earth. During the
same week, in December, 1934, he and Wallace Thurman both died.

> Langston Hughes, *The Big Sea: An Autobiography* (New York: Alfred A. Knopf, 1940),
> pp. 240–41

ROBERT BONE   In essence there are two Rudolph Fishers: a con-
forming and rebelling self. The conformist is the middle-class child who
obeys his parents when they warn him not to play with roughnecks. He is
the brilliant student who is Class Day Orator at Brown, who graduates
summa cum laude from Howard, and establishes his professional identity as
Dr. Fisher. The rebel is Bud Fisher, frequenter of speakeasies and cabarets,
who has always envied the bad kids on the block and who writes about
them in his fiction. The rebel self, however, is more mischievous than
dangerous, and after a period of bohemian adventures settles into middle-
class routine. Such is the psychodrama at the heart of Fisher's cruder tales.

In a second group of Fisher tales, the theme of breach and reconciliation
is projected outward on the social plane. Here the author strives to repair
various divisions that threaten to destroy the black community. Thus "Ringtail" is concerned with the enmity between West Indian and native-born
American; "High Yaller," with the potentially disruptive force of a light
complexion; "Blades of Steel" and "Common Meter" with the social class
division that separates the "rat" from the "dicty." In each of these contexts,
Fisher's aim is to exorcise the demons of disruption and cement the ties of
racial solidarity. 〈. . .〉

A third group of Fisher stories is explicitly concerned with the Great
Migration. As the author's imagination reaches out to embrace the historical
experience of millions, his art assumes a greater density of texture and
complexity of vision. On the plane of history, moreover, Fisher's divided
self proves to be an asset: it enables him to project and then to mediate
the central value conflict of his age. For the split personality of the Baptist
preacher's son mirrors the divided soul of the Southern migrant. Both are
torn between a set of standards that are traditional, religious, and puritanical,
and a series of temptations that are novel, secular, and hedonistic.

Fisher's strength lies in the fact that he is genuinely torn between these value systems. His very ambivalence allows him to achieve a delicate balance of rural and urban, traditional and modern values. His divided psyche generates a powerful desire to mediate, or reconcile, or find a middle ground, which is the source of pastoral. He is therefore able to encompass the paradoxes of change and continuity, of spiritual loss and gain, which are the essence of the Great Migration. He is able to record the disappointments and defeats of the Southern migrants, and yet to celebrate the hope which survives their disillusionment.

> Robert Bone, *Down Home: A History of Afro-American Short Fiction from Its Beginnings to the End of the Harlem Renaissance* (New York: G. P. Putnam's Sons, 1975), pp. 153–54, 156

LEONARD J. DEUTSCH   The Harlem Renaissance was occasioned, as observers have remarked, by a "demographic shift of the Black population that is perhaps the most crucial fact of Afro-American history in the twentieth century" 〈Richard Barksdale and Keneth Kinnamon〉. Fisher took a lively look at this "crucial fact" and explored many of its consequences and manifestations in his short stories. 〈. . .〉

Fisher's various concerns include the adjustments blacks were called upon to make after the Great Migration from the South; Harlem's complex and ambiguous meaning for black people—as mecca and hell; and Harlem's spirit of joy and competitiveness as reflected in its jazz. His concerns also include the intraracial and interracial problems and the identity crises fomented by differences in pigmentation. Serious as these themes are, all of Fisher's stories combine a characteristic balance of folk humor and ironic commentary. Taken together, they provide some of the basic documents—both historical and literary—of the period. 〈. . .〉

Fisher's language is the medium of a rich style which informs while it entertains and elates. The author had appended a glossary of Harlemese to *The Walls of Jericho* but the stories burst with definitions too—some serious and helpful, others wry and ironic. If the reader does not know what a *dicty*, the *dozens*, a *rent party*, the *camel walk*, and other artifacts of black culture are, he will be enlightened by reading the stories in which they are explicitly defined. *Lodi*, the reader learns, is an urban game played by flicking bottle caps across a chalked-up sidewalk. An *airshaft* is "a horrible channel that separates one tall house from the next, a place of unpleasant noises and odors." Fisher makes distinctions: *cabarets*, for example, are "not like theatres or concert halls. You don't just go to a cabaret and sit back and wait to be entertained. You get out on the floor and join the pow-wow and help entertain yourself." With sardonic wit, Fisher informs the reader that *trap-windows* on a door are "designed against rent-collectors and other robbers." And along with Eben in "The Backslider," the reader learns that a *police raid* was a "legalized rampage upon blind pigs and gambling dens; that a blind pig was a place where you could buy bootleg liquor if you were wealthy enough; yes, that Harlem as a whole might be considered a prolific sow without eyes"—a wry definition and social commentary all rolled into one. ⟨. . .⟩

In 1933 Fisher averred: "Outsiders know nothing of Harlem life as it really is. What one sees in a night club or a dance hall is nothing, doesn't scratch the surface—is in fact presented solely for the eyes of outsiders. . . . But what goes on behind the scenes and beneath the dark skins of Harlem folk—fiction has not found much of that yet." Fisher was an insider who scratched deeply. The stories reveal his love for the people of Harlem and the diversity of talents they represent. They also help us to understand the quality of life of Harlem during the Renaissance period.

Leonard J. Deutsch, " 'The Streets of Harlem': The Short Stories of Rudolph Fisher,"
Phylon 40, No. 2 (June 1979): 159–60, 170–71

CHIDI IKONNÉ   Most of Rudolph Fisher's short stories are raw slices of life cut from a parcel of life not far from where Carl Van Vechten was to cut his *Nigger Heaven* later. Perhaps that was why, after the appearance of his novel *The Walls of Jericho* in 1928 *The Crisis* charged that "Mr. Fisher does not yet venture to write of himself and his own people; of Negroes like his mother, his sister and his wife." Thinking mainly of his short story "High Yaller," Allison Davis had earlier placed him among writers whom he called "Van Vechtenites." Fisher's pre–August 1926 stories, therefore, are important to our study not only because of their Negro self-expressiveness, but also because they offer an insight into how easy it is to exaggerate the white influence—especially Carl Van Vechten's—on the young Harlem Renaissance writers.

Rudolph Fisher's "High Yaller," which won the first prize for fiction in *The Crisis* literary contest of 1925, is a realistic approach to an aspect of the emotional mulatto theme. There is no attempt on the part of the author to sell the near-white Evelyn Brown as an angel. Her inclination towards men of lighter color is made obvious and understandable. Once she can no longer bear the burden of the label "colored," she does the logical thing: she passes.

Commenting on "High Yaller," Charles Waddell Chesnutt said, "its atmosphere may be a correct reflection of Negro life in Harlem, with which I am not very familiar." A self-confident portrayal of the less sophisticated Negro life by a member of the Negro race, "High Yaller" contains elements and intraracial problems which were as unacceptable to some black assimilationists as they were unnoticeable to the non-initiated observer. These include (1) the subconscious envy underneath the molestation of the so-called "high yaller"; (2) the secret desire of some of the darker Negroes to be fairer, as revealed in Jay's cynical remarks:

> Point is, there aren't any more dark girls. Skin bleach and rouge have wiped out the stain. The blacks have turned sealskin, the sealskin are light-brown, the light-browns are all yaller, and the yallers are pink.

(3) the unscrupulousness of some Negroes who thickened the color-line, as in Hank's, in the interest of their personal advancement; and (4) the Harlem parlance, including the "gutter-talk" of people like the boy whom Jay throws out of a room for being disorderly.

The prize mentioned above was awarded to "High Yaller" in October 1925. Before then, however, Walter White, starting from 10 February 1925, had tried unsuccessfully to place it with *American Mercury*, *Harper's* and the *Century* whose editors were his friends. It will be difficult, therefore, to accuse Fisher of having written "High Yaller" to please white faddists.

Chidi Ikonné, *From Du Bois to Van Vechten: The Early New Negro Literature, 1903–1926* (Westport, CT: Greenwood Press, 1981), pp. 179–81

JOHN McCLUSKEY, JR.   As a Harlem Renaissance writer, Rudolph Fisher is unique in his dramatizations of encounters that still shape the personalities of urban black communities and their institutions. The impact of black migration on the cities and the impact of the cities on blacks have been profound. Despite the seeming euphoria of the white night-visitors and both black and white publicists for Harlem cabarets and the Renaissance, there were sides of Harlem life that were not so well-known. In his first autobiography, *The Big Sea*, Langston Hughes said, ". . . ordinary Negroes hadn't heard of the Negro Renaissance. And if they had, it hadn't raised their wages any." We are indebted to Fisher for giving us a glimpse of that side far from the glitter, indeed for showing both the anguish and the comedy of new arrivals trying to find their balance and seek clarity and purpose in a new and often indifferent city.

⟨. . .⟩ Rudolph Fisher treats the concerns of the workaday Harlemite. As a fiction writer he joins Langston Hughes in shaping a significant body of work which consistently reflects the trials and triumphs of the early urbanization of Black America. In Fisher's more mature short fiction, bridges are sought and a dialogue develops. In the dialogue between young and old, between traditional and modern, the result can be understanding and growth.

> John McCluskey, Jr., " 'Aim High and Go Straight': The Grandmother Figure in the Short Fiction of Rudolph Fisher," *Black American Literature Forum* 15, No. 2 (Summer 1981): 59

ELEANOR Q. TIGNOR   In 1925, Rudolph Fisher broke into the predominantly white publishing world with his short story "City of Refuge," a triumph commented upon in this letter from Arna Bontemps:

> I saw and talked with Rudolph Fisher frequently between the date of publication of his story "City of Refuge" in the *Atlantic Monthly* and August 1931 when I left New York. Earlier Countee Cullen had told me that someone had told him about a young writer from Washington who had just sold two stories to the *Atlantic*. This news had gone around literary circles in Harlem, because up to that time none of the young writers of the New Negro Movement had been able to break into that magazine. So the stage was set, and "City of Refuge" created something of a sensation.

Bontemps further remarked:

> I met Bud, as we called Fisher, some months later, and I remember when he set up his practice on 7th Avenue. . . . Bud was clever, facile. . . . His health seemed exceptional, so his early death was more than shocking. He was indeed part of the spirit of the Harlem Renaissance.

Before his premature death at the age of thirty-seven, seventeen other of Dr. Fisher's short stories had been published, five of which are vignettes with the all-inclusive title "South Lingers On" (called by Alain Locke "Vestiges, Harlem Sketches" and given four subtitles: "Shepherd, Lead Us," "Majutah," "Learnin'," and "Revival"), published in the 1925 special issue of *Survey Graphic* and two of which are little known children's stories with the same young boy (Ezekiel) as the central character, published in *Junior Red Cross News*. The other published stories came out in subsequent issues of *The Atlantic*, in *McClure's*, *The New York News*, *Opportunity*, *Crisis*, and *Story*. Through a communication with Rudolph Fisher's sister, Pearl Fisher, I discovered four unpublished stories: "The Lost Love Blues," a three-part, 46-page story; "The Lindy Hop," a story in three versions (an incomplete handwritten manuscript of fourteen pages, with many revisions, and two typewritten manuscripts of three parts each, with major differences only in the ending, one having twenty-five pages and the other, which seemed to be Fisher's preference, having twenty-three); a 19-page story, "Across the Airshaft," and the 24-page "The Man Who Passed" or "False Face" (with both titles and a third undecipherable one deleted). These manuscripts, as well as a slightly modified version of "Miss Cynthie," better known in its published form, all are undated but were typed by the same Broadway typing and mimeographing service.

Thematically, Fisher's short fiction might be grouped in five somewhat overlapping categories: vestiges of the South and the promise of Harlem ("City of Refuge," "Lost Love Blues," and the five-part "South Lingers On," including "Shepherd, Lead Us," the Jake Crimshaw sketch, "Majutah," "Learnin'," and "Revival"); the conflict of generations ("Fire by Night," "The Lindy Hop," and "Miss Cynthie"); foul play in Harlem ("Guardian of the Law," "The Backslider," "Blades of Steel," "Across the Airshaft," and "Common Meter"); problems of prejudice ("High Yaller," "The Man Who Passed" or "False Face," "Dust," and "Ringtail"); the child in Harlem ("Ezekiel" and "Ezekiel Learns"). ⟨. . .⟩

Rudolph Fisher moved most of his short stories toward a happy or optimistic resolution, frequently with an O. Henry-style surprise twist. Detached but at the same time accepting of human foibles and able to see the comic side of human nature, Fisher was a sympathetic recorder and translator of Harlem life of the 1920s and early 1930s. As Arna Bontemps stated, "He was indeed part of the spirit of the Harlem Renaissance."

Eleanor Q. Tignor, "The Short Fiction of Rudolph Fisher," *Langston Hughes Review* 1, No. 1 (Spring 1982): 18–19, 24

JOHN McCLUSKEY, JR.   The sacred-secular tension, the grandmother figure who symbolizes the Southern tradition hoping to transplant human concerns in Harlem, the lyric which drives the plot toward a wholesome resolution—all of these are brought together in one of Fisher's last

published pieces, the popular "Miss Cynthie." The story was published in
Story magazine in June 1933 and reprinted in *Best American Short Stories,
1934*. Since that time, the piece has been included in numerous anthologies
of Afro-American literature. In the opening scene, Miss Cynthie arrives in
New York to visit her grandson Dave Tappen. She has never been to New
York; indeed, she has never traveled far from her hometown in North
Carolina. She has learned that Dave is a success and she anticipates his
achievement within a respectable profession. When he invites her to the
theater to watch the musical review in which he stars, she is disappointed.
A stage career is not her idea of a respectable profession. Her disappointment
quickly shifts to shock as she watches Dave and her girl friend cavort on
the stage much to the delight of the crowd. After a thundering ovation,
Dave reappears on stage. He taps out a rhythm and sings a song taught to
him years ago by Miss Cynthie. The song is instantly recognized by the
audience. He then quiets the crowd to explain the true source of his success:
the feisty Miss Cynthie, who has instructed him to do "like a church
steeple—aim high and go straight."

As Dave sang his childhood song, Miss Cynthie has watched the lyric's
effect on the crowd. The young men and women have been transformed
from a loud and sin-loving crowd to children, children who share in Dave's
memory and perhaps recall a similar song and caring from their pasts. The
movement is from the throes of decadence to relative innocence. Miss
Cynthie concludes that "they didn't mean no harm" in their fervent appreci-
ation of the musical revue. In addition, the song seems to have unlocked
a door to Miss Cynthie's secular past, for as she moves out of the theatre,
she pats her foot in time to the jazz rhythms of the orchestra's recessional.

The transformational and binding aspect of black music functions credibly
in this place, since it operates through an agent who comprises the dual
aspect in dynamic, comic, and moving ways. Miss Cynthie's thinking is not
so rigid that she cannot accept an aspect of her own past. Incidentally,
there were at least two other models for Miss Cynthie in two earlier, though
less successful, stories. Grammie in "Guardian of the Law" takes matters
into her own hands and rescues her nephew, a rookie policeman, from the
clutches of two thugs. In an alternative ending in an unpublished story,
"Lindy Hop" (c. 1932–33), Grandma wins a dance contest in order to
indirectly dissuade her granddaughter from working as a ballroom hostess.
She dances the traditional dances (reel, cake-walk, etc.) while her much
younger partner dances the modern dances (Charleston and turkey trot).
Youth is balanced by age here. For both stories, the older female figure is
driven to seemingly unlikely actions through love.

It is Miss Cynthie's love that insists on forgiving both Dave for his choice of profession and simultaneously the young crowd for their seeming fixation with decadence. The snatch of children's rhyme is part of an informing tradition that can open up a different aspect of their lives, can deflect them from a headlong flight to moral chaos, can summon the memory and possibility of love.

John McCluskey, Jr., "Healing Songs: Secular Music in the Short Fiction of Rudolph Fisher," CLA Journal 26, No. 2 (December 1982): 200–202

BERNARD W. BELL   The Walls of Jericho is a satirical treatment of prejudice and self-delusion. Structured around a remote, incongruous analogy between the biblical legend of Joshua and the legendary Joshua Jones, a black furniture mover, the novel reveals Fisher's ironic view of the walls people build around their neighborhoods and themselves. In its modern context the legend signifies the external reality of the color line that encircled the growing Harlem colony during the 1920s and the disparity between the surface behavior and deeper self of the characters. The main theme is dramatically introduced early in the first of the six major sections of the novel. Fred Merrit, a fair-skinned lawyer, assaults the color line when he buys a house on Court Avenue, the most exclusive white residential street adjacent to black Harlem. A racial chauvinist, Merrit confesses that though " 'I'd enjoy this house, if they let me alone, purely as an individual, just the same I'm entering it as a Negro. I hate fays. Always have. Always will. Chief joy in life is making them uncomfortable. And if this doesn't do it— I'll quit the bar.' " Color and class prejudice are therefore the chief objects of Fisher's satire. Because white resistance to black neighbors had resulted in riots and terrorism, Merrit hires the toughest furniture movers in Harlem to move him into the hostile white neighborhood. The moving crew is Jinx Jenkins and Bubber Brown, minor comic characters, and is supervised by big, strong Joshua Jones, a legendary piano mover and the main character, whose surface toughness conceals a compassionate heart ⟨. . .⟩

Midway through the novel the legend of Joshua and its modern interpretation are explained, first in the black vernacular of Joshua and then in the formal words of Tod Bruce, an Episcopal minister. Joshua's folk version of the formal sermon actually serves a double function for the omniscient author-narrator. First, it establishes the intellectual distance between author-narrator and main character, and second, it reveals the author-narrator's sympathy for the working class by burlesquing the pomp and ceremony of middle-class religious rituals. In colorful, irreverent dialect, Joshua tells about " 'a bird named Joshua' " who " 'thought he was the owl's bowels, till one day he run up against a town named Jericho.' " Fisher undercuts his hero's intelligence by pointing out that although Joshua knew the story, its "meaning was a little too deep" for him. In contrast, the Rev. Tod Bruce, aware of the continuing struggle for literacy of many of his congregation, explains the modern lesson of the Jewish legend in plain, standard English: " 'Self-revelation is the supreme experience, the chief victory, of a man's life. In all the realm of the spirit, in all the Canaan of the soul, no conquest yields so miraculous a reward.' " Two battles are clearly being fought in the novel: one for living space and the other for self-revelation.

As a friend and guide, the author-narrator cultivates the exotic appeal of Harlem for his white readers. ⟨. . .⟩ Slang, idiom, syntax, physical gestures, and the dozens all contribute to the surface realism and satirical effect of their dialogue on the anticipated race war triggered by Merrit's move to a white neighborhood. But instead of allowing their dialogue to stand on its own, Fisher proceeds to explain its sociopsychological significance to his mainly white readers. By interpreting the verbal insults and aggression between Jinx and Bubber as an effort to suppress the mutual affection that their class considers unmanly and unnatural, Fisher reinforces the ironic thrust of the plot and characters while simultaneously revealing his ambivalence toward the comic pair. An uneven blend of biblical legend, satire, and comedy, *The Walls of Jericho* reveals the bitter-sweet truths of color and class prejudice beneath the surface reality of Harlem.

Bernard W. Bell, *The Afro-American Novel and Its Tradition* (Amherst: University of Massachusetts Press, 1987), pp. 138–40.

MARGARET PERRY   The short stories of Rudolph Fisher have a sense of literary history behind them, for he ploughed the same fields as the masters of this art, such as Poe, Gogol, and James. There are times, indeed, when Fisher gives the impression that he went from studying the nineteenth-century writers directly to his desk to write, ignoring practitioners of the art who were his own contemporaries. In an earlier review of Fisher's work I noted that "Both stories ['City of Refuge' and 'Miss Cynthie'] illustrate Fisher's ability to transform life into art through control of characterization, plot, and diction, and insistence on a single effect at the story's conclusion." Fisher was a traditionalist in form, then; but he was also one in point of view, in his themes, and in the values he stressed through the major characters he created. One might also venture to say that Fisher often wrote in the mode of dramatic comedies, eschewing tragedy in any case even in the stories that end unhappily.

Fisher writes comedy in the classical sense, as Gilbert Murray states in *The Classical Tradition in Poetry*, comedy that has as its core "a union of lovers." This re-creation of acts and emotions, mimesis, moves from conflict to resolution within the very special milieu of Black Harlem. The over-all impression one gets of Fisher's use of the short story form is that he engages the reader in a positive, comic view of life which arises from the lyric impulse to sing mainly about triumph, about the possibility of being saved or renewed. Once again, to quote Murray: "Tragedies end in death. Comedies end in marriage." Murray is not referring to marriage as a legal procedure, but is alluding to the joy that issues from a harmonious end to the strife and conflict within the imaginative work. It seems he is seeking not only the melody but also the harmony, as Shelley wrote in his famous *Defence of Poetry*. One is always conscious of an ordered universe in Fisher's world; he writes about the ruptures that are brought on by disharmony, the disjointedness that must be replaced at the denouement by order.

> Margaret Perry, "A Fisher of Black Life: Short Stories by Rudolph Fisher," *The Harlem Renaissance Re-examined*, ed. Victor A. Kramer (New York: AMS Press, 1987), pp. 255–56

Bibliography

The Walls of Jericho. 1928.
The Conjure-Man Dies: A Mystery Tale of Dark Harlem. 1932.
Short Fiction. Ed. Margaret Perry. 1987.

Langston Hughes
1902–1967

JAMES LANGSTON HUGHES was born in Joplin, Missouri, on February 1, 1902. His mother, Carrie Langston Hughes, had been a schoolteacher; his father, James Nathaniel Hughes, was a storekeeper. James left for Mexico while his son was still an infant, and the latter was raised mostly by his grandmother, Mary Langston. Hughes lived for a time in Illinois with his mother, who remarried, and went to high school in Cleveland. He spent the summer of 1919 in Mexico with his father, then taught for a year in Mexican schools. He entered Columbia University in September 1921, a few months after his poem, "The Negro Speaks of Rivers," appeared in the *Crisis* for June 1921.

After a year of schooling, Hughes took on various jobs in New York, on trans-Atlantic ships, and in Paris. He returned to America in 1925, and while working as a busboy in Washington, D.C., he slipped three poems beside Vachel Lindsay's plate. Lindsay was impressed and began promoting the young poet. In 1925 Hughes won a literary contest in *Opportunity*, and his writing career was launched. His first collection of poems, *The Weary Blues*, was published in 1926. Another volume, *Fine Clothes to the Jew*, appeared the next year. A benefactor sent Hughes to Lincoln University, from which he received a B.A. in 1929.

Hughes subsequently supported himself as a poet, novelist, and writer of stories, screenplays, articles, children's books, and songs. His first novel, *Not without Laughter*, appeared in 1930. His first short-story collection was *The Ways of White Folks* (1934). He wrote a children's book in collaboration with Arna Bontemps, *Popo and Fifina, Children of Haiti* (1932), based on a trip Hughes took to Haiti in 1931. He also collaborated with Zora Neale Hurston on a folk comedy, *Mule Bone*, but it was not published until 1991.

Having received several literary awards and fellowships in the 1930s, including a Guggenheim Fellowship in 1935, Hughes was able to write without financial worries. He promoted black theatre in both Harlem and Los Angeles, and himself wrote a number of plays, the most famous of which

is *Tambourines to Glory* (1958). In 1940 he published his first autobiography, *The Big Sea*.

Hughes moved to California in 1939, settling in Hollow Hills Farm near Monterey. Two years later he moved to Chicago, and from 1942 onward he lived in Harlem. Such volumes as *Shakespeare in Harlem* (1942) and *Fields of Wonder* (1947) established him as the leading black poet in America. Hughes's Communist leanings, initially triggered by a trip to the Soviet Union in 1931, caused him to be summoned before the House Un-American Activities Committee (HUAC), where, fearful of being imprisoned or black-balled, he repudiated any Communist or socialist tendencies and maintained that his repeated calls for social justice for black Americans, expressed in his earlier work, were not incompatible with American political ideals.

In the 1950s and 1960s, Hughes gained popularity through the recurring protagonist of his stories, Jesse B. Semple, or "Simple." These stories were collected in four volumes: *Simple Speaks His Mind* (1950), *Simple Takes a Wife* (1953), *Simple Stakes a Claim* (1957), and *Simple's Uncle Sam* (1965). A selection, *The Best of Simple*, appeared in 1961. Story collections not involving Simple are *Laughing to Keep from Crying* (1952) and *Something in Common and Other Stories* (1963). A second autobiography, *I Wonder as I Wander*, was published in 1956.

In his later years Hughes devoted himself to promoting black literature by compiling anthologies of black American poetry, fiction, and folklore, and by writing nonfiction books for children, including *The First Book of Negroes* (1952), *The First Book of Jazz* (1955), and *The First Book of Africa* (1960). He received the NAACP's Spingarn Medal in 1960 and was elected to the National Institute of Arts and Letters in 1961. Hughes never married. He died of congestive heart failure in New York City on May 22, 1967.

▣ *Critical Extracts*

LANGSTON HUGHES   ⟨. . .⟩ there is, for the American Negro artist who can escape the restrictions the more advanced among his own group would put upon him, a great field of unused material ready for his art. Without going outside his race, and even among the better classes with their "white" culture and conscious American manners, but still Negro enough to be different, there is sufficient matter to furnish a black artist with a lifetime of creative work. And when he chooses to touch on the relations between Negroes and whites in this country with their innumerable overtones and undertones, surely, and especially for literature and the drama, there is an inexhaustible supply of themes at hand. To these the Negro artist can give his racial individuality, his heritage of rhythm and warmth, and his incongruous humor that so often, as in the Blues, becomes ironic laughter mixed with tears. But let us look again at the mountain.

A prominent Negro clubwoman in Philadelphia paid eleven dollars to hear Raquel Meller sing Andalusian popular songs. But she told me a few weeks before she would not think of going to hear "that woman," Clara Smith, a great black artist, sing Negro folksongs. And many an upper-class Negro church, even now, would not dream of employing a spiritual in its services. The drab melodies in white folks' hymnbooks are much to be preferred. "We want to worship the Lord correctly and quietly. We don't believe in 'shouting.' Let's be dull like the Nordics," they say, in effect.

The road for the serious black artist, then, who would produce a racial art is most certainly rocky and the mountain is high. Until recently he received almost no encouragement for his work from either white or colored people. The fine novels of Chesnutt go out of print with neither race noticing their passing. The quaint charm and humor of Dunbar's dialect verse brought to him, in his day, largely the same kind of encouragement one would give a sideshow freak (A colored man writing poetry! How odd!) or a clown (How amusing!).

The present vogue in things Negro, although it may do as much harm as good for the budding colored artist, has at least done this: it has brought him forcibly to the attention of his own people among whom for so long, unless the other race had noticed him beforehand, he was a prophet with little honor. I understand that Charles Gilpin acted for years in Negro theaters without any special acclaim from his own, but when Broadway gave him eight curtain calls, Negroes, too, began to beat a tin pan in his honor. I know a young colored writer, a manual worker by day, who had been writing well for the colored magazines for some years, but it was not until he recently broke into the white publications and his first book was accepted by a prominent New York publisher that the "best" Negroes in his city took the trouble to discover that he lived there. Then almost immediately they decided to give a grand dinner for him. But the society ladies were careful to whisper to his mother that perhaps she'd better not come. They were not sure she would have an evening gown.

The Negro artist works against an undertow of sharp criticism and misunderstanding from his own group and unintentional bribes from the whites. "O, be respectable, write about nice people, show how good we are," say the Negroes. "Be stereotyped, don't go too far, don't shatter our illusions about you, don't amuse us too seriously. We will pay you," say the whites. Both would have told Jean Toomer not to write *Cane*. The colored people did not praise it. The white people did not buy it. Most of the colored people who did read *Cane* hate it. They are afraid of it. Although the critics gave it good reviews the public remained indifferent. Yet (excepting the work of Du Bois) *Cane* contains the finest prose written by a Negro in America. And like the singing of Robeson, it is truly racial. ⟨. . .⟩

Let the blare of Negro jazz bands and the bellowing voice of Bessie Smith singing Blues penetrate the closed ears of the colored near-intellectuals until they listen and perhaps understand. Let Paul Robeson singing Water Boy, and Rudolph Fisher writing about the streets of Harlem, and Jean Toomer holding the heart of Georgia in his hands, and Aaron Douglas drawing strange black fantasies cause the smug Negro middle class to turn from their white, respectable, ordinary books and papers to catch a glimmer of their own beauty. We younger Negro artists who create now intend to express our individual dark-skinned selves without fear or shame. If white people are pleased we are glad. If they are not, it doesn't matter. We know we are beautiful. And ugly too. The tom-tom cries and the tom-tom laughs. If colored people are pleased we are glad. If they are not, their displeasure doesn't matter either. We build our temples for tomorrow, strong as we know how, and we stand on top of the mountain, free within ourselves.

Langston Hughes, "The Negro Artist and the Racial Mountain" (1926), *Langston Hughes Review* 4, No. 1 (Spring 1985): 2–4

SHERWOOD ANDERSON   *The Ways of White Folks* is something to puzzle you. If Mr. ⟨Carl⟩ Carmer goes one way, Mr. Langston Hughes goes another. You can't exactly blame him. Mr. Hughes is an infinitely better, more natural, story teller than Mr. Carmer. To my mind he gets the ball over the plate better, has a lot more on the ball but there is something missed. Mr. Carmer is a member of the Northern white race gone South, rather with jaws set, determined to please and be pleased, and Mr. Hughes might be taken as a member of the Southern colored race gone North, evidently not determined about anything but with a deep-seated resentment in him. It is in his blood, so deep-seated that he seems himself unconscious of it. The Negro people in these stories of his are so alive, warm, and real and the whites are all caricatures, life, love, laughter, old wisdom all to the Negroes and silly pretense, fakiness, pretty much all to the whites. ⟨. . .⟩

Mr. Hughes, my hat off to you in relation to your own race but not to mine. ⟨. . .⟩

The truth is, I suspect, that there is, back of all this, a thing very little understood by any of us. It is an individualistic world. I may join the Socialist or the Communist Party but that doesn't let me out of my own individual struggle with myself. It may be that I can myself establish something between myself and the American Negro man or woman that is sound. Can I hold it? I am sitting in a room with such a man or woman and we are talking. Others, of my own race, come in. How can I tell what is asleep in those others? Something between the Negro man and myself gets destroyed . . . it is the thing D. H. Lawrence was always speaking of as "the flow." My neighbor, the white man, coming in to me as I sit with my Negro friend, may have qualities I value highly but he may also stink with old prejudice. "What, you have a damn nigger in here?" In the mind of the Negro: "Damn the whites. You can't trust them." That, fed constantly by pretense of understanding where there is no understanding. Myself and Mr. Carmer paying constantly for the prejudices of a whole race. Mr. Hughes paying too. Don't think he doesn't pay.

But story telling is something else, or should be. It too seldom is. There are always too many story tellers using their talents to get even with life. There is a plane to be got on—the impersonal. Mr. Hughes gets on it perfectly with his Negro men and women. He has a fine talent. I do not see how anyone can blame him for his hatreds. I think "Red-Headed Baby" is a bum story. The figure of Oceola Jones in the story, "The Blues I'm Playing," is the most finely drawn in the book. The book is a good book.

Sherwood Anderson, "Paying for Old Sins," *Nation*, 11 July 1934, pp. 49–50

ARNA BONTEMPS   Few people have enjoyed being Negro as much as Langston Hughes. Despite the bitterness with which he has occasionally indicted those who mistreat him because of his color (and in this collection of sketches and stories ⟨*Laughing to Keep from Crying*⟩ he certainly does not let up), there has never been any question in this reader's mind about his basic attitude. He would not have missed the experience of being what he is for the world.

The story "Why, You Reckon?," which appeared originally in *The New Yorker*, is really a veiled expression of his own feeling. Disguised as a young Park Avenue bachelor who comes with a group of wealthy friends for a night of colorful, if not primitive, entertainment in a Harlem night club, the Langston Hughes of a couple of decades ago can be clearly detected. He too had come exploring and looking for fun in the unfamiliar territory north of 125th Street. The kidnapping and robbing of the visitor in the story is of course contrived, but the young man's reluctance to rejoin his friends or to go back to the safety of his home downtown reflects the author's own commentary. "This is the first exciting thing that's ever happened to me," he has the white victim say to the amazement of his abductors as he stands in a coal bin stripped of his overcoat and shoes, his wallet and studs. "This was real."

Over this tale, as over most of the others in *Laughing to Keep from Crying*, the depression of the Thirties hangs ominously, and it serves as more than just an indication of the dates of their writing. It provides a kind of continuity. After a while it begins to suggest the nameless dread which darkens human lives without reference to breadlines and relief agencies. ⟨. . .⟩

Langston Hughes has practiced the craft of the short story no more than he has practiced the forms of poetry. His is a spontaneous art which stands or falls by the sureness of his intuition, his mother wit. His stories, like his poems, are for readers who will judge them with their hearts as well as their heads. By that standard he has always measured well. He still does.

Arna Bontemps, "Black & Bubbling," *Saturday Review*, 5 April 1952, p. 17

JULIAN C. CAREY   Simple's greatest challenge to his *négritude* comes from his friend and bourgeois foil, "I." An articulate, sophisticated, educated Negro liberal, the antagonist questions Simple's militancy and simple solutions to his problem. Simple, for example, is amazed that "white folks is scared to come to Harlem," when it is he who should be afraid of them: "The white race drug me over from Africa, slaved me, freed me, lynched me, starved me during the depression, jim crowed me during the war—then they come talking about they is scared of me!" "I" reminds him that he sounds just like a Negro nationalist, "someone who wants Negroes to be on top." Simple replies, "when everybody else keeps me on the bottom, I don't see why I shouldn't want to be on top. I will, too, someday." The antagonist asks Simple to have an open mind about white people, to separate the good ones from the bad, to which he replies, "I have near about lost my mind worrying with them. . . . In fact, they have hurt my soul." "I" then reminds him that white people "blasted each other down with V-bombs during the war." However equally distributed the white man's brutality, "to be shot down is bad for the body," says Simple, "but to be Jim Crowed is worse for the spirit."

Simple, however, is not entirely antagonistic to white people. He would just like for them to experience and endure his life; he wants to "share and share alike." He believes that if the "good white friends" that "I" mentions would share a hot old half-baggage jim crow train car with him or use a "COLORED" toilet in a Southern town, they would stop resolving and start solving. "I" tells Simple that it is against the law for white people to use colored facilities down South and asks if he wants "decent white folks to get locked up just to prove they love [him]?" "I get locked up for going in their waiting rooms," responds Simple, "so why shouldn't they get locked up for going in mine." "Your explanation depresses me," "I" states. "Your nonsense depresses me," replies Simple.

There is yet another conflict involving his *négritude* that Simple has with "I," and it is an intellectual one. Being educated and "observing life for literary purposes," "I" finds fault with Simple's verse when the latter expresses himself poetically. It would seem that the antagonist is trying to make a poet out of a Negro, but Simple would just as soon remain a Negro poet. After spending a creative week-end at Orchard Beach, but being sure that the "violent rays" did not tamper with his complexion, Simple shows his "colleged" friend a poem: "Sitting under the trees / With the birds and the bees / Watching the girls go by." Recalling his literary training, "I" states that Simple "ought to have another rhyme. . . . 'By' ought to rhyme with 'sky' or something." Simple fails to see the reasoning behind the request, for he "was not looking up at no sky. . . . [He] was looking at the girls." When Simple tries to imitate Elizabethan verse (he pronounces it "Lizzie Beasley"), he is told his lyric is doggerel; but not discouraged by his friend's remarks, he reminds "I" that "you don't learn everything in books." Though the men, at times, strain the bonds of their friendship, their discussions, no matter how heated, usually end with Simple ordering "two beers for two steers" and then saying, "Pay for them, chum!"

Julian C. Carey, "Jesse B. Semple Revisited and Revised," *Phylon* 32, No. 2 (Summer 1971): 160–61

FAITH BERRY   The House Un-American Activities Committee (HUAC) was reaching out like an octopus and, by 1950, was referring to Hughes in its documents. ⟨. . .⟩

Hughes did not know what the repercussions would be when he appeared before the McCarthy Committee on March 26, 1953. He did know that some witnesses, in order to save themselves, had destroyed others by "naming names," which he was determined not to do. He knew, too, that others who had taken the Fifth Amendment had ended up in jail or, worse, as suicides. Having seen enough careers broken, he could not be sure that the same would not happen to him. ⟨. . .⟩

When McCarthy sounded the gavel at the public hearing and came face to face with Hughes and his lawyer for this encounter, Frank D. Reeves, it appeared they were meeting for the first time. In fact, they had already met privately in executive session—first with ⟨Roy⟩ Cohn and ⟨G. David⟩ Schine, and then in the Senator's office. Cohn, a harsher interrogator than Schine, had grilled Hughes about some of his writings. McCarthy, however, was anxious that a renowned American author should not become a "hostile witness." He had worked out an arrangement whereby Hughes would not be asked to "name names" of known Communists, but only in order to admit tacitly his own pro-Communist sympathies and writings. Having been indecisive about whether he would testify at all, after much private discussion with Reeves, he finally agreed to cooperate in the McCarthy scenario. He feared the worst if he didn't. Raising his right hand, he said, "I do," when the Senator asked him, "Do you swear to tell the whole truth and nothing but the truth, so help you God?"

On the witness stand, Hughes confessed that "there was such a period" when Cohn asked whether he had been a believer in the Soviet form of government; and "I certainly did," when questioned whether he wrote poetry which reflected his feelings during that time; and "That is correct, sir," when Cohn added, "I understand your testimony to be that you never actually joined the Communist Party." But so hard did he try to tell the truth about his past Soviet sympathies and at the same time sound like a patriotic American that he was only a shadow of himself. "A complete reorientation of my thinking and feelings occurred roughly four or five years ago," he offered, but Cohn quickly interjected "I notice that in 1949 you made a statement in defense of the Communist leaders who were on trial, which was in the *Daily Worker*." Hughes said he believed "one can and does" get a fair trial in America. Pressed to defend "When a Man Sees Red" and other works, he got away with, "They do not represent my current thinking," and "I have more recent books I would prefer." Asked to explain his "complete change in ideology," he affirmed, "I have always been a believer in the American form of government." There were moments when, pulverized into submission, he did disparage the Soviet Union. Praised by Southern Senator John McClellan for his "refreshing and comforting testimony," Hughes finally asked McCarthy, after about an hour of the inquisition, "Am I excused now, sir?" McCarthy finally let him go, after announcing he had "included in the record, on request," Hughes's earlier poem, "Goodbye, Christ" "to show the type of thinking of Mr. Hughes at that time." To show he also had been a "friendly witness," he sought assurance from the poet that he had not been "in any way mistreated by the staff or by the Committee." The capitulation was complete, from beginning to end.

> Faith Berry, *Langston Hughes: Before and Beyond Harlem* (Westport, CT: Lawrence Hill, 1983), pp. 317–19

STEVEN C. TRACY   Langston Hughes was ⟨. . .⟩ a "New Negro," part of the Harlem Renaissance movement that investigated African ties, affirmed African beauty, and elevated the cultural harvest of the "lowdown" folks—the blues, jazz, oral sermons, and folk tales that provide potent links to Africa—to a level that began to assert the importance that had been denied both the creator and creation. Throughout Hughes's work there is an affirmation of African-Americanism, both in style and content. Very often to understand his work one must know blues and jazz in particular. One must meet Hughes on his own ground, as African-Americans have had to meet whites on theirs.

This was naturally a very serious subject, one that had been dealt with seriously by many African-American authors, Hughes among them. Hughes, however, recognized the importance of humor in African-American cultural identity:

> There is so much richness in Negro humor, so much beauty in
> black dreams, so much dignity in our struggle, and so much
> universality in our problems, in us—in each living human being
> of color—that I do not understand the tendency today that
> some Negro artists have of seeking to run away from themselves,
> of running away from us, of being afraid to sing our songs,
> paint our own pictures, write about ourselves. ("Spingarn Medal
> Acceptance Speech," NAACP Convention, St. Paul,
> Minnesota, June 26, 1960.)

Hughes did not run away from humor; he was not afraid to laugh. Instead he went about creating a realistic comic figure with which his audience could identify: Jesse B. Semple, a native of Harlem, Negro capital of America.

In dialect the name blurs into an exhortation to "just be simple," a role into which many African-Americans were forced by circumstance, albeit often ironically and for self-preservation, given America's racial situation. Under those circumstances, simple is complex, and so is Simple.

Steven C. Tracy, "Simple's Great African-American Joke," *CLA Journal* 27, No. 3 (March 1984): 242–43

SHERLEY ANNE WILLIAMS   Perhaps the reason why the Harlem Renaissance paid so little homage to the monumental works of the past was that the older literature, represented by the works of Paul Laurence Dunbar, Pauline Hopkins, Sutton Griggs, and the earlier W. E. B. Du Bois, had been so hostile to the emerging new value system. *Home to Harlem* represented to both Du Bois and to ⟨Marcus⟩ Garvey the very epitome of "insult to the race," but it was, nonetheless, the quintessential novel of the "Harlem Renaissance," in ways that a novel like *Cane*, with its Southern, rural setting, could not be.

The new generation, of which Hughes was a member, revelled in the very things that the old "New Negroes" had rejected. It is clear that they viewed themselves and their art in connection with twentieth century modernism. They rejected the out-of-hand, heavy academic romanticism and empire building fantasies of the nineteenth century. But this was exactly the universe of Du Bois and Garvey, who wanted to create a sphinxlike and majestic black nationalism. Much of what they admired, Hughes considered stuffy, dry, artificial, and ridiculously old-fashioned. The grandeur that Du Bois strained after in his novels and pageants was similar to what Garvey staged in his street demonstrations. On a symbolic level they were almost identical, despite their mutual hatred. And these monumental symbols of civilization that they exalted were, in their view, the truest expression of what black people should be striving for—dignity, stability, formality, a princely hierarchy, and a cult of respectability. The presentation of this mythology dominates the last pages of Du Bois' *Dark Princess*. It is also to be seen in the Garveyite practice of conferring princely titles.

Hughes was an interested observer, but no active participant, in this "melanomaniac" pageantry. To him it was clear that the black American experience must be symbolized by the working class rejection of bourgeois pretentiousness. If it may be said that the values of Josephine St. Pierre Ruffin and Alexander Crummell had been corrupted by the ethics of Victorian gentility, it may be said that Langston Hughes and Claude McKay were caught up in the 1920s fashions of cultural relativism, proletarianism, and modern primitivism. To Hughes, Harlem was "like a Picasso painting in his cubistic period." Indeed, he shared at least one thing with the white jazz musician, Mezz Mezzrow, who viewed black culture as "a collective nose thumbing . . . one big Bronx cheer for the righteous squares everywhere." I doubt, however, that Hughes ever forgot, even if the Carl Van Vechtens and the Mezz Mezzrows sometimes did, that the backbone of the black community is the righteous square, the plain ol' workin' stiff like Jesse B. Semple.

> Sherley Anne Williams, "Langston Hughes and the Negro Renaissance," *Langston Hughes Review* 4, No. 1 (Spring 1985): 44–45

ARNOLD RAMPERSAD   Between Hughes, on the one hand, and ⟨James⟩ Baldwin and ⟨Ralph⟩ Ellison, on the other, was one difference far greater than any between the latter writers. While Langston psychologically needed the race in order to survive and flourish, their deepest needs as artists and human beings were evidently elsewhere. He wanted young black writers to be objective about the race, but not to scorn or to flee it. And all around him he saw young blacks confused by the rhetoric of integration and preparing to flee the race even when they made excoriating cries as exquisitely as Baldwin did in his essays. Baldwin's second novel had contained no black characters; his third would include blacks, but as characters secondary to his hero, a white American writer. To some extent, Baldwin was much more concerned with the mighty and dangerous challenge of illuminating—as a virtual pioneer in modern American fiction—the homosexual condition than with the challenge of writing about race, which by contrast had been exhaustively treated.

Although Langston did not dispute the right of black authors to tell any story they chose, a black writer's place was at home, which in Manhattan was Harlem—a perfectly fine place if not deserted by its human talent. At the end of ⟨. . .⟩ 1960, when he spoke on the WABC television program "Expedition: New York," he stressed the positive. Harlem a congested area? "It is. Congested with people. All kinds. And I'm lucky enough to call a great many of them my friends." This cheerful, uncritical acceptance of Harlem was anathema to the tortured James Baldwin, whose "Fifth Avenue Uptown," his portrait of the Harlem community in *Esquire* magazine the previous July, had showed warts and only warts: poverty, degradation, filth, and "the silent, accumulating contempt and hatred of a people."

In the half-decade of integration since 1954, and despite stirring essays on race by Baldwin and other blacks, Langston was one of the few black writers of any consequence to champion racial consciousness as a source of inspiration for black artists. No such call came from Richard Wright, Gwendolyn Brooks, Melvin Tolson, Robert Hayden, Ralph Ellison, Chester Himes, or—to be sure—Frank Yerby, by far the most financially successful Afro-American author, as a writer of avidly read Southern romances. And, as the youngest writers began slowly to perceive an emptiness in their art and lives in spite of the afflated rhetoric of integration, they would turn to Hughes more than to any other living author. "Oh if the nurse would let me travel through Harlem with you as the guide," Conrad Kent Rivers wrote to him, "I, too, could sing of black America." "The Negro Speaks of Rivers," Rivers admitted, "changed my outlook toward myself as a Negro." Lorraine Hansberry, writing to Langston to dissociate herself from an *Esquire* attack on him by Baldwin which she allegedly had sanctioned, confirmed her regard for him "not only as my mentor but the poet laureate of our people." (As for Baldwin's attack on Langston, she told a journalist, "Jimmy shows Langston no *respect*. . . . He refers to Langston in public the way we niggers usually talk in private to each other.")

Arnold Rampersad, *The Life of Langston Hughes* (New York: Oxford University Press, 1988), Vol. 2, pp. 297–98

ALICE WALKER   When I started thinking about this piece on Langston I was surprised to find his presence so much further away than I imagined it ever could be. For Langston's spirit is one that stayed around, after his death, for many of us. Five years after he died I could still "feel" him, as if he were sitting in my living room or at the top of a tree in my yard. Even now, every once in a while, he floats quite vividly through my dreams, teaching me as a spirit in much the same way he did as a person. What, I sometimes wonder, does this mean?

I think it means that some of us, as we grow and suffer and struggle and age—turn into love. We may continue to be our ordinary selves, but in fact, a transformation occurs. I suspect we let go of everything that does not matter, even our own names, sometimes, so that when a bright hopeful face of anything greets us, we are ready to bestow a smile. The radiance of which lasts an entire life.

By the time I met him, Langston Hughes had turned into love. That is what I met. That is what continues to comfort me through various nights.

That is what continues to be a sun. This is true, I believe, for many people.

And now the only question is: How can we honor this?

I think we can honor Langston's memory by remembering that in this life, the Christian church notwithstanding, we are not really required to attain perfection, which is impossible, but to learn to love, which is.

This is almost as hard as attaining perfection, but that is only because we are afraid. I like to think of something Mahatma Gandhi did, in pondering our situation. There was a Hindu man who had killed a Moslem child, and he came to Gandhi in his grief and asked what he could do to atone. Gandhi said: adopt a Moslem child, and raise him as a Moslem. This is a brilliant response, and becomes more profound the longer one studies it.

In this context, I think of a line in Langston's autobiography where he dismisses Zora Neale Hurston with the line: "Girls are funny creatures." I am thankful that twenty-five years after writing that line Langston, on meeting me, showed no trace of thinking "Girls are funny creatures," but rather responded to me as if I were his own child, my future as a person and a writer his own concern.

> Alice Walker, "Turning into Love: Some Thoughts on Surviving and Meeting Langston Hughes," *Callaloo* 12, No. 4 (Fall 1989): 665

HANS OSTROM　　　⟨. . .⟩ Hughes's stories implicitly define a kind of story that is different from modernist modes crafted by James Joyce, Katherine Mansfield, Ernest Hemingway, and others. In this as in other matters, Hughes was something of an anomaly; he was an "old-fashioned innovator." He was old-fashioned in the sense that he was drawn to the story-as-tale or the story-as-sketch and preferred a style less polished and less elliptical than that of most modernists. ⟨. . .⟩ But he was an innovator in the way he boldly handled issues of race and class in short fiction, made use of an oral tradition, and especially in the way he developed the very brief, dialogue-dependent Simple stories.

Examining a cross section of the narrative modes within Hughes's short fiction, at least three main forms emerge: the traditional dramatic story with a clear plot, conflict, and resolution; the sketch, with a journalistic or nonfiction texture and muted dramatic action; and the "oral" story, heavily dependent on monologue and dialogue and often featuring different kinds of wordplay. ⟨. . .⟩

Hughes's narrative counterrevolution in favor of plot did not spring from literary conservatism, however, nor from an antipathy to Joyce, Mansfield, or any of the writers who would later be termed modernists. Hughes's main link to the modernists, after all, is D. H. Lawrence, himself an odd-person-out with regard to narrative style and structure. In part because he was inspired by Lawrence's direct, socially alert stories, Hughes started writing short fiction with social critique uppermost in mind. A lyrical, elliptical, subtle mode would not have served the purpose of presenting "the ways of white folks" and the collisions in society that racism caused. In other words, Hughes was often if not always drawn to the relatively uncomplicated narrative vehicle exemplified by Lawrence's fiction because it enabled him to dramatize racial friction. Ironically, what is so original about his short fiction, its economic and social critique of the racial "landscape," is exactly the element that drew him in many instances to a tried-and-true, conservative narrative mode. By contrast, Joyce, Mansfield, Hemingway, and Stein all seemed nearly obsessed with the stylistic "surface" of their stories, even if these writers offer social critique of a different kind. ⟨. . .⟩

Because the Simple stories embody many of the critical tenets Hughes defined early in his career, it may be tempting to overlook how different they are from his other short fiction; but if only *The Ways of White Folks* and *Laughing to Keep from Crying* were examined, Hughes would not be judged a master of the dialogue-based short story. The Simple stories clearly allowed him to link the orality of his plays and poetry with the short-fiction genre, without abandoning other elements which had made his earlier stories successful: his political and social alertness; his eye for dramatic situations; his allegiance to everyday subjects; and his psychological acumen.

Certainly, Hughes's milieu, his preoccupations, were significantly different from those of Ernest Hemingway, but in the Simple stories, Hughes equaled the Hemingway of "Hills Like White Elephants" or "A Clean, Well-Lighted Place," in his capacity to base a narrative almost entirely on dialogue and make it succeed. The Simple stories bringing Hughes acclaim for their humor, accessibility, and topicality, also earn him a place among the best innovators of short fiction.

> Hans Ostrom, *Langston Hughes: A Study of the Short Fiction* (New York: Twayne, 1993), pp. 56–57, 59

▣ *Bibliography*

The Weary Blues. 1926.
Fine Clothes to the Jew. 1927.
Not without Laughter. 1930.

The Negro Mother and Other Dramatic Recitations. 1931.

Dear Lovely Death. 1931.

The Dream Keeper and Other Poems. 1932.

Popo and Fifina, Children of Haiti (with Arna Bontemps). 1932.

Scottsboro Limited: Four Poems and a Play in Verse. 1932.

The Ways of White Folks. 1934.

A New Song. 1938.

The Big Sea: An Autobiography. 1940.

Shakespeare in Harlem. 1942.

Freedom's Plow. 1943.

Jim Crow's Last Stand. 1943.

Lament for Dark Peoples and Other Poems. Ed. H. Driessen. 1944.

This Is My Land (with Toy Harper and La Villa Tullos). c. 1945.

Fields of Wonder. 1947.

Street Scene (adapter; with Kurt Weill). 1948.

Cuba Libre: Poems by Nicolás Guillén (translator; with Ben Frederic Carruthers). 1948.

Troubled Island (adapter; with William Grant Still). 1949.

One-Way Ticket. 1949.

The Poetry of the Negro 1746–1949 (editor; with Arna Bontemps). 1949, 1970.

Simple Speaks His Mind. 1950.

Montage of a Dream Deferred. 1951.

The First Book of Negroes. 1952.

Laughing to Keep from Crying. 1952.

Simple Takes a Wife. 1953.

Famous American Negroes. 1954.

The First Book of Rhythms. 1954.

Famous Negro Music Makers. 1955.

The First Book of Jazz. 1955.

The Sweet Flypaper of Life (with Roy De Carava). 1955.

The First Book of the West Indies. 1956.

I Wonder as I Wander: An Autobiographical Journey. 1956.

A Pictorial History of the Negro in America (with Milton Meltzer). 1956, 1963, 1968.

Selected Poems of Gabriela Mistral (translator). 1957.

Simple Stakes a Claim. 1957.

The Book of Negro Folklore (editor; with Arna Bontemps). 1958.

Famous Negro Heroes of America. 1958.

The Langston Hughes Reader. 1958.

Tambourines to Glory. 1958.

Simply Heavenly: A Comedy with Music (with David Martin). 1959.

Selected Poems. 1959.

An African Treasury (editor). 1960.

The First Book of Africa. 1960, 1964.

Ask Your Mama: Twelve Moods for Jazz. 1961.

The Best of Simple. 1961.

Fight for Freedom: The Story of NAACP. 1962.

Five Plays. Ed. Webster Smalley. 1963.

Poems from Black Africa (editor). 1963.

Something in Common and Other Stories. 1963.

New Negro Poets U.S.A. (editor). 1964.

Simple's Uncle Sam. 1965.

The Book of Negro Humor (editor). 1965.

The Best Short Stories by Negro Writers: Anthology from 1899 to the Present (editor). 1967.

Black Magic: A Pictorial History of the Negro in American Entertainment (with Milton Meltzer). 1967.

The Panther and the Lash: Poems of Our Times. 1967.

Black Misery. 1969.

Don't You Turn Back: Poems. Ed. Lee Bennett Hopkins. 1969.

Good Morning, Revolution: Uncollected Social Protest Writings. Ed. Faith Berry. 1973.

Langston Hughes in the Hispanic World and Haiti. Ed. Edward J. Mullen. 1977.

Arna Bontemps–Langston Hughes Letters 1925–1967. Ed. Charles H. Nichols. 1980.

Mule Bone: A Comedy of Negro Life (with Zora Neale Hurston). Ed. George Houston Bass and Henry Louis Gates, Jr. 1991.

⊞ ⊞ ⊞

Zora Neale Hurston
c. 1891–1960

ZORA NEALE HURSTON was born probably on January 7, 1891, although she frequently gave her birth date as 1901 or 1903. She was born and raised in America's first all-black incorporated town, Eatonville, Florida. Her father, John Hurston, was a former sharecropper who became a carpenter, preacher, and three-term mayor in Eatonville. Her mother, Lucy Hurston, died in 1904; two weeks after her death, Hurston was sent to Jacksonville, Florida, to school, but wound up neglected by her remarried father and worked a variety of menial jobs. A five-year gap in her personal history at this time has led some biographers to conjecture that she was married; however, no evidence exists to support or disprove this speculation. In 1917 she began studies at Morgan Academy in Baltimore and in 1918 attended Howard University, where her first short story appeared in the college literary magazine. She later won a scholarship to Barnard College to study with the eminent anthropologist Franz Boas.

While living in New York Hurston worked as a secretary to the popular novelist Fannie Hurst. Though she only lived in New York for a short time, Hurston is considered a major force in the Harlem Renaissance of the 1920s and 1930s. She was an associate editor for the one-issue avant-garde journal *Fire!!* and she collaborated on several plays with various writers, including *Mule Bone: A Comedy of Negro Life*, written with Langston Hughes. Boas arranged a fellowship for Hurston that allowed her to travel throughout the South and collect folklore. The result of these travels was the publication of Hurston's first collection of black folk tales, *Mules and Men* (1935). Hurston is thought to be the first black American to have collected and published Afro-American folklore, and both of her collections have become much used sources for myths and legends of black culture. Her interest in anthropology took her to several Latin American countries, including Jamaica, Haiti, and Honduras. Her experiences in Jamaica and Haiti appear in her second collection of folk tales, *Tell My Horse* (1938).

Hurston's first novel, *Jonah's Gourd Vine* (1934), is loosely based on the lives of her parents in Eatonville. It was written shortly after *Mules and Men* (although it was published first) and has been criticized as being more of an anthropological study than a novel. Her best-known work, the novel *Their Eyes Were Watching God*, was published in 1937. Written after a failed love affair, *Their Eyes Were Watching God* focuses on a middle-aged woman's quest for fulfillment in an oppressive society. Hurston also wrote *Moses, Man of the Mountain* (1939), an attempt to fuse biblical narrative and folk myth. In addition to her life as a writer, Hurston worked temporarily as a teacher, a librarian at an Air Force base, a staff writer at Paramount Studios, and as a reporter for the *Fort Pierce* (Florida) *Chronicle*.

Her autobiography, *Dust Tracks on a Road*, won the 1943 Annisfield Award. Her final novel, *Seraph on the Suwanee*, appeared in 1948. An attempt to universalize the issues addressed in *Their Eyes Were Watching God*, *Seraph* is Hurston's only novel to feature white protagonists. Hurston's other honors include Guggenheim Fellowships in 1936 and 1938. She wrote for various magazines in the 1950s, but her increasingly conservative views concerning race relations effectively alienated her from black intellectual culture. She died on January 28, 1960, in Fort Pierce, Florida.

❖ *Critical Extracts*

H. I. BROCK   The writer has gone back to her native Florida village—a Negro settlement—with her native racial quality entirely unspoiled by her Northern college education. She has plunged into the social pleasures of the black community and made a record 〈*Mules and Men*〉 of what is said and done when Negroes are having a good gregarious time, dancing, singing, fishing, and above all, and incessantly, talking. 〈. . .〉

The book is packed with tall tales rich with flavor and alive with characteristic turns of speech. Those of us who have known the Southern Negro from our youth find him here speaking the language of his tribe as familiarly as if it came straight out of his own mouth and had not been translated into type and transmitted through the eye to the ear. Which is to say that a very tricky dialect has been rendered with rare simplicity and fidelity into symbols so little adequate to convey its true values that the achievement is remarkable.

H. I. Brock, "The Full, True Flavor of Life in a Negro Community," *New York Times Book Review*, 18 November 1935, p. 4

STERLING A. BROWN   Janie's grandmother ⟨in *Their Eyes Were Watching God*⟩, remembering how in slavery she was used "for a work-ox and a brood sow," and remembering her daughter's shame, seeks Janie's security above all else. But to Janie, her husband, for all his sixty acres, looks like "some old skull-head in de graveyard," and she goes off down the road with slack-talking Jody Sparks. In Eatonville, an all-colored town, Jody becomes the "big voice," but Janie is first neglected and then brow-beaten. When Jody dies, Tea-Cake, with his contagious high spirits, whirls Janie into a marriage, idyllic until Tea-Cake's tragic end. Janie returns home, grief-stricken but fulfilled. Better than her grandmother's security, she had found out about living for herself.

Filling out Janie's story are sketches of Eatonville and farming down "on the muck" in the Everglades. On the porch of the mayor's store "big old lies" and comic-serious debates, with the tallest of metaphors, while away the evenings. The dedication of the town's first lamp and the community burial of an old mule are rich in humor but they are not cartoons. Many incidents are unusual, and there are narrative gaps in need of building up. Miss Hurston's forte is the recording and the creation of folk-speech. Her devotion to these people has rewarded her; *Their Eyes Were Watching God* is chock-full of earthy and touching poetry. ⟨. . .⟩

But this is not *the* story of Miss Hurston's own people, as the foreword states, for *the* Negro novel is as unachievable as the Great American Novel. Living in an all-colored town, these people escape the worst pressures of class and caste. There is little harshness; there is enough money and work to go around. The author does not dwell upon the "people ugly from ignorance and broken from being poor" who swarm upon the "muck" for short-time jobs. But there is bitterness, sometimes oblique, in the enforced folk manner, and sometimes forthright. The slave, Nanny, for bearing too light a child with gray eyes, is ordered a terrible beating by her mistress, who in her jealousy is perfectly willing to "stand the loss" if the beating is fatal. And after the hurricane there is a great to-do lest white and black victims be buried together. To detect the race of the long-unburied corpses, the conscripted grave-diggers must examine the hair. The whites get pine coffins; the Negroes get quick-lime. "They's mighty particular how dese dead folks goes tuh judgment. Look lak they think God don't know nothin' 'bout de Jim Crow law."

Sterling A. Brown, " 'Luck Is a Fortune,' " *Nation*, 16 October 1937, pp. 409–10

RICHARD WRIGHT   *Their Eyes Were Watching God* is the story of Zora Neale Hurston's Janie who, at sixteen, married a grubbing farmer at the anxious instigation of her slave-born grandmother. The romantic Janie, in the highly charged language of Miss Hurston, longed to be a pear in blossom and have a "dust-bearing bee sink into the sanctum of a bloom; the thousand sister-calyxes arch to meet the love embrace." Restless, she fled from her farmer husband and married Jody, an up-and-coming Negro business man who, in the end, proved to be no better than her first husband. After twenty years of clerking for her self-made Jody, Janie found herself a frustrated widow of forty with a small fortune on her hands. Tea Cake, "from in and through Georgia," drifted along and, despite his youth, Janie took him. For more than two years they lived happily; but Tea Cake was bitten by a mad dog and was infected with rabies. One night in a canine rage Tea Cake tried to murder Janie, thereby forcing her to shoot the only man she had ever loved.

Miss Hurston can write; but her prose is cloaked in that facile sensuality that has dogged Negro expression since the days of Phillis Wheatley. Her dialogue manages to catch the psychological movements of the Negro folk-mind in their pure simplicity, but that's as far as it goes.

Miss Hurston *voluntarily* continues in her novel the tradition which was *forced* upon the Negro in the theater, that is, the minstrel technique that makes the "white folks" laugh. Her characters eat and laugh and cry and work and kill; they swing like a pendulum eternally in that safe and narrow orbit in which America likes to see the Negro live: between laughter and tears.

⟨. . .⟩ The sensory sweep of her novel carries no theme, no message, no thought. In the main, her novel is not addressed to the Negro, but to a white audience whose chauvinistic tastes she knows how to satisfy. She exploits the phase of Negro life which is "quaint," the phase which evokes a piteous smile on the lips of the "superior" race.

> Richard Wright, "Between Laughter and Tears," *New Masses*, 5 October 1937, p. 25

ZORA NEALE HURSTON   ⟨. . .⟩ I see nothing but futility in looking back over my shoulder in rebuke at the grave of some white man who has been dead too long to talk about. That is just what I would be doing in trying to fix the blame for the dark days of slavery and the Reconstruction. From what I can learn, it was sad. Certainly. But my ancestors who lived and died in it are dead. The white men who profited by their labor and lives are dead also. I have no personal memory of those times, and no responsibility for them. Neither has the grandson of the man who held my folks. I see no need in Button-holing that grandson like the Ancient Mariner did the wedding guest and calling for the High Sheriff to put him under arrest.

I am not so stupid as to think that I would be bringing this descendant of a slave-owner any news. He has heard just as much about the thing as I have. I am not so humorless as to visualize the grandson falling out on the sidewalk before me, and throwing an acre of fits in remorse because his old folks held slaves. No, indeed! If it happened to be a fine day and he had had a nice breakfast, he might stop and answer me like this:

"In the first place, I was not able to get any better view of social conditions from my grandmother's womb than you could from your grandmother's. Let us say for the sake of argument that I detest the institution of slavery and all that it implied, just as much as you do. You must admit that I had no more power to do anything about it in my unborn state than you had in yours. Why fix your eyes on me? I respectfully refer you to my ancestors, and bid you a good day."

If I still lingered before him, he might answer me further by asking questions like this:

> "Are you so simple as to assume that the Big Surrender
> (Southerners, both black and white speak of Lee's surrender to Grant
> as the Big Surrender) banished the concept of human slavery
> from the earth? What is the principle of slavery? Only the
> literal buying and selling of human flesh on the block? That was
> only an outside symbol. Real slavery is couched in the desire
> to and the efforts of any man or community to live and advance
> their interests at the expense of the lives and interests of
> others. All of the outward signs come out of that. Do you not
> realize that the power, prestige and prosperity of the greatest
> nations on earth rests on colonies and sources of raw materials?
> Why else are great wars waged? If you have not thought,
> then why waste time with your vapid accusations? If you have,
> then why single *me* out?" And like Pilate, he will light a
> cigar, and stroll on off without waiting for an answer.

Anticipating such an answer, I have no intention of wasting my time beating on old graves with a club. I know that I cannot pry aloose the clutching hand of Time, so I will turn all my thoughts and energies on the present. I will settle for from now on.

And why not? For me to pretend that I am Old Black Joe and waste my time on his problems, would be just as ridiculous as for the government of Winston Churchill to bill the Duke of Normandy the first of every month, or for the Jews to hang around the pyramids trying to picket Old Pharaoh.

While I have a handkerchief over my eyes crying over the landing of the first slaves in 1619, I might miss something swell that is going on in 1942. Furthermore, if somebody were to consider my grandmother's ungranted wishes, and give {it}me what *she* wanted, I would be too put out for words.

Zora Neale Hurston, *Dust Tracks on a Road: An Autobiography* (1942; rpt. New York: HarperPerennial, 1991), pp. 206–8

WORTH TUTTLE HEDDEN   Though *Seraph on the Suwanee* is the love story of a daughter of Florida Crackers and of a scion of plantation owners, it is no peasant-marries-the-prince tale. Arvay Henson, true Cracker in breeding, is above her caste in temperament; James Kenneth Meserve is plain Jim who speaks the dialect and who has turned his back on family, with its static living in the past, to become foreman in a west Florida turpentine camp. Neither is it a romance of the boy-meets-girl school. Beginning conventionally enough with a seduction (a last minute one when Arvay is in her wedding dress), it ends twenty-odd years later when the protagonists are about to be grandparents. In this denouement the divergent lines of Miss Hurston's astonishing, bewildering talent meet to give us a reconciliation scene between a middle-aged man and a middle-aged woman that is erotically exciting and a description of the technique of shrimping that is meticulously exact. Emotional, expository; meandering, unified; naive, sophisticated; sympathetic, caustic; comic, tragic; lewd, chaste—one could go on indefinitely reiterating this novel's contradictions and still end helplessly with the adjective unique. ⟨. . .⟩

Reading this astonishing novel, you wish that Miss Hurston had used the scissors and smoothed the seams. Having read it, you would like to be able to remember every extraneous incident and every picturesque metaphor.

Worth Tuttle Hedden, "Turpentine and Moonshine: Love Conquers Caste Between Florida Crackers and Aristocrats," *New York Herald Tribune Books*, 10 October 1948, p. 2

ROBERT BONE   The genesis of a work of art may be of no moment to literary criticism but it is sometimes crucial in literary history. It may, for example, account for the rare occasion when an author outclasses himself. *Their Eyes Were Watching God* (1937) is a case in point. The novel was written in Haiti in just seven weeks, under the emotional pressure of a recent love affair. "The plot was far from the circumstances," Miss Hurston writes in her autobiography, "but I tried to embalm all the tenderness of my passion for him in *Their Eyes Were Watching God.*" Ordinarily the prognosis for such a novel would be dismal enough. One might expect immediacy and intensity, but not distance, or control, or universality. Yet oddly, or perhaps not so oddly, it is Miss Hurston's best novel, and possibly the best novel of the period, excepting *Native Son.*

The opening paragraph of *Their Eyes Were Watching God* encompasses the whole of the novel's meaning: "Ships at a distance have every man's wish on board. For some they come in with the tide. For others they sail forever on the horizon, never out of sight, never landing, until the Watcher turns his eyes away in resignation, his dreams mocked to death by Time. That is the life of man" (p. 9). For women, the author continues, the dream is the sole reality. "So the beginning of this was a woman, and she had come back from burying the dead."

Janie has been gone for almost two years as the action of the novel commences. The townspeople know only that she left home in the company of a lover much younger than herself, and that she departed in fine clothes but has returned in overalls. Heads nod; tongues wag; and the consensus is that she has played the fool. Toward the gossiping women who, from the safety of a small-town porch "pass notions through their mouths," Janie feels only contempt and irritation: "If God don't think no mo' 'bout 'em than Ah do, they's a lost ball in de high grass." To Phoeby, her kissing-friend, she tells the story of her love for Tea-Cake, which together with its antecedents comprises the main body of the novel.

Robert Bone, *The Negro Novel in America* (New Haven: Yale University Press, 1958), pp. 127–28

ROBERT HEMENWAY   What I should like to conclude with is the hypothesis that one reason Zora Neale Hurston was attracted to the scientific conceptualization of her racial experience during the late twenties and early thirties was its *prima facie* offering of a structure for black folklore. That is, it offered a pattern of meaning for material that white racism consistently distorted into "Negro" stereotypes. A folk singer was a cultural object of considerable scientific importance to the collecting anthropologist precisely because his folk experience affirms his humanity, a fact that Hurston could know subjectively as she proved it scientifically. The scientific attraction became so strong that she was led into seriously planning a career as a professional anthropologist, and it continued to affect her writing even after she had rejected such a possibility. When she used Eatonville as fiction in *Jonah's Gourd Vine* (1934), and folklore as personal narrative in her collection, *Mules and Men* (1935), she was in the process of rejecting the scientific conceptualization, but had not yet reached the aesthetic resolution in fiction that characterized her two masterpieces of the late thirties, *Their Eyes Were Watching God* (1937), and *Moses, Man of the Mountain* (1939). Hurston never denied the usefulness of the Barnard training, but she made it clear that something more was needed for the creation of art. As she once told a reporter: "I needed my Barnard education to help me see my people as they really are. But I found that it did not do to be too detached as I stepped aside to study them. I had to go back, dress as they did, talk as they did, live their life, so that I could get into my stories the world I knew as a child."

In sum, then, Zora Neale Hurston was shaped by the Harlem Renaissance, but by Boas as well as by Thurman and Hughes, by Barnard as well as by Harlem. This should not necessarily suggest that the Boas experience was of a superior quality; in many ways it seriously hindered her development as an artist. Nor should it suggest that the aesthetic excitement among the Harlem literati failed to influence her thought. It does mean that the attraction of scientific objectivity was something Hurston had to work through to arrive at the subjective triumphs of her later books. But the ferment of the Harlem Renaissance should also not be underestimated. Hughes, in particular, showed Hurston the poetic possibilities of the folk idiom and she was continually impressed when a reading from Hughes's poems would break the ice with dock loaders, turpentine workers, and jook singers. The mutual effort involved in the creation of *Fire*, the nights at Charles S. and James Weldon Johnson's, the *Opportunity* dinners, even the teas at Jessie Fauset's helped make Zora Hurston aware of the rich block of material which was hers by chance of birth, and they stimulated her thinking about the techniques of collecting and presenting it.

Robert Hemenway, "Zora Neale Hurston and the Eatonville Anthropology," *The Harlem Renaissance Remembered*, ed. Arna Bontemps (New York: Dodd, Mead, 1972), pp. 212–13

S. JAY WALKER   It comes as something of a shock to discover that Zora Neale Hurston's neglected 1937 masterpiece, *Their Eyes Were Watching God*, deals far more extensively with sexism, the struggle of a woman to be regarded as a person in a male-dominated society, than racism, the struggle of blacks to be regarded as persons in a white-dominated society. It is a treatment virtually unique in the annals of black fiction, and in her handling of it, Ms. Hurston not only shows an aching awareness of the stifling effects of sexism, but also indicates why the feminist movement has failed, by and large, to grasp the imaginations of black womanhood.

Janie Killicks Starks Woods, the heroine of the novel, is followed through three marriages, the first of which brings her safety, the second wealth and prestige, and the third love. On the surface, it sounds indistinguishable from the woman's-magazine fiction which has been denounced as the most insidious form of sexism. Yet a great deal goes on beneath the surface of Hurston's novel, leading to a final interpretation of love that denies not sexuality but sex-role stereotypes. The love that completes the novel is one that the previous marriages had lacked because it is a relationship between acknowledged equals. Janie and "Tea Cake," her husband, share resources, work, decisions, dangers, and not merely the marriage bed.

It is something less than a primer of romanticized love. At one point, Tea Cake, jealous of a suspected rival, beats Janie; at another, Janie, having the same suspicion, beats Tea Cake. Each has weaknesses, fears; but in the final analysis each respects the other as a person, and it is that respect that allows them to challenge the world's conventions and to find each other, and themselves.

S. Jay Walker, "Zora Neale Hurston's *Their Eyes Were Watching God:* Black Novel of Sexism," *Modern Fiction Studies* 20, No. 4 (Winter 1974–75): 520–21

ALICE WALKER   It has been pointed out that one of the reasons Zora Neale Hurston's work has suffered neglect is that her critics never considered her "sincere." Only after she died penniless, still laboring at her craft, still immersed in her work, still following *her* vision and *her* road, did it begin to seem to some that yes, perhaps this woman *was* a serious artist after all, since artists are known to live poor and die broke. But you're up against a hard game if you have to die to win it, and we must insist that dying in poverty is an unacceptable extreme.

We live in a society, as blacks, women, and artists, whose contests we do not design and with whose insistence on ranking us we are permanently at war. To know that second place, in such a society, has often required more work and innate genius than first, a longer, grimier struggle over greater odds than first—and to be able to fling your scarf about dramatically while you demonstrate that you know—is to trust your own self-evaluation in the face of the Great White Western Commercial of white and male supremacy, which is virtually everything we see, outside and often inside our own homes. That Hurston held her own, literally, against the flood of whiteness and maleness that diluted so much other black art of the period in which she worked is a testimony to her genius and her faith.

As black women and as artists, we are prepared, I think, to keep that faith. There are other choices, but they are despicable.

Zora Neale Hurston, who went forth into the world with one dress to her name, and who was permitted, at other times in her life, only a single pair of shoes, rescued and recreated a world which she labored to hand us whole, never underestimating the value of her gift, if at times doubting the good sense of its recipients. She appreciated us, in any case, *as we fashioned ourselves*. That is something. And of all the people in the world to be, she chose to be herself, *and more and more of herself*. That, too, is something.

Alice Walker, "On Refusing to Be Humbled by Second Place in a Contest You Did Not Design: A Tradition by Now," *I Love Myself When I Am Laughing . . . and Then Again When I Am Looking Mean and Impressive: A Zora Neale Hurston Reader*, ed. Alice Walker (New York: The Feminist Press, 1979), p. 4

HENRY LOUIS GATES, JR.   Hurston's achievement in *Dust Tracks* is twofold. First, she gives us a *writer's* life—rather than an account of "the Negro problem"—in a language as "dazzling" as Mr. Hemenway says it is. So many events in the book were shaped by the author's growing mastery of books and language, but she employs both the linguistic rituals of the dominant culture and those of the black vernacular tradition. These two speech communities are the sources of inspiration for Hurston's novels and autobiography. This double voice unreconciled—a verbal analogue of her double experiences as a woman in a male-dominated world and as a black person in a non-black world—strikes me as her second great achievement.

Many writers act as if no other author influenced them, but Hurston freely describes her encounter with books, from Xenophon in the Greek through Milton to Kipling. Chapter titles and the organization of the chapters themselves reflect this urge to testify to the marvelous process by which the writer's life has been shaped by words. "The Inside Search" and "Figure and Fancy" reveal the workings of the youthful Hurston's mind as she invented fictional worlds, struggled to find the words for her developing emotions and learned to love reading. "School Again," "Research" and

"My People! My People!"—printed in the original form for the first time—
unveils social and verbal race rituals and customs with candor that shocks
even today. Hurston clearly saw herself as a black woman writer and thinker
first and as a specimen of Negro progress last. What's more, she structured
her autobiography to make such a reading inevitable.

>   Henry Louis Gates, Jr., " 'A Negro Way of Saying,' " *New York Times Book Review*,
>   21 April 1985, pp. 43, 45

JOHN LOWE   Humor is a basic, continuing component in Hurston;
to her, laughter was a way to show one's love for life, and a way to bridge
the distance between author and reader. But more than this, she was determined to create a new art form based on the Afro-American cultural tradition, something she helped recover and define, as an anthropologist. ⟨. . .⟩
It now seems clear that humor played a crucial role in her initial reception
by, and later relations with, the other members of the Harlem Renaissance;
in her sense of folklore and its functions; in the anthropological aspect of
Hurston's humor, which grew out of her training as a professional folklorist;
and in the ever changing and increasing role humor played in her fiction,
including her masterworks, *Their Eyes Were Watching God* and *Moses, Man
of the Mountain*. ⟨. . .⟩

Dust Tracks never bores the reader, largely because the book, in celebrating
Zora Neale Hurston, also salutes the culture that made her. The text is
larded with humor, both as structure and adornment. Hurston uses comic
expressions, jokes, and entire collections of humorous effects, to amplify,
underline, and sharpen the points she makes. These deceptively delightful
words often contain a serious meaning, just as the slave folktales did. Hurston
skillfully trims and fits folk saying into integral parts of her narrative; on
the first page, for instance, she describes her hometown by saying "Eatonville
is what you might call hitting a straight lick with a crooked stick. The town
. . . is a by-product of something else." This type of description becomes
more pungent when she combines these materials with her own imaginative
coinages, as in the following description of her father's family: "Regular
hand-to-mouth folks. Didn't own pots to pee in, nor beds to push 'em
under. . . . No more to 'em than the stuffings out of a zero." This utterance
alone gives utterance to Hurston's assertion that the Negro's greatest contri-
butions to the language were (1) the use of metaphor and simile ("hand-
to-mouth folks"); (2) the use of the double descriptive ("pot . . . nor beds");
and (3) the use of verbal nouns ("stuffings"). It also reveals the way such

tools can be used to revitalize language by working simultaneously in the comic mode.

> John Lowe, "Hurston, Humor, and the Harlem Renaissance," *The Harlem Renaissance Re-examined*, ed. Victor A. Kramer (New York: AMS Press, 1987), pp. 284–85, 289

KARLA F. C. HOLLOWAY   Hurston develops her character Janie to the point that she is an assertive, self-fulfilled woman. Weaving her maturity through the natural imagery of the pear tree, through a fertile farmland with Logan Killicks where her spirit is spoiled, and into a town grown out of wilderness tamed, Hurston's word destroys sexual and natural fertility. Her word sweeps through with the force of a hurricane destroying all the structures so carefully framed from the opening pages of the novel. Hurston's text has warned the reader from the same early pages of its potential for destruction, teasing itself with the "ships at a distance" puzzle that sets the narrative tone. This often-quoted paragraph (perhaps so much so because its ambiguity invites a variety of critical comment) is a linguistic trope, a tease. It is language used to tell on, to signify upon, itself. It warns the reader through such signification that here is a text that talks its own structure into existence. I think it is less important to try to discover what Hurston's opening paragraphs mean than it is to point out that these paragraphs signal a text with an internal force that will gather strength through its manipulations of language. ⟨Henry Louis⟩ Gates's observation of the importance of this text's structure clarifies its importance:

> Hurston . . . has made *Their Eyes Were Watching God* into a paradigmatic signifying text, for this novel resolves that implicit tension between the literal and the figurative contained in standard English usages of the term "signifying." *Their Eyes* represents the black trope of signifying both as thematic matter and as a rhetorical strategy of the novel itself.

I would take Gates's point further and assert that *Eyes* represents a vocal structure that is something more basic than "strategy." He observes that Janie, the protagonist, "gains her voice, as it were, in her husband's store not only by engaging with the assembled men in the ritual of signifying . . . but also by openly signifying upon her husband's impotency." I support this statement with an emendation important to my thesis of voice: Janie gains her voice from the available voice of the text and subsequently learns to share it with the narrator 〈. . .〉 This is a vital extension of Gates's discussion of *Eyes*. I must credit the voice gained to the structure itself. Certainly the traditions of signifying belong to a black community, but Hurston has made them belong to a literary text in ways that empower them to take on their own life forms. This is a tradition of voice let loose in *Jonah* and re-merged to the literary text in *Eyes*. I think it is the same voice because Hurston uses it as character—investing it with active power. Sometimes her "word" is a teasing ambiguity; other times, it is an innocent bystander. But lest we fail to take it seriously, it returns in a whirlwind to exact its due on the very world it had created in the beginning. We know this is so because in the final pages of the novel, which are really the opening pages because the novel is a flashback (another show of power by the recursive word), Janie talks to her friend Phoeby, telling her what she must tell those who criticize what she has done with her life. "Then you must *tell* [emphasis added] them," Janie says, and if we have attended to that power of the word to speak itself into being, we know that Janie too has learned that through telling her spirit will rest fulfilled. "Love is lak de sea," she tells Phoeby, while the narrative voice finishes the image that opened the novel and speaks of Janie pulling "in her horizon like a great fish-net" and calling her soul "to come and see." The images of water and air collapse in these final pages; the wind turns peaceable and waits for its next embodiment.

Karla F. C. Holloway, The Character of the Word: The Texts of Zora Neale Hurston (Westport, CT: Greenwood Press, 1987), pp. 39–40

JENNIFER JORDAN   Despite her lack of veracity, critics like Alice Walker, Robert Hemenway, and Mary Helen Washington have managed to maintain both a certain objectivity about Hurston's weaknesses and a respectful fondness for her daring and talent. This same openmindedness and tolerance for ambivalence are not always reflected in the critical responses to her greatest work, *Their Eyes Were Watching God*. Hurston's independence, her refusal to allow her love interests and marriages to hamper her career, and her adventuresomeness in confronting the dangers of anthropological research in the violent turpentine camps of the South and in the voodoo temples of Haiti make her a grand candidate for feminist sainthood. Difficulties arise, however, when critics transfer their narrow conception of Hurston's personal attitudes and history to their readings of *Their Eyes Were Watching God*, a novel that reflects Hurston's ambiguity about race, sex, and class. The result is the unsupportable notion that the novel is an appropriate fictional representation of the concerns and attitudes of modern black feminism. ⟨. . .⟩

Their Eyes Were Watching God is a novel that examines with a great deal of artistry the struggle of a middle-class woman to escape the fetters of traditional marriage and the narrow social restrictions of her class and sex. But Janie Killicks Starks Woods never perceives herself as an independent, intrinsically fulfilled human being. Nor does she form the strong female and racial bonds that black feminists have deemed necessary in their definition of an ideologically correct literature. The novel fails to meet several of the criteria defined by black feminist criticism. Perhaps the acceptance and glorification of this novel as the bible of black women's liberation speak to the unconscious conflicts about emotional and financial dependence, sexual stereotyping, intraracial hostilities, and class interests inherent within the black feminist movement. In its very ambivalences Hurston's *Their Eyes Were Watching God* may serve as a Rorschach test by which these conflicts are revealed and thus is an appropriate manifesto for black feminism.

But the novel's success or failure as an ideological document does not diminish its aesthetic worth. It remains one of the great novels of black literature—a novel that is laughing out-loud funny, that allows black people to speak in their own wonderful voices, and that portrays them in all their human nobility and pettiness.

Jennifer Jordan, "Feminist Fantasies: Zora Neale Hurston's *Their Eyes Were Watching God*," *Tulsa Studies in Women's Literature* 7, No. 1 (Spring 1988): 106–7, 115

NELLIE McKAY   Unlike the solitary but representative hero of male autobiography, Janie Starks and Zora Neale Hurston join voices to produce a personal narrative that celebrates an individual and collective black female identity emerging out of the search for an autonomous self. Although the structure of this text is different, the tradition of black women celebrating themselves through other women like themselves began with their personal narratives of the nineteenth century. Female slave narratives, we know, generally had protagonists who shared their space with the women who instilled pride of self and love of freedom in them. The tradition continued into the twentieth century. For instance, much of the early portion of Hurston's autobiography, *Dust Tracks on a Road*, celebrates the relationship she had with her mother and the lessons she learned, directly and indirectly, from other women in the community. Thus, Hurston's structure for Janie's story expands that already existing tradition to concretize the symbolic rendering of voice to and out of the women's community by breaking away from the formalities of conventional autobiography to make Janie's text an autobiography about autobiographical storytelling, in the tradition of African and Afro-American storytelling. Hurston, struggling with the pains and ambivalences she felt toward the realities of a love she had to reject for the restraints it would have placed on her, found a safe place to embalm the tenderness and passion of her feelings in the autobiographical voice of Janie Crawford, whose life she made into a very fine crayon enlargement of life.

> Nellie McKay, " 'Crayon Enlargements of Life': Zora Neale Hurston's *Their Eyes Were Watching God* as Autobiography," *New Essays on* Their Eyes Were Watching God, ed. Michael Awkward (New York: Cambridge University Press, 1990), pp. 68–69

MAYA ANGELOU   Zora Neale Hurston chose to write her own version of life in *Dust Tracks on a Road*. Through her imagery one soon learns that the author was born to roam, to listen and to tell a variety of stories. An active curiosity led her throughout the South, where she gathered up the feelings and the sayings of her people as a fastidious farmer might gather eggs. When she began to write, she used all the sights she had seen, all the people she encountered and the exploits she had survived. One reading of Hurston is enough to convince the reader that Hurston had dramatic adventures and was a quintessential survivor. According to her own account in *Dust Tracks on a Road*, a hog with a piglet and an interest in some food Hurston was eating taught the infant Hurston to walk. The sow came snorting toward her, and Zora, who had never taken a step, decided that the time had come to rectify her reluctance. She stood and not only walked but climbed into a chair beyond the sow's inquisitive reach.

That lively pragmatism which revealed itself so early was to remain with Hurston most of her life. It prompted her to write and rewrite history. Her books and folktales vibrate with tragedy, humor and the real music of Black American speech.

⟨. . .⟩ Is it possible that Hurston, who had been bold and bodacious all her life, was carrying on the tradition she had begun with the writing of *Spunk* in 1925? That is, did she mean to excoriate some of her own people, whom she felt had ignored or ridiculed her? The *New Yorker* critic declared the work a "warm, witty, imaginative, rich and winning book by one of our few genuine grade A folk writers."

There is, despite its success in certain quarters, a strange distance in this book. Certainly the language is true and the dialogue authentic, but the author stands between the content and the reader. It is difficult, if not impossible, to find and touch the real Zora Neale Hurston. The late Larry Neal in his introduction to the 1971 edition of *Dust Tracks on a Road* cited, "At one moment she could sound highly nationalistic. Then at other times she might mouth statements which in terms of the ongoing struggle for Black liberation were ill conceived and were even reactionary."

There is a saying in the Black community that advises: "If a person asks you where you're going, you tell him where you've been. That way you neither lie nor reveal your secrets." Hurston called herself the "Queen of the Niggerati." She also said, "I like myself when I'm laughing." *Dust Tracks on a Road* is written with royal humor and an imperious creativity. But then all creativity is imperious, and Zora Neale Hurston was certainly creative.

> Maya Angelou, "Foreword," *Dust Tracks on a Road* (New York: HarperPerennial, 1991), pp. viii–xii

❖ *Bibliography*

Jonah's Gourd Vine. 1934.

Mules and Men. 1935.

Their Eyes Were Watching God. 1937.

Tell My Horse. 1938, 1939 (as *Voodoo Gods: An Inquiry into Native Myths and Magic in Jamaica and Haiti*).

Moses, Man of the Mountain. 1939.

Dust Tracks on a Road: An Autobiography. 1942.

Caribbean Melodies for Chorus of Mixed Voices and Soloists by William Grant Still (editor). 1947.

Seraph on the Suwanee. 1948.

I Love Myself When I Am Laughing . . . and Then Again When I Am Looking Mean and Impressive: A Zora Neale Hurston Reader. Ed. Alice Walker. 1979.

The Sanctified Church. 1981.

Spunk: Selected Stories. 1985.

Mule Bone: A Comedy of Negro Life (with Langston Hughes). Ed. George Houston Bass and Henry Louis Gates, Jr. 1991.

Nella Larsen
1891–1964

NELLA MARIE LARSEN was the daughter of an African–West Indian father and a Danish mother. Though the year of 1893 has been cited as the year of her birth, official working records reveal it to be April 13, 1891. Her father died when she was two; two years later her mother married a Danish man. Larsen was raised in an all-white household, in predominantly white surroundings, attending school in the primarily German and Scandinavian suburbs of Chicago. Larsen entered all-black Fisk University Normal School (high school) in 1907, attending for one year.

Larsen studied as a nurse in New York and later worked in that profession in Tuskegee, Alabama, and in New York. She quit nursing in 1921, but years later returned to the profession after abandoning all involvement in the literary world. In 1919 she married Dr. Elmer S. Imes, a physicist and a notorious womanizer. (Larsen always published either under her maiden name or a pseudonym.) Their rocky relationship finally ended in divorce in 1932 amidst great public scandal.

In 1922 Larsen became a librarian at the New York Public Library, in charge of children's books at the Countee Cullen branch. In 1926 the first of Larsen's two novels, *Quicksand,* was begun and, in 1928, published by Alfred A. Knopf. The book dealt with the then-unconventional theme of the mulatto in society. Although some critics cite fame and popularity as Larsen's guiding ambition, *Quicksand*'s treatment of bourgeois black Americans was a significant and financially risky departure from the most popular black American novels of the time, which dealt with lower-class nightlife in Harlem. Larsen was awarded the Harmon Foundation bronze medal for literature in 1928, and after the publication of her second novel, *Passing,* in 1929, she received the first Guggenheim Fellowship ever given to a black American woman.

In 1930 Larsen traveled to Mallorca to work on a new novel, but it was never published. She was accused of plagiarism in her short story "Sanctuary," which was published in *Forum* in 1930; although exonerated, she was profoundly disturbed by the incident. Owing to financial difficulties and her divorce, Larsen quit writing altogether and worked as a nurse in Brooklyn, New York, until her death on March 30, 1964. She is buried in Brooklyn's Cypress Hills Cemetery.

❖ *Critical Extracts*

ROARK BRADFORD   The real charm of ⟨*Quicksand*⟩ lies in Miss Larsen's delicate achievement in maintaining for a long time an indefinable, wistful feeling—that feeling of longing and at the same time a conscious realization of the impossibility of obtaining—that is contained in the idea of Helga Crane. (Helga is an idea more than she is a human being: drawing character does not seem to be one of Miss Larsen's major accomplishments.) ⟨. . .⟩

It leads directly to a splendid emotional climax. The brief scene is at a party in Harlem. Helga is alone for a moment with the man who first understood that strange emotions swelled within her bosom. (That was years before at Naxos. Now he is the husband of her best friend.) Her nerves are tuned to a high pitch; her soul is stirred; savagery tears at her heart; the black blood chokes the white, and Africa rumbles through her veins. And the man—suddenly the veneers of civilization crackle about him and—well, the reader is as tense as the two actors in the drama.

But alas! Without knowing just where it comes from, the reader suddenly catches a faint odor of talcum powder. And from that point on the book—in this reviewer's opinion—suffers from odors . . . Burnt cork, mostly.

In spite of its failure to hold up to the end, the book is good. No doubt it will be widely read and discussed. The reader, to get the maximum enjoyment, should begin with a mind as free as possible of racial prejudices and preconceived notions and conclusions. Miss Larsen seems to know much about the problems that confront the upper stratum of Negroes, and happily, she does not get oratorical about what she knows. She is quite sensitive to Negro life, but she isn't hysterical about it. There is a saneness about her writing that, in these hysterical literary times, more than compensates for her faults.

> Roark Bradford, "Mixed Blood," *New York Herald Tribune Books*, 13 May 1928, p. 22

W. E. B. DU BOIS   Nella Larsen's *Passing* is one of the finest novels of the year. If it did not treat a forbidden subject—the inter-marriage of a stodgy middle-class white man to a very beautiful and selfish octoroon—it would have an excellent chance to be hailed, selected and recommended. As it is, it will probably be given the "silence," with only the commendation of word of mouth. But what of that? It is a good close-knit story, moving along surely but with enough leisure to set out seven delicately limned characters. Above all, the thing is done with studied and singularly successful art. Nella Larsen is learning how to write and acquiring style, and she is doing it very simply and clearly. ⟨. . .⟩

Nella Larsen ⟨. . .⟩ explains just what "passing" is: the psychology of the thing; the reaction of it on friend and enemy. It is a difficult task, but she attacks the problem fearlessly and with consummate art. The great problem is under what circumstances would a person take a step like this and how would they feel about it? And how would their fellows feel?

W. E. B. Du Bois, [Review of *Passing*], *Crisis* 36, No. 7 (July 1929): 234–35

ROBERT BONE   The key to the narrative structure of *Quicksand* is contained in a passage toward the end of the novel in which Helga Crane rebels against her lot as a brood mare: "For she had to admit it wasn't new, this feeling of dissatisfaction, of asphyxiation. Something like it she had experienced before. In Naxos. In New York. In Copenhagen. This differed only in degree." Helga's quest for happiness has led her, floundering, through a succession of minor bogs, until she is finally engulfed by a quagmire of her own making. The basic metaphor of the novel, contained in its title, is supported throughout by concrete images of suffocation, asphyxiation, and claustrophobia. Associated always with Helga's restlessness and dissatisfaction, these symbols of a loathsome, hostile environment are at bottom projections of Negro self-hatred: "It was as if she were shut up, boxed up with hundreds of her race, closed up with that something in the racial character which had always been, to her, inexplicable, alien. Why, she demanded in fierce rebellion, should she be yoked to these despised black folk?"

On one level, *Quicksand* is an authentic case study which yields readily to psychoanalytic interpretation. Each of the major episodes in Helga's life is a recapitulation of the same psychological pattern: temporary enthusiasm; boredom, followed by disgust; and finally a stifling sense of entrapment. Then escape into a new situation, until escape is no longer possible. Race is functional in this pattern, for it has to do with Helga's initial rejection and therefore with her neurotic withdrawal pattern. Her tendency to withdraw from any situation which threatens to become permanent indicates that she is basically incapable of love or happiness. No matter how often she alters her situation, she carries her problems with her.

Deserted by her colored father and rejected by her white stepfather, Helga's quest may be viewed as the search for a father's love. The qualities of balance and security which she finds so appealing in Danish society; her attraction for Dr. Anderson, an older married man; her desire for "nice things" as a substitute for the security of parental love; and her belated return to religion can all be understood in these terms. Her degrading marriage to a jackleg preacher who "fathers" her in a helpless moment plainly has its basis in the Oedipal triangle. Her unconscious need to be debased is in reality the need to replace her mother by marrying a "no-account" colored man not unlike her gambler father. ⟨. . .⟩

The dramatic tension of the novel can be stated in terms of a conflict between Helga's sexuality and her love for "nice things." Her desire for material comfort is static; it is the value premise on which the novel is based: "Always she had wanted . . . the things which money could give, leisure, attention, beautiful surroundings. Things. Things. Things." Helga's sexuality, on the other hand, is dynamic; its strength increases until she is overwhelmed and deprived of the accouterments of gracious living forever. ⟨. . .⟩

⟨. . .⟩ Helga's tragedy, in Larsen's eyes, is that she allows herself to be declassed by her own sexuality. The tone of reproach is unmistakable. It is this underlying moralism which differentiates *Quicksand* from the novels of the Harlem School. It is manifested not in Helga's behavior, which is "naturalistic" and well motivated, even inevitable, but in the symbols of luxury which are counterposed to the bog, in the author's prudish attitude toward sex, and in her simple equation of "nice things" with the pursuit of beauty.

Robert Bone, *The Negro Novel in America* (New Haven: Yale University Press, 1958), pp. 103–6

CLAUDIA TATE   Race ⟨. . .⟩ is not ⟨*Passing's*⟩ foremost concern, but is merely a mechanism for setting the story in motion, sustaining the suspense, and bringing about the external circumstances for the story's conclusion. The real impetus for the story is Irene's emotional turbulence, which is entirely responsible for the course that the story takes and ultimately accountable for the narrative ambiguity. The problem of interpreting *Passing* can, therefore, be simplified by defining Irene's role in the story and determining the extent to which she is reliable as the sole reporter and interpreter of events. We must determine whether she accurately portrays Clare, or whether her portrait is subject to, and in fact affected by, her own growing jealousy and insecurity. In this regard, it is essential to ascertain precisely who is the tragic heroine—Irene who is on the verge of total mental disintegration or Clare whose desire for excitement brings about her sudden death.

Initially, *Passing* seems to be about Clare Kendry, inasmuch as most of the incidents plot out Clare's encounters with Irene and Black society. Furthermore, Irene sketches in detail Clare's physical appearance down to "[her] slim golden feet." Yet, she is unable to perceive the intangible aspects of Clare's character, and Larsen uses Irene's failure as a means of revealing disturbing aspects of her own psychological character. ⟨. . .⟩

Irene is literally obsessed with Clare's beauty, a beauty of such magnitude that she seems alien, impervious, indeed inscrutable. ⟨. . .⟩ Irene repeatedly describes Clare in hyperbole—"too vague," "too remote," "so dark and deep and unfathomable," "utterly strange," "incredibly beautiful," "utterly beyond any experience. . . ." These hyperbolic expressions are ambiguous. They create the impression that Clare is definitely, though indescribably, different from and superior to Irene and other ordinary people.

Irene's physical appearance, on the other hand, is drawn sketchily. We know that she has "warm olive skin" and curly black hair. Though Irene is not referred to as a beauty, given her confidence and social grace, we are inclined to believe that she is attractive. Despite the fact that little attention is given to Irene's physical portrayal, her encounter with Clare provides the occasion for the subtle revelation of her psychological character. Hence, the two portraits are polarized and mutually complementary—one is purely external, while the other is intensely internal.

Claudia Tate, "Nella Larsen's *Passing*: A Problem of Interpretation," *Black American Literature Forum* 14, No. 4 (Winter 1980): 143–44

MARY HELEN WASHINGTON   Larsen's failure in dealing with ⟨. . .⟩ marginality is implicit in the very choice of "passing" as a symbol or metaphor of deliverance for her women. It is an obscene form of salvation. The woman who passes is required to deny everything about her past—her girlhood, her family, places with memories, folk customs, folk rhymes, her language, the entire long line of people who have gone before her. She lives in terror of discovery—what if she has a child with a dark complexion, what if she runs into an old school friend, how does she listen placidly to racial slurs? And more, where does the woman who passes find the equanimity to live by the privilege status that is based on the oppression of her own people?

Larsen's heroines are all finally destroyed somewhere down the paths they choose. Helga Crane loses herself in a loveless marriage to an old black preacher by whom she has five children in as many years. She finally retreats into illness and silence, eventually admitting to herself a suppressed hatred for her husband. *Passing*'s Irene Redfield suspects an affair between her friend Clare (recently surfaced from the white world) and her black physician husband. This threatens her material and psychological security. In the novel's melodramatic ending, she pushes Clare off the balcony of a seventeenth-floor apartment and sinks into unconsciousness when she is questioned about Clare's death.

And Nella Larsen, who created Helga and Irene, chose oblivion for herself. From the little we know of the last 30 years of her life, she handled the problem of marginality by default, living entirely without any racial and cultural identity. Her exile was so complete that one of her biographers couldn't find an obituary for her: "I couldn't even bury Nella Larsen," she said.

But unlike the women in her novels, Larsen did not die from her marginality. She lived 70 years, was an active part of the high-stepping Harlem Renaissance, traveled abroad, and worked as a nurse for 40 years. She was an unconventional woman by 1920s standards: she wore her dresses short, smoked cigarettes, rejected religion, and lived in defiance of the rules that most black women of her education and means were bound by. She lived through the conflicts of the marginal woman and felt them passionately. Why didn't she leave us the greater legacy of the mature model, the perceptions of a woman who confronts the pain, alienation, isolation, and grapples with these conundrums until new insight has been forged from the struggle? Why didn't she continue to write after 1929? ⟨. . .⟩

She did not solve her own problems, but Larsen made us understand as no one did before her that the image of the middle-class black woman as a coldly self-centered snob, chattering irrelevantly at bridge club and sorority meetings, was as much a mask as the grin on the face of Stepin Fetchit. The women in her novel, like Larsen, are driven to emotional and psychological extremes in their attempts to handle ambivalence, marginality, racism, and sexism. She has shown us that behind the carefully manicured exterior, behind the appearance of security is a woman who hears the beating of her wings against a walled prison.

Mary Helen Washington, "Nella Larsen: Mystery Woman of the Harlem Renaissance," Ms. 9, No. 6 (December 1980): 50

CHERYL A. WALL   The novels ⟨Larsen⟩ left behind prove that at least some of her promise was realized. Among the best written of the time, her books comment incisively on issues of marginality and cultural dualism that engaged Larsen's contemporaries, such as Jean Toomer and Claude McKay, but the bourgeois ethos of her novels has unfortunately obscured the similarities. However, Larsen's most striking insights are into psychic dilemmas confronting certain black women. To dramatize these, Larsen draws characters who are, by virtue of their appearance, education, and social class, atypical in the extreme. Swiftly viewed, they resemble the tragic mulattoes of literary convention. On closer examination, they become the means through which the author demonstrates the psychological costs of racism and sexism.

For Larsen, the tragic mulatto was the only formulation historically available to portray educated middle-class black women in fiction. But her protagonists subvert the convention consistently. They are neither noble nor long-suffering; their plights are not used to symbolize the oppression of blacks, the irrationality of prejudice, or the absurdity of concepts of race generally. Larsen's deviations from these traditional strategies signal that her concerns lie elsewhere, but only in the past decade have critics begun to decode her major themes. Both *Quicksand* and *Passing* contemplate the inextricability of the racism and sexism which confront the black woman in her quest for a wholly integrated identity. As they navigate between racial and cultural polarities, Larsen's protagonists attempt to fashion a sense of self free of both suffocating restrictions of ladyhood and fantasies of the exotic female Other. They fail. The tragedy for these mulattoes is the impossibility of self-definition. Larsen's protagonists assume false identities that ensure social survival but result in psychological suicide. In one way or another, they all "pass." Passing for white, Larsen's novels remind us, is only one way this game is played.

Cheryl A. Wall, "Passing for What? Aspects of Identity in Nella Larsen's Novels," *Black American Literature Forum* 20, Nos. 1–2 (Spring–Summer 1986): 97–98

DEBORAH E. McDOWELL   Although Irene is clearly deluded about her motives, her racial loyalty, her class, and her distinctness from Clare, the narrative suggests that her most glaring delusion concerns her feelings for Clare. 〈. . .〉 The narrative traces this developing eroticism in spatial terms. It begins on the roof of the Drayton hotel (with all the suggestions of the sexually illicit), intensifies at Clare's tea party, and, getting proverbially "close to home," explodes in Irene's own bedroom. Preoccupied with appearances, social respectability, and safety, however, Irene tries to force these emerging feelings underground. The narrative dramatizes that repression effectively in images of concealment and burial. Significantly, the novel's opening image is an envelope (a metaphoric vagina) which Irene hesitates to open, fearing its "contents would reveal" an "attitude toward danger." 〈. . .〉 Irene tries to preserve "a hardness from feeling" about the letter, though "brilliant red patches flamed" in her cheeks. Unable to explain her feelings for Clare, "for which she could find no name," Irene dismisses them as "Just somebody walking over [her] grave." The narrative suggests pointedly that Clare is the body walking over the grave of Irene's buried sexual feelings.

Lest the reader miss this eroticism, Larsen employs fire imagery—the conventional representation of sexual desire—introducing and instituting this imagery in the novel's opening pages. Irene begins her retrospective account of her reunion with Clare, remembering that the day was "hot," the sun "brutal" and "staring," its rays "like molten rain." Significantly, Irene, feeling "sticky and soiled from contact with so many sweating bodies," escapes to the roof of the Drayton Hotel where she is reunited with Clare, after a lapse of many years. (Irene is, ironically, "escaping" to the very thing she wants to avoid.) 〈. . .〉

Although the ending is ambiguous and the evidence circumstantial, I agree with Cheryl Wall that, "Larsen strongly implies that Irene pushes Clare through the window" 〈. . .〉 To suggest the extent to which Clare's death represents the death of Irene's sexual feelings for Clare, Larsen uses a clever objective correlative: Irene's pattern of lighting cigarettes and snuffing them out. Minutes before Clare falls from the window to her death, "Irene finished her cigarette and threw it out, watching the tiny spark drop slowly down to the white ground below." Clearly attempting a symbolic parallel, Clare is described as "a vital glowing thing, like a flame of red and gold" who falls from (or is thrown out of) the window as well. Because Clare is a reminder of that repressed and disowned part of Irene's self, Clare must be banished, for, more unacceptable than the feelings themselves is the fact that they find an object of expression in Clare. In other words,

Clare is both the embodiment and the object of the sexual feelings that Irene banishes.

Larsen's becomes, in effect, a banishing act as well. Or put another way, the idea of bringing a sexual attraction between two women to full narrative expression is likewise, too dangerous a move ⟨. . .⟩ Larsen's clever narrative strategies almost conceal it. In *Passing* she uses a technique found commonly in narrative by Afro-American and women novelists with a "dangerous" story to tell: "safe" themes, plots, and conventions are used as the protective cover underneath which lie more dangerous subplots. Larsen envelops the subplot of Irene's developing if unnamed and unacknowledged desire for Clare in the safe and familiar plot of racial passing. Put another way, the novel's clever strategy derives from its surface theme and central metaphor—passing. It takes the form of the act it describes. Implying false, forged, and mistaken identities, the title functions on multiple levels: thematically, in terms of the racial and sexual plot; and strategically, in terms of the narrative's disguise.

> Deborah E. McDowell, "Introduction," *Quicksand and Passing* (New Brunswick, NJ: Rutgers University Press, 1986), pp. xxvi–xxvii, xxix–xxx

---

HAZEL V. CARBY   Social relations which objectified the body permeate ⟨*Quicksand*⟩. Helga herself was represented as a consumer, a woman who defined a self through the acquisition of commercial products, consumer goods, and commodities. As a woman, she is at the center of a complex process of exchange. Money was crucial to Larsen's narrative, structuring power relations, controlling social movement, and defining the boundaries of Helga's environment. Money replaces kinship as the prime mediator of social relations: Helga's white uncle sent her money as he could not afford to acknowledge her relationship to him. This money allowed her social movement; she bought her way out of a Jim Crow car and eventually out of Harlem. In Chicago, Helga spent money, buying and consuming rather than facing her desperate conditions. While the possession of money disguises her real social predicament, the lack of money forced degradation and the recognition that in the job market her social position as a black woman was narrowly defined as domestic worker.

Although money permitted Helga's movement within the text, the direction of her journey reproduces the tensions of migration into a structure of oppositions between country and city. Helga's first movement in the text is from South to North, from the rural outskirts of Atlanta to industrial

Chicago.   Immediately upon arrival in Chicago, Helga became one of a crowd. Her initial identification was with the anonymity of the city, where she had the appearance of freedom but no actual home or friends. This anonymity brought brief satisfaction and contentment, while Helga could maintain her position as consumer, but she discovered her vulnerability as an object of exchange when her money ran out. Larsen represented the city as a conglomeration of strangers, where social relations were structured through the consumption of both objects and people. The imagery of commerce and this process of exchange dominated the text as it moved to New York and Copenhagen. This polarity between rural and urban experience frames the text; in the closing pages, all cities are finally abandoned and Helga is metaphorically and, the reader is led to assume, literally buried in the rural South. ⟨. . .⟩

⟨. . .⟩ Larsen's representation of both race and class are structured through a prism of black female sexuality. Larsen recognized that the repression of the sensual in Afro-American fiction in response to the long history of the exploitation of black sexuality led to the repression of passion and the repression or denial of female sexuality and desire. But, of course, the representation of black female sexuality meant risking its definition as primitive and exotic within a racist society. Larsen attempted to embody but could not hope to resolve these contradictions in her representation of Helga as a sexual being, making Helga the first truly sexual black female protagonist in Afro-American fiction. Racist sexual ideologies proclaimed the black woman to be a rampant sexual being, and in response black women writers either focused on defending their morality or displaced sexuality onto another terrain. Larsen confronted this denial directly in her fiction. Helga consistently attempted to deny her sensuality and repress her sexual desires, and the result is tragedy. Each of the crises of the text centered on sexual desire until the conclusion of the novel, where control over her body was denied Helga and her sexuality was reduced to its biological capacity to bear children. Helga's four children represented her entrapment as she was unable to desert them; her fifth child represented her certain death.

Hazel V. Carby, *Reconstructing Womanhood: The Emergence of the Afro-American Woman Novelist* (New York: Oxford University Press, 1987), pp. 173–74

ELIZABETH AMMONS   Clearly, Irene and Clare are doubles. Clare represents for Irene the dangerous side of herself—foreign, outlawed— that she as a respectable middle-class black woman has successfully denied.

Clare is sexual, daring, creative. She has moved out of African American bourgeois culture; she roams free of its demands for conformity and social service and endless attention to familial and community uplift.

But where has this "freedom" taken Clare? Her life as a white woman is hollow and self-destructive; it represents a pact with self-loathing, a project in self-erasure. Her true self is so unknown to the white man she has married and with whom she has had a child that she lives daily with his racist and hideously ironic nickname for her, "Nig." To tell him why the appellation is particularly offensive would be to lose the position of "freedom" she has created for herself. To remain silent is to acquiesce in the system of self-degradation that she has bought into. ⟨. . .⟩

Complicating these conflicting possibilities even further, Larsen allows us to know Clare's story only through another woman no less conflicted, dishonest, or cowardly than Clare. Dutiful, repressed, correct, Irene clearly *needs* Clare dead. ⟨. . .⟩ She pushes Clare out the window.

Or does Clare jump? We cannot say. We can surmise either possibility— or, paradoxically, in this novel about split and conflicting identities and possibilities—both. If Clare and Irene, finally, are alienated parts of one potentially whole identity, to say that Clare jumped is the same as to say that Irene pushed her, and vice versa. In either case, Larsen's story about the black woman artist in *Passing* ends in permanent silence. The divisions between respectable middle-class feminine status and the woman artist, between heterosexual and lesbian desire, and between acceptance in white and black America are unbridgeable.

> Elizabeth Ammons, "Jumping out the Window: Nella Larsen's *Passing* and the End of an Era," *Conflicting Stories: American Women Writers at the Turn into the Twentieth Century* (New York: Oxford University Press, 1991), pp. 190–91.

JONATHAN LITTLE   Larsen, obviously aware of the traditions before her, chooses not to depict such serene returns ⟨to the African-American community⟩ for her ⟨mulatto⟩ characters in *Passing*. Even after returning back across the color line into the Black community, Clare Kendry finds no peace, rest, loyalty—or any real security. Clare's racial origins are revealed to her white racist husband at a party held at the Freelands' apartment. The "freeland" is free in one respect. Clare is finally "let out" of her marriage by the discovery. Earlier she had told her friend, Irene Redfield, " 'But if Jack [her husband] finds out, if our marriage is broken, that lets me out. Doesn't it?' " The freeland Clare attains is finally ironic, however, since she promptly falls to her death, pushed by the same friend in whom she had so closely confided. In killing Clare off, Larsen does not depict any "freeland" or supportive community that will embrace Clare in her process of returning. Larsen undermines romantic convention, substituting ironic tragedy where there had been joy.

Even further, Larsen implies that there is no longer a Black community anywhere in the world to return to. Oddly enough, in *Passing*, Brazil, instead of Africa, is evoked as the quintessential text of racial equality and haven from North American white oppression. Irene Redfield, the narrative consciousness in *Passing*, reports that her husband Brian is enamored with Brazil and longs to escape there, away from racist Harlem, away from what he calls " 'this hellish place.' " Even this vision, however, is ironized, showing the extent of Brian's romantic delusions. By the end of the twenties, the hopes of a Brazilian paradise, the "Eldorado" of the South, were shattered. Thus Larsen chose Brazil instead of Africa for a reason: By the time she wrote *Passing* in 1929, Brazil symbolized a deflated and ironic hope for an alternative community that was more a romantic dream than a reality. Larsen's irony, then, extends beyond the confines of her text to show how the weave of disillusionment runs through the global environment, and not just through bourgeois Black Harlem.

Larsen's letters (1925–1932) to Carl Van Vechten (to whom, along with his wife, Fania Marinoff, Larsen dedicated *Passing*) affirm the view of Larsen as a skeptic. Consistent with her distance from the cause of racial uplift shown in her novels, she wrote to Van Vechten that she "wanted very much the pleasure of refusing" an invitation to the Women's Auxiliary of the NAACP tea held in her honor in 1928. At the same time, however, she also attacked misguided and perhaps unintentionally racist white liberal thinking 〈. . .〉

In her fiction and in her letters, Larsen does not offer any final messages or final Truth(s) that will clear away racial and social difficulties. This orientation prevents Larsen from portraying a triumphant character or social utopia. Every direction she offers is quickly undercut by a counter-dilemma— e.g., Brazil is no longer available as a social and racial utopia. Even the traditional passing for white plot is undermined. There is no supportive "birthright" to which her passers may serenely return.

Jonathan Little, "Nella Larsen's *Passing*: Irony and the Critics," *African American Review* 26, No. 1 (1992): 174–75

DAVID L. BLACKMORE   The implications of Larsen's "flirtation" 〈in *Passing*〉 with both female and male homosexuality are radical. For Irene, lesbianism offers an alternative to repressive middle-class marriages. As an African-American woman, Irene must inevitably confront the stereotype that women of her race are Jezebels. White American culture tells her that black female identity centers around desire, that in fact an African American woman is nothing but a beast driven by irrepressible sexuality. The key, then, to combating this stereotype lies in the repression of sexuality, in the confinement of desire to the constricted realm of the respectable marriage. Doing her part to dispel the Jezebel myth, Irene plays the role of the eminently respectable, asexual mother/wife. In focusing her energies and identity on her husband and sons, she deflects attention away from her own sexual nature. ⟨. . .⟩

It is unclear whether Larsen's suggestion of a lesbian relationship as an alternative to Irene's repressive marriage reflects a sexual decision she made or contemplated in her own life. However, her literary experimentation with non-traditional sexuality mirrors a larger trend in 1920s' Harlem, where lesbianism and particularly female bisexuality received a great deal of attention as naughty but exciting options for adventurous, "modern" women. As Lillian Faderman details in her recent book *Odd Girls and Twilight Lovers*, a visible black lesbian subculture was established in Harlem early in the century. Furthermore, large numbers of whites flocked to Harlem in the '20s "to experience homosexuality as the epitome of the forbidden." The perception of upper Manhattan as a center of laissez-faire sexuality drew both blacks and whites who wished to observe or participate in sexual practices deemed immoral by the white establishment. ⟨. . .⟩

Just as a romance with Clare would provide an alternative to Irene's emotionally empty existence, so leading a homosexual life in Brazil would free Brian from his own unsatisfying role in bourgeois Harlem society. In Brazil he would face less pressure to " 'care for ladies.' " He could express more openly his attraction to other men; he could, in fact, engage in sexual activity that would not be the " 'joke' " that straight sex is to him. He would be free of his unwanted role as sexual overlord to his wife, and free to determine for himself the role a man should play in sexual and social relationships. No longer the "empowered" yet burdened provider for a family, he would also no longer be the segregated subordinate in a white man's world. Brian's Brazil provides an alternate vision of an Afro-centric sphere in which a man need not provide for a woman and where men may love each other freely. This, surely, is a radical vision on Larsen's part.

David L. Blackmore, " 'That Unreasonable Restless Feeling': The Homosexual Sub-texts of Nella Larsen's *Passing*," *African American Review* 26, No. 3 (1992): 478–79, 481

▨ *Bibliography*

Quicksand. 1928.

Passing. 1929.

An Intimation of Things Distant: Collected Fiction. Ed. Charles R. Larson. 1992.

◈ ◈ ◈

Claude McKay
1890–1948

CLAUDE MCKAY was born in Sunny Ville, Jamaica, on September 15, 1890. After being apprenticed to a wheelwright in Kingston, he emigrated to the U.S. in 1912 and studied agriculture at the Tuskegee Institute and at Kansas State University. He abandoned his studies in 1914 and moved to Harlem, where he became a leading radical poet. Before coming to America, McKay had published a collection of poetry entitled *Songs of Jamaica* (1912). While in Harlem he frequently wrote under the pseudonym Eli Edwards, a name derived from that of his wife, Eulalie Imelda Edwards. This marriage ended in 1914 after only six months; McKay's wife gave birth to a daughter whom he never saw.

"If We Must Die," perhaps McKay's best-known poem, was published in Max Eastman's magazine, the *Liberator*, in 1919. This stirring call to arms was written after the race riots that followed the end of World War I. McKay lived in London from 1919 to 1921; during this time he first read Karl Marx and worked for the Marxist periodical *Worker's Dreadnought*. In 1922—the year he published his celebrated poetry collection *Harlem Shadows*—he made a "magic pilgrimage" to the USSR where he was warmly welcomed by the Communist leaders and addressed the Third Communist International. He wrote two works that were translated into Russian by P. Okhrimenko in 1923: *Sudom Lincha,* a collection of three stories, and the treatise *Negry v Amerike*. These works were translated into English by Robert Winter, the first (as *Trial by Lynching: Stories about Negro Life in America*) in 1977, the second (as *The Negroes in America*) in 1979. McKay's interest in Marx seems to have been based on his perception of its calls for a return to agrarian values and for racial equality. However, McKay never joined the Communist party and by the 1930s he had completely renounced all association with communism.

From 1923 to 1934 McKay lived overseas, having left the United States as a result of his alienation from the black American intelligentsia and from the leaders of the Harlem Renaissance. In Paris he came to feel that racial barriers separated him from "the lost generation"; he subsequently moved to Marseilles and later to Morocco. In Marseilles he wrote his first two novels, *Home to Harlem* (1928) and *Banjo* (1929). On its publication, *Home to Harlem* became the most popular novel ever written by a black author. In 1932 McKay published a collection of short stories, *Gingertown*, followed by a third novel, *Banana Bottom* (1933).

Returning to the U.S. in 1934, McKay worked briefly as a laborer in a welfare camp. In 1938 he wrote *A Long Way from Home*, an account of his life since first coming to America. In 1944 he was baptized into the Roman Catholic church and wrote essays on Christian faith. He died in Chicago on May 22, 1948.

◈ Critical Extracts

W. E. B. DU BOIS   Claude McKay's *Home to Harlem* 〈. . .〉 for the most part nauseates me, and after the dirtier parts of its filth I feel distinctly like taking a bath. This does not mean that the book is wholly bad. McKay is too great a poet to make any complete failure in writing. There are bits of *Home to Harlem*, beautiful and fascinating: the continued changes upon the theme of the beauty of colored skins; the portrayal of the fascination of their new yearnings for each other which Negroes are developing. The chief character, Jake, has something appealing, and the glimpses of the Haitian, Ray, have all the materials of a great piece of fiction.

But it looks as though, despite this, McKay has set out to cater for that prurient demand on the part of white folk for a portrayal in Negroes of that utter licentiousness which conventional civilization holds white folk back from enjoying—if enjoyment it can be called. That which a certain decadent section of the white American world, centered particularly in New York, longs for with fierce and unrestrained passions, it wants to see written out in black and white, and saddled on black Harlem. This demand, as voiced by a number of New York publishers, McKay has certainly satisfied, and added much for good measure. He has used every art and emphasis to paint drunkenness, fighting, lascivious sexual promiscuity and utter absence of restraint in as bold and as bright colors as he can.

If this had been done in the course of a well-conceived plot or with any artistic unity, it might have been understood if not excused. But *Home to Harlem* is padded. Whole chapters here and there are inserted with no connection to the main plot, except that they are on the same dirty subject. As a picture of Harlem life or of Negro life anywhere, it is, of course, nonsense. Untrue, not so much as on account of its facts, but on account of its emphasis and glaring colors. I am sorry that the author of *Harlem Shadows* stooped to this. I sincerely hope that he will some day rise above it and give us in fiction the strong, well-knit as well as beautiful theme, that it seems to me he might do.

W. E. B. Du Bois, "Two Novels," *Crisis* 35, No. 6 (June 1928): 202

FREDA KIRCHWEY   I read *Banjo* with the same mixture of joy and discomfort that comprised my feeling about *Home to Harlem*. Here is an unforgettable picture of waterfront life in Marseilles where seamen and drifters of all races and nations live in a conglomerate mass "bumming a day's work, a meal, a drink, existing from hand to mouth, anyhow, any way, between box car, tramp ship, bistro, and bordel." " 'Hot damn,' cried Banjo, 'What a town this heah is to spread joy in!' " Careless love and jazz and the warm, red wine that flows from the barrels on the docks; fights and sudden death and hunger and disease, mingled without order or restraint or end—this is the life of the Provençal port. All of it Claude McKay pours richly into the pages of the book. He has achieved a fine piece of characterization and description, depending for its effect upon a sure mastery of the material rather than on any particular sense of direction or of form. As life sprawls in the Ditch and on the breakwater, so does Claude McKay's story sprawl. But larded in between image and episode is the inevitable commentary. Always intelligent, it nevertheless seems an intrusion, perhaps because the author, in the role of analyst, sounds self-conscious and a little ill at ease.

Freda Kirchwey, "Black and White," *Nation*, 22 May 1929, p. 614

RUDOLPH FISHER   The first six stories ⟨of *Gingertown*⟩ are laid in Negro Harlem, which has apparently fascinated Mr. McKay, himself a British West Indian, precisely as it might fascinate any other outside observer. These scenes, however, are not definitely Harlem as they are definitely Negro; that is, while these things could not have happened to anybody but Negroes, they could have happened in any Negro community—any black belt. Merely to capitalize the "b" and call Harlem the "Belt" is not a sufficient distinction. But the themes have one commendably distinctive feature. Most stories about Negroes could just as well have been told about Jews, Swedes or Chinamen. The complexion or other racial characteristic, physical or mental, is not ordinarily the essence of the theme but merely an attribute. Such a story is "Truant," the sixth in this collection, describing a restless spirit which happened to be a Negro's but might just as well have been anybody's. Such also are the sketches following "Truant." But the five tales preceding it present difficulties which arise specifically out of the most obvious Negro characteristic—skin-color. And simple as this device is, it undeniably gives the first five narratives a flavor which the others lack. Accordingly, though the setting is not made unmistakable, and though the more general aspects of the themes are familiar, there is still a specifically complexional essence which sets these five apart as definitely Negro. These too, despite their distracting inaccuracies of dialect—strange West-Indianisms issue from the mouths of American blacks on occasion—are by far the most dramatic scenes of the collection. In all twelve, however, there is a robust vigor characteristic of all Mr. McKay's work.

Rudolph Fisher, "White, High Yellow, Black," *New York Herald Tribune Books*, 27 March 1932, p. 3

CLAUDE McKAY   I was surprised when I discovered that many of the talented Negroes regarded their renaissance more as an uplift organization and a vehicle to accelerate the pace and progress of smart Negro society. It was interesting to note how sharply at variance their artistic outlook was from that of the modernistic white groups that took a significant interest in Negro literature and art. The Negroes were under the delusion that when a lady from Park Avenue or from Fifth Avenue, or a titled European, became interested in Negro art and invited Negro artists to her home, that was a token of Negroes breaking into upper-class white society. I don't think that it ever occurred to them that perhaps such white individuals were searching for a social and artistic significance in Negro art which they could not find in their own society, and that the radical nature and subject of their interest operated against the possibility of their introducing Negroes further than their own particular homes in coveted white society.

Also, among the Negro artists there was much of that Uncle Tom attitude which works like Satan against the idea of a coherent and purposeful Negro group. Each one wanted to be the first Negro, the one Negro, and the only Negro *for the whites* instead of for their group. Because an unusual number of them were receiving grants to do creative work, they actually and naïvely believed that Negro artists as a group would always be treated differently from white artists and be protected by powerful white patrons.

Some of them even expressed the opinion that Negro art would solve the centuries-old social problem of the Negro. That idea was vaguely hinted by Dr. ⟨Alain⟩ Locke in his introduction to *The New Negro*. Dr. Locke's essay is a remarkable chocolate *soufflé* of art and politics, with not an ingredient of information inside.

They were nearly all Harlem-conscious, in a curious synthetic way, it seemed to me—not because they were aware of Harlem's intrinsic values as a unique and popular Negro quarter, but apparently because white folks had discovered black magic there. I understood more clearly why there had been so much genteel-Negro hostility to my *Home to Harlem* and to Langston Hughes's primitive Negro poems.

I wondered after all whether it would be better for me to return to the new *milieu* of Harlem. Much as all my sympathy was with the Negro group and the idea of the Negro renaissance, I doubted if going back to Harlem would be an advantage. I had done my best Harlem stuff when I was abroad, seeing it from a long perspective. I thought it might be better to leave Harlem to the artists who were on the spot, to give them their chance to produce something better than *Home to Harlem*. I thought that I might as well go back to Africa.

Claude McKay, *A Long Way from Home* (1937; rpt. New York: Harcourt, Brace & World, 1970), pp. 321–23

ST. CLAIR DRAKE   Claude McKay came to this country from Jamaica in 1912, four years before Marcus Garvey, the organizer of the Universal Negro Improvement Association. He, like Garvey, had left the West Indies in search of wider opportunities for self-expression. Garvey's destiny led him toward a mass-leadership role, then to imprisonment and deportation to Jamaica. Claude McKay eventually won international acclaim as a writer; then came poverty, chronic illness, and finally his death—almost unnoticed.

His autobiography had contemporary relevance for a number of reasons. Black intellectuals are still involved in the quest for an identity and an ideology, and under circumstances similar to those of the period through which McKay lived. Present-day pilgrimages of black Americans, West Indians, and Africans to China and Cuba are reminiscent of the Moscow journeys of an earlier period. The dilemmas and contradictions that accompany attempts to reconcile Marxism and black nationalism are as perplexing to the intellectuals of the 1960s as they were to those of the 1920s and 1930s. Stokely Carmichael, Eldridge Cleaver, and James Forman find themselves confronted with the same type of problems that faced Paul Robeson, Richard Wright, and Langston Hughes. McKay came to grips with them earlier than any of the others, and his autobiography documents the processes of discovery, growth, inner conflict, and disillusionment that all sensitive black intellectuals experience in a world where racism is a pervasive reality.

A Long Way from Home, like the autobiography of other black writers since World War I, falls into a literary tradition that begins with the narratives of runaway slaves, including The Life and Times of Frederick Douglass, and continues in Booker T. Washington's Up from Slavery and W. E. B. Du Bois' Dusk of Dawn. The genre is one in which more intimate aspects of the autobiographer's personal experiences are subordinated to social commentary and reflections upon what it means to be a Negro in a world dominated by white men. There have been no black Marcel Prousts and André Gides. The traumatic effects of the black experience seem to have made confessional writing an intellectual luxury black writers cannot afford.

McKay's narrative is unique in one aspect. Other accounts by prominent black men of their encounter with America have been written by those who were born and bred in the United States. Claude McKay was one of the more talented individuals in the stream of immigrants from the British West Indies who have been seeking their fortune in the United States since the turn of the century. They were refugees from a poverty exacerbated by overpopulation, and from a social system in which British settlers and their mixed-blood descendants had kept most blacks in a subordinate position. During the twenties and thirties West Indians played an active role in the hectic politics of Harlem, a phenomenon that has been analyzed with insight and perception (and also some bias) by Harold Cruse in The Crisis of the Negro Intellectual.

McKay's life was a single episode in the 500-year-old drama of the black diaspora, that massive dispersal of millions of men and women out of the great African homeland to the Caribbean islands and onto the American continents. He symbolizes their wanderings backward and forward between Africa and the New World, and from both of these areas to Britain and Europe. They have become detribalized in the process and have developed a pan-African consciousness. McKay does not emphasize his West Indianness but rather his blackness, his solidarity with Afro-Americans and Africans.

He was keenly conscious of being a child of the diaspora, revealing sentiments similar to those in the Negro spiritual: "Sometimes I feel like a motherless child, a long way from home." ⟨. . .⟩

McKay was a complex man who himself had enjoyed the hospitality of many a "fine white house." Compassionate and valuing his relations with specific white friends, he realized the danger of racial solidarity sliding over into hate, but he thought it was a risk that had to be taken. The last chapter of the autobiography is a plea for black unity, and it led him to the position that Dr. Du Bois had espoused in 1934 at the cost of his position on the board of the NAACP, and that the youth in the civil-rights movement came to thirty years later. We have no way of knowing how he would have reacted to the Deacons for Defense, Malcolm X's Afro-American Unity Organization, the Black Panthers, or the Republic of New Africa. But what he has to say about the general forms of organization that black communities should adopt have a startlingly contemporary ring.

> St. Clair Drake, "Introduction," *A Long Way from Home* (New York: Harcourt, Brace & World, 1970), pp. ix–xi, xvii

---

GEORGE E. KENT   The story of McKay's poetry is also the story of such novels as *Home to Harlem*, *Banjo*, and *Banana Bottom*, both with respect to the soul's embattlement and the quality of the fiction. In *Home to Harlem*, the soulful way is expressed through Jake, a former longshoreman who has returned to Harlem after deserting an American army intent upon exploiting him as a laborer instead of a fighter against Germans, and Ray, an educated Black whose alienation from both Blacks and Whites blocks him from the uncomplicated celebration of joy that Jake easily achieves. Ray's main function in the novel is to represent a contrast to Jake and to articulate a criticism of Western culture, Jake's to assert an incorruptible innocence while celebrating the joys of the flesh, comradeship, and love. His natural innocence is his salvation, no matter what situation he confronts: the army's attempt to reduce him, living with an English woman who unsuccessfully attempts to keep him tethered, living with a black woman who requires brutality as an ingredient of love, dealing with a labor situation that offers either scabbing or an insincere labor union.

The greatest threat to his sense of innocence derives from the thin plot of the novel. Returning to Harlem, he discovers in Felice, a woman who returns the money he has paid for sexual favors, a natural soulmate. After discovering their natural affinity, Jake loses her for most of the duration of the novel, a fact which allows McKay to explore Harlem joy life. When Jake finds her, she has become the common-law partner of Jake's comrade Zeddy—but has not taken him into the inner citadel of her heart. Zeddy, angered at the threatened loss of Felice, draws a razor, and Jake confronts him with a pistol. Thus the snake has entered the edenic garden of comradeship—but not for long. Both men suffer quick remorse over the threatened corruption of their souls. Zeddy apologizes, and his apology is quickly accepted by Jake. Jake's realization of the threat to his innocence is expressed as follows:

> His love nature was generous and warm without any vestige
> of the diabolical or sadistic.
>   Yet here he was caught in the thing that he despised so
> thoroughly . . . Brest, London, and his America. Their vivid brutality
> tortured his imagination. Oh, he was infinitely disgusted with
> himself to think that he had just been moved by the same
> savage emotions as those vile, vicious, villainous white men who,
> like hyenas and rattlers, had fought, murdered, and clawed
> the entrails out of black men over the common commercial flesh
> of women.

The form of soul in *Home to Harlem* is really romantic bohemianism. The reader can admire the superiority of Jake and Felice's natural normality, but cannot forget that the real test comes when Jake has given hostages to fortune in the form of a wife and children, a situation in which the vibrations of the black man's condition in Western culture are not so easily brushed aside.

George E. Kent, "The Soulful Way of Claude McKay," *Blackness and the Adventure of Western Culture* (Chicago: Third World Press, 1972), pp. 46–48

JAMES S. GILES   When discussing McKay, one is tempted to fall into a fallacy comparable to that which has plagued much Scott Fitzgerald criticism—the obvious temptation to write about what both men might have done, rather than what they did. Perhaps McKay offers even more tragic possibilities for this kind of criticism than Fitzgerald, for the "waste" was much less McKay's own fault than Fitzgerald's. The author of *Home to Harlem* can be seen as a classic case of a black writer's being destroyed by the impossible pressures of his situation. He wrote a book during a period in which some Negroes were an intellectual "fad" and became famous. At a less fortuitous time, he wrote a better book which "failed." He continued to write during the worst of times for black writers and had difficulty in even getting published. One of his poems signaled the emergence of "the New Negro" in America; and, for the rest of his career, he attempted to reconcile black militancy with a personal concept of poetry which was heavily influenced by traditional concepts of form. He wished to be both a voice of black political and social ideas, and a lyric poet. Finally, he attempted to publish verse proclaiming the hypocrisy of the United States' fighting a war against Hitler while remaining a racist nation. Still, this "tragic failure" approach is as wrong for McKay as for Fitzgerald. What is finally important is that both men did produce a significant body of lasting work.

As the 1940s progressed, McKay's letters concerning ultimate racial justice in America became increasingly hopeless. In a letter of August 28, 1946, he asserted to Eastman that he did not want ". . . to go sour on humanity even after living in this awful land of the U.S.A." It is not surprising, then, that "Boyhood in Jamaica's" emphasis is upon an international black movement. There is a special irony in finding the man who had seemed to personify the concept of the American "New Negro" in 1919 advocating a new international black movement almost thirty years later, but one should not be too surprised by this fact. From the beginning, McKay was aware of the philosophical limitations of the 1920s Renaissance. From the beginning, he was searching for an aesthetic and philosophical principle based upon the concept of a unique black identity; he was never going to be limited to the boundaries of the United States in his quest for such a principle, for he did not regard himself as primarily an American or as a Jamaican, but as a black man. In A Long Way from Home, he stressed the importance of such a racial identity to everything he wrote, even to the poetry which does not seem to be overtly black in form or content. Moreover, despite the painful evidence of his own life, he did not finally forfeit his faith that a new, and a better, world was coming for the black man. The last two sentences of "Boyhood in Jamaica" emphasize that faith: "Happily, as I move on, I see that adventure [of the black man in white society] changing for those who will come after me. For this is the century of the coloured world."

James R. Giles, *Claude McKay* (Boston: Twayne, 1976), pp. 157–58

MARIAN B. McLEOD   Though it is a slim volume, *The Negroes in America* aids materially in understanding McKay's outlook on American society and culture and explains, in part at least, the reasons for his alienation from the black intelligentsia, from the liberal political movement, and ultimately from the left-wing groups through which he had long hoped to witness a fundamental change in the status of Negroes in the United States.

McKay shared a draft copy of his book's initial chapters with ⟨Max⟩ Eastman, who was also in Moscow for the meeting of the Comintern. Eastman recommended revisions, and McKay responded to him in these words:

> You assert that I say that the Negro problem is the chief problem
> of the Revolution in America. When you come to read my book,
> you will find that I have said no such thing. What I say is that
> the Negro problem is an integral part and one of the chief
> problems of the class struggle in America, and I stand by that
> declaration.

The Negroes in America is essentially a propagandist tract, but in McKay's view—as in Dr. Du Bois's—such literature had the highest rank, since its goal was social transformation rather than merely the creation of a pleasing entertainment or the expression of inconsequential petulance. Furthermore, he was supported by Trotsky, who emphasized that "The training of black propagandists is the most imperative and extremely important revolutionary task of the present time." The whole work has the tone of didactic journalism, and at times it becomes rather less than cogent in its development of an argument or demolition of some popular shibboleth. It is repetitious of its central theme; the structure is not always wholly admirable; some chapters are little more than extended quotations strung together loosely by commentary that lacks penetration, and the final chapter is merely a reprint of a contribution to the October 1922 issue of *The Liberator*. Yet, notwithstanding these shortcomings, *The Negroes in America* provides one of the few examples of a genuinely thoughtful and committed black creative writer acting as social critic and polemicist.

Marian B. McLeod, "Claude McKay's Russian Interpretation: *The Negroes in America*," *CLA Journal* 23, No. 3 (March 1980): 340–41

WAYNE F. COOPER   In *A Long Way from Home*, McKay projected a very definite picture of himself as first and foremost a literary artist in the romantic mold. His first objective had always been to experience life directly in order to communicate the truth of his experience in his art. This urge for new experiences as nourishment for his creative expression is a theme sustained throughout A Long Way from Home. Whatever stifled man's potential to experience fully nature's free gifts, McKay rejected.

By defining himself simply as an independent, free-spirited poet, McKay avoided almost entirely any close examination of those deep inner motivations that had moved him to choose the particular paths he had taken from Jamaica to New York, to Moscow, to Paris, and to Tangier. By becoming simply The Poet, he avoided, above all, any real discussion of how deeply involved he had truly been, both emotionally and intellectually, with communism between 1919 and 1923. As a consequence, A Long Way from Home became, as McKay intended it should be, a pleasantly impressionistic book, a seemingly effortless account of his travels and his encounters with the great and near-great of international communism and the literary world of Europe and America. Through it all, he portrayed himself as a black man intent upon remaining true to himself, yet accepting, too, the inescapable obligation to write truthfully about those qualities within himself and his race that both set blacks apart as unique and made them one with the rest of mankind. It was not a dishonest or ignoble goal; McKay had never been an introspective writer. But A Long Way from Home failed to convey the complexity of his life.

> Wayne F. Cooper, Claude McKay: Rebel Sojourner in the Harlem Renaissance (Baton Rouge: Louisiana State University Press, 1987), pp. 317–18

MELVIN DIXON   ⟨. . .⟩ in Banjo Ray rejects civilization as vehemently as he feels rejected by it. The extremity of this position leads to a self-righteous tone in Ray's proclamation, which is compromised by Ray's lack of productivity. McKay backs himself into such a corner that he all but extinguishes any hope that intellect and instinct, education and passion, can coexist for black writers as they have for Russian novelists like Tolstoy, whose art, Ray believes, grew from the soil. The quest McKay began with Ray meeting Jake on a moving train—an overground railroad—and continued until Ray's ultimate break with civilization and embrace of vagabonding finds a more balanced conclusion in Banana Bottom. In the earlier novels McKay attempted to survey the wilderness of black alienation and displacement. In his last novel, McKay finds peace with himself through his female protagonist Bita Plant who, uprooted from Jamaica and grafted with a European education, manages to transplant herself back in the native soil.

McKay's choice of a female protagonist to complete his quest shows his desire for regeneration. Bita fulfills the potential of McKay's bachelor wanderers. Her procreative union with her peasant husband Jubban, in which both are "nourished by the same soil," resolves McKay's dilemma of unification with land, culture, and self. McKay previously depicted divided sensibilities through oppositional friendships between men, which limit creativity to the realm of art. This is not to say that Jake and Banjo fail as mates for Ray, but that the union goes only so far. Through the "offspring" of literature Ray represents his racial ambivalence or displacement. And Ray does locate Harlem and the Ditch as places for the performance of his identity. Bita Plant, however, embodies regeneration.

By returning in *Banana Bottom* to the time and place of his West Indian upbringing, McKay frees himself from the overwhelming cultural tradition of Europe and from American myths of racial uplift through face-saving art (a dominant ideology during the Harlem Renaissance). McKay is also free to explore the range of characters, situations, and life opportunities a predominantly black environment provides. Readers encounter a similar ease in Zora Neale Hurston's fiction, which takes place in the all-black town of Eatonville, Florida. McKay and Hurston luxuriate in lavish descriptions of quotidian events, customs, and the various features of the land. Yet McKay worried about the possibility of exaggeration and imprecision in his writing. He once commented disparagingly in a letter to his longtime friend Max Eastman, "Whether poetry or prose, my writing is always most striking and true when it is a little reminiscent and nostalgic. The vividness of *Home to Harlem* was due to my being removed just the right distance from the scene. Doing *Banjo* I was too close to it. *Banana Bottom* was a lazy dream, the images becoming blurred from overdoing long-distance photography." The imagery, no matter how imprecise, clearly helped McKay resolve some long-standing, as well as long-distance, conflicts, for the novel celebrates Bita's successful reintegration into her home society.

Melvin Dixon, "To Wake the Nations Underground: Jean Toomer and Claude McKay," *Ride Out the Wilderness: Geography and Identity in Afro-American Literature* (Urbana: University of Illinois Press, 1987), pp. 52–53.

ELMER LUETH   At the time of McKay's novel ⟨*Home to Harlem*⟩, the tendency to look at Blacks as savage-like had, of course, a long tradition. Especially in the racial debates of the nineteenth century, Blacks were repeatedly considered "noble savages" or "exotic primitives" who may be equipped with positive characteristics like innate goodness or physical prowess, but would ultimately remain inferior to whites because of "natural" intellectual limitations. In 1926, elements of this debate had gained renewed currency, mostly in reaction to Carl Van Vechten's novel *Nigger Heaven*, which was heavily accused of exploiting such stereotypes. In this context, McKay's decision to create a character like Ray who combines traits of a savage with the abilities of a refined intellectual becomes significant. McKay makes a conscious effort to invest the term "savage" with a different connotation and to deprive it of its traditionally derogatory meaning. In *Home to Harlem*, the term still stands for a definite set of traits that Blacks share, but McKay no longer perceives it as intellectually limiting. One can be a savage equipped with unusual emotional and physical powers and still reach out for whatever knowledge one wants to acquire. The term "savage" loses its negative determinism, but remains intact as a description of racial characteristics. McKay therefore implicitly argues in favor of a non-limiting racial identity for Blacks. Ironically, Ray himself has totally discarded this concept of race without realizing how much he is part of it.

Such a reading of McKay's presentation of Ray and his understanding of the term "savage" naturally casts a very different light on the presentation of Jake and other Blacks mentioned earlier. What seems like an unfortunate perpetuation of negative stereotypes about Blacks at first glance turns, at second glance, into a self-confident claim for racial idiosyncrasies. In this reading of the novel, McKay presents a Harlem that is definitely shaped by something typically "black." Somewhere in the midst of all that music, that desire for different forms of physical expression, and that fast-paced interaction of human beings, the never clearly defined racial identity of Blacks finds an expression. However, as mentioned above, this entails no limitation of the potential of Blacks. There remains room for individual development in all directions, and whether an individual turns into an intellectual like Ray or into a "sweetman" and gambler like Zeddy, has nothing to do with color.

Elmer Lueth, "The Scope of Black Life in Claude McKay's *Home to Harlem*," *Obsidian II* 5, No. 3 (Winter 1990): 49–50

TYRONE TILLERY   The reason ⟨McKay⟩ had chosen Marseilles as his setting ⟨for *Banjo*⟩ and had created such an episodic plot was rooted in the very criticism he challenged. His assertion that he knew more about African-American life than most American-born blacks was an exaggeration.

In fact, McKay had little more experience among American blacks than some bohemian and radical whites. His relationship with the ordinary blacks celebrated in his poems and prose always remained perfunctory. He had worked alongside blacks in America only from 1916 to 1920, when he had left the United States to travel to his "spiritual homeland," England. From 1922 until 1934, he spent all of his time abroad. But even during the years when he had worked among lower-class American blacks, McKay managed to remain aloof from his environment.

His association with the black masses had never been voluntary; it had occurred as a result of his own failure to succeed at middle-class pursuits. By McKay's own admission, he had gleaned all he could from his Harlem experiences. Writing to Eastman after the publication of *Home to Harlem*, he had lamented that "all [his] hankering for the United States had disappeared," and, more important, "all of it [Harlem] had gone out in the first novel." Of the future projects he outlined for Eastman, none mentioned Harlem as a background.

The hostile reaction of Du Bois, White, and other blacks to McKay's books stemmed in part from their disappointment with the black settings and characters he chose to depict (low-life instead of middle-class life), in part from hostility to McKay as a West Indian who presumed to be an authority on American blacks, and in part from anger at his assault on middle-class blacks. By 1929, the year of *Banjo*'s publication, middle-class blacks had grown even more sensitive to the depiction of black Americans in fiction; the black audience who borrowed books from the library or who bought books for their homes wanted to see positive portraits of blacks. Thus, it is not surprising that the *New York Amsterdam News*, one of the few black newspapers to praise *Home to Harlem*, was outraged at *Banjo*, complaining that it was full of things that would please white readers, "Coon stuff."

Black writers and critics had logical reasons to be sensitive about literature that seemed to perpetuate old stereotypes concerning blacks. McKay tried to argue that the black middle class was offended by his subject matter because it identified more with whites and had no sympathy for the black lower class. But it is not true that the small black middle class turned its back on poorer blacks. Middle-class blacks during the twenties did not lead a life separated from lower-class black life. All blacks, whatever their economic circumstances, lived in the same neighborhoods, attended the same churches, shopped in the same stores, and so on. Even the Harvard-educated Du Bois, who occupied the heights of black society, had what today would seem a surprising amount of contact with lower-class African-

Americans. According to George Kent, author of *Blackness and the Adventure of Western Culture*, many of the Renaissance writers and critics brought to their "task" a cosmopolitan range of experiences that protected them from a simple, myopic middle-class perspective. ⟨. . .⟩

In *Banjo*, McKay poured out much of what he was struggling to achieve in his own life: an understanding of his own identity. Too much of the person Claude McKay peered through the pages of *Banjo* for it to succeed as a dramatization of the conflict between the unspoiled folk and Western civilization. The catharsis so evident in *Banjo* represents McKay's personal journey to answer the question "Who am I?" At best, he was only able to respond in the manner of his black characters in *Banjo* who, when foreign officials asked for their papers, were distinguished by the official phrase: "Nationality Doubtful."

Tyrone Tillery, *Claude McKay: A Black Poet's Struggle for Identity* (Amherst: University of Massachusetts Press, 1992), pp. 112–13, 125

▓ *Bibliography*

Constab Ballads. 1912.

Songs of Jamaica. 1912.

Spring in New Hampshire and Other Poems. 1920.

Harlem Shadows. 1922.

Sudom Lincha. Tr. P. Okhrimenko. 1923.

Negry v Amerike. Tr. P. Okhrimenko. 1923.

Home to Harlem. 1928.

Banjo: A Story without a Plot. 1929.

Gingertown. 1932.

Banana Bottom. 1933.

A Long Way from Home. 1937.

Harlem: Negro Metropolis. 1940.

Selected Poems. 1953.

The Dialect Poetry. 1972.

The Passion of Claude McKay: Selected Prose and Poetry 1912–1948. Ed. Wayne Cooper. 1973.

My Green Hills of Jamaica and Five Jamaican Short Stories. 1979.

◈ ◈ ◈

Wallace Thurman
1902–1934

WALLACE HENRY THURMAN was born on August 16, 1902, in Salt Lake City, Utah, the son of Oscar and Beulah Thurman. Little is known of his early life in the American West. He attended the University of Utah in 1919, but left after a year; in 1922 he entered the University of Southern California in Los Angeles, but left after a year and attempted to establish a career in journalism. Although he founded a journal, *Outlet*, in 1924, it lasted only six months and in 1925 Thurman went to New York and became a reporter for the *Looking Glass*, the managing editor of the *Messenger* (where he published the work of Langston Hughes and Zora Neale Hurston), and circulation manager of *World Tomorrow*, a white-owned paper.

In 1926 Hughes asked Thurman to edit a new journal, *Fire!!*, whose subtitle proclaimed it to be "Devoted to younger Negro artists." Thurman lent considerable financial assistance to the enterprise, but only one issue, dated November 1926, emerged; it contained, however, the work of Hughes, Hurston, Arna Bontemps, Countee Cullen, and other prominent writers. Two years later Thurman established a slightly less radical magazine, *Harlem: A Forum of Negro Life*, but it too folded after one issue.

Thurman began his literary career as a playwright, although none of his plays have been published. His first play, *Harlem: A Melodrama of Negro Life in Harlem*, was written in collaboration with William Jourdan Rapp and premiered on Broadway on February 20, 1929. It received mixed reviews, as some critics felt that it focused excessively on the seamier sides of black life in Harlem, but it brought Thurman immediate fame. He collaborated with Rapp on another play, *Jeremiah, the Magnificent* (1930), but received only one posthumous performance. Neither of these plays has been published.

The Blacker the Berry (1929) was Thurman's first novel. It is a searing portrayal of racism within the black community, as its protagonist, Emma Lou, experiences prejudice from lighter-skinned blacks. *Infants of the Spring* (1932), Thurman's next novel, appears to be a *roman à clef* in which the pretentious writers of a Harlem literary commune are based upon Hughes,

Hurston, Cullen, and other leading figures of the Harlem Renaissance. Thurman's last novel, *The Interne* (1932), written in collaboration with Abraham L. Furman, is not explicitly about black themes, but treats of the corruption and inefficiency of an urban hospital.

Although he attained prominence in the world of New York publishing— he worked on the editorial staff of Macfadden Publications and later became an editor at the Macaulay Publishing Company—Thurman returned to California in 1934. He wrote two screenplays, "Tomorrow's Children" (1934) and "High School Girl" (1935), the former of which was banned in New York because of its sexually daring content. Thurman, who was notorious for a lifestyle full of decadence and alcohol, developed tuberculosis and returned to New York in May 1934. He collapsed at his reunion party and spent the last six months of his life in City Hospital on Welfare Island, New York, where he died on December 22, 1934.

▣ *Critical Extracts*

UNSIGNED   There are no passages in *The Blacker the Berry* to indi- cate that Mr. Thurman is out to astound people. He makes no effort to display the swiftly acquired erudition of a Van Vechten, but sticks to his main thesis. That thesis is the conflict a "coal-black nigger" is subjected to now that color prejudice has crossed the line into the black belts. Emma Lou, born in Boise, Idaho, of a light-skinned mother and a blue-black no- good father, is made to feel from her birth that she has betrayed her race. Her grandparents, scions of good Confederate stock through miscegenation in slavery days, have formed the Blue Vein circle of Boise, so called because its members are light enough in color to see the purple blood beat through the arteries in their wrists. Emma Lou, of course, is outside the pale. Her hair is not kinky; but there her good points stop. And no creams, no bleaching agencies, no lotions will purge her of her unfortunate niggerish color. ⟨. . .⟩

All this might have made a poignant story. As it is, Mr. Thurman writes prose in imitation of the white "genteel" tradition without ever making you certain that he is composing his novel from within the vantage point of Emma Lou's "genteel" brain. He gives the effect of objectivity where subjectivity is demanded, chiefly because he reports where he should be dramatizing the world as it appeared to Emma Lou.

Unsigned, " 'Dynasty' and Some Other Recent Works of Fiction," *New York Times Book Review*, 17 March 1929, p. 6

V. F. CALVERTON   The whole novel ⟨*The Blacker the Berry*⟩ turns upon color distinctions among the Negroes themselves. Emma Lou, the heroine, a Negress of very dark complexion, finds that her whole life among her own people is hampered and harnessed by the fact that she is not of a lighter color. Everywhere she discovers it is the mulatto, quadroon, and octoroon who are favored. Her type is scorned with the epithets of "spade," "inkspitter," "dark meat," and "black cat." "Color-conscious," she cries to her brown-skinned lover, "who wouldn't be color-conscious when everywhere you go people are always talking about color?" In providing a picture of this phase of Negro life, this color-conflict and prejudice among Negroes themselves, the novel is worth while. As a literary effort it is without distinction. At no point does it arrest or grip the reader, or sweep him along with its movement. It lacks the very dynamics that should be most conspicuous in the life which Mr. Thurman sets out to depict.

V. F. Calverton, "The Negro Writer," *New York Herald Tribune Books*, 26 May 1929, p. 14

RUDOLPH FISHER   As nearly as one can make out, the title of Mr. Thurman's second book ⟨*Infants of the Spring*⟩ means "nipped in the bud." The theme is the early demise of the so-called New Negro, whose literary and artistic renaissance enjoyed a fair bit of publicity five years ago, but in the course of the novel there is so much expositional and argumentative prattle on race prejudice and communism that one can not be sure at the end just what the book started out to say.

There actually was, about three years ago, a dwelling in Harlem where a number of young colored artistic aspirants lived, argued and caroused. This house is the model for Mr. Thurman's Niggeratti Manor, and its former habitues the prototypes of the figures he now sketches. Among these are Raymond Taylor, a young writer, Stephen Jorgenson, Raymond's friend, a white graduate student who comes to live at the Manor and remains remarkably color-blind until his eyes become used to the darkness; Eustace Savoy,

Pelham Gaylord and Paul Arblan, who is the one engaging, though far too lightly drawn, personality in the book. There are three girls, two of whom fall out over Stephen, and the third who finally becomes Raymond's mistress, and a landlady.

There is Samuel, a white uplifter, and Dr. Parkes, a black one, and various more or less successful Negroes, who fortunately do not live in the Manor but are brought in from time to time for the author's praise or blame. And there are two major parties, one a donation party to which all guests bring groceries, the other a "salon," to which come all the young writers, painters and hangers-on and burst into violent disagreements.

It does not take the illusioned landlady long to come to her senses and institute a general artistic exodus.

Perhaps the new Negro is dead. Or perhaps in the warm sunlight of publicity, he stretched himself out and dozed off to sleep. In either case, this novel is no evidence that the brownskinned brother is either roused or revived.

Rudolph Fisher, "Harlem Manor," New York Herald Tribune Books, 21 February 1932, p. 16

MARTHA GRUENING   There is no mistaking ⟨in *Infants of the Spring*⟩ the grimness of his attitude toward artistic and literary Harlem, the Negro Renaissance, and those on both sides of the color line who have made it possible. Once again Mr. Thurman has written an ironic, mordant, and deeply honest book. I know of no other story of Negro life, unless it is Claude McKay's *Banjo*, which reflects with such authenticity the clash of views among Colored People themselves as to the function and achievements of Negro artists in a white world. If one excepts George Schuyler, Thurman is the only Negro writer who has made any attempt to debunk the Negro Renaissance. There is need of such debunking. The Negro Renaissance has produced some first-rate work. It has also produced a great deal which is mediocre and pretentious and which has been almost ludicrously overpraised and ballyhooed. ⟨. . .⟩

The narrative framework of the story is slight, a series of episodes in the life of a group of artists and dilettantes who, for a while, occupy the same house in Harlem and who all, in one way or another, find frustration. Their experiences are revealed to a large extent in the give and take of conversation and it is in these conversations that the virtue of the book largely resides. The disillusion it reflects is not due wholly to problems of color, nor does the author see it as confined to colored artists. The color line is merely an added element of exasperation in a world in which artists inevitably suffer and in which all but the strongest of them are doomed. "I may get moody once in a while and curse my fate," says Ray, "but so does any other human being with an ounce of intelligence. The odds are against me ... well ... so are they against every other man who dares to think for himself."

Infants of the Spring is not a great book but it is an important one. Like Mr. Thurman's earlier *The Blacker the Berry*, and unlike much of the output of contemporary Harlem, it is written with no weather eye on a possible white audience. There have been a few other books equally honest in their description of certain phases of Negro life—Langston Hughes's *Not Without Laughter* and Claude McKay's *Home to Harlem* come to mind in this connection—but no other Negro writer has so unflinchingly told the truth about color snobbery within the color line, the ins and outs of "passing" and other vagaries of prejudice.

Martha Gruening, "Two Ways to Harlem," *Saturday Review of Literature*, 12 March 1932, p. 585

LANGSTON HUGHES   He was a strangely brilliant black boy, who had read everything, and whose critical mind could find something wrong with everything he read. I have no critical mind, so I usually either like a book or don't. But I am not capable of liking a book and then finding a million things wrong with it, too—as Thurman was capable of doing.

Thurman had read so many books because he could read eleven lines at a time. He would get from the library a great pile of volumes that would have taken me a year to read. But he would go through them in less than a week, and be able to discuss each one at great length with anybody. That was why, I suppose, he was later given a job as a reader at Macaulay's—the only Negro reader, so far as I know, to be employed by any of the larger publishing firms.

Later Thurman became a ghost writer for *True Story*, and other publications, writing under all sorts of fantastic names, like Ethel Belle Mandrake or Patrick Casey. He did Irish and Jewish and Catholic "true confessions." He collaborated with William Jordan Rapp on plays and novels. Later he ghosted books. In fact, this quite dark young Negro is said to have written *Men, Women, and Checks.* ⟨. . .⟩

⟨. . .⟩ He was a strange kind of fellow, who liked to drink gin, but *didn't* like to drink gin; who liked being a Negro, but felt it a great handicap; who adored bohemianism, but thought it wrong to be a bohemian. He liked to waste a lot of time, but he always felt guilty wasting time. He loathed crowds, yet he hated to be alone. He almost always felt bad, yet he didn't write poetry.

Once I told him if I could feel as bad as he did *all* the time, I would surely produce wonderful books. But he said you had to know how to *write*, as well as how to feel bad. I said I didn't have to know how to feel bad, because, every so often, the blues just naturally overtook me, like a blind beggar with an old guitar:

> You don't know,
> You don't know my mind—
> When you see me laughin',
> I'm laughin' to keep from cryin'.

About the future of Negro literature Thurman was very pessimistic. He thought the Negro vogue had made us all too conscious of ourselves, had flattered and spoiled us, and had provided too many easy opportunities for some of us to drink gin and more gin, on which he thought we would always be drunk. With his bitter sense of humor, he called the Harlem literati, the "niggerati."

Langston Hughes, *The Big Sea: An Autobiography* (New York: Alfred A. Knopf, 1940), pp. 234, 238

HUGH M. GLOSTER   Perhaps the most interesting sections of *Infants of the Spring* are those containing satirical comments on the Negro Renascence. Though the so-called "New Negro" was acclaimed and patronized throughout the United States as a phenomenon in art, Thurman observes that very little "was being done to substantiate the current fad, to make it the foundation for something truly epochal." Through Taylor he protests "that the average Negro intellectual and artist has no goal, no standards, no elasticity, no pregnant germ plasm." Again using Taylor as a medium, he contends that Jean Toomer is the "only one Negro who has the elements of greatness" and that the others are without genuine ability:

> "The rest of us are mere journeymen, planting seed for someone else to harvest. We all get sidetracked sooner or later. The older ones become warped by propaganda. We younger ones are mired in decadence. None of us seem able to rise above our environment."

Taylor attributes the emphasis upon abnormality in the literature of the Negro Renascence to the vogue of Faulkner and Hemingway. To make his satire of the Negro Renascence more personal, Thurman assembles the leading writers—Sweetie Mae Carr (Zora Neale Hurston?), Tony Crews (Langston Hughes?), DeWitt Clinton (Countee Cullen?), Cedric Williams (Eric Walrond?), Dr. Manfred Trout (Rudolph Fisher?), and others—at Niggerati Manor upon the request of Dr. Parkes (Alain Locke?) to establish a salon and a concerted artistic movement. The purpose of the meeting is lost, however, in a heated debate concerning whether the "New Negro" should cultivate his African heritage, espouse full rights of citizenship, join the proletariat in an effort to overthrow capitalism, or strive for individual self-expression. Through Taylor, Thurman recommends the last-named choice:

> "Individuality is what we should strive for. Let each seek his own salvation. To me, a wholesale flight back to Africa or a wholesale allegiance to Communism or a wholesale adherence to an antiquated and for the most part ridiculous propagandistic program are all equally futile and unintelligent."

Hugh M. Gloster, *Negro Voices in American Fiction* (Chapel Hill: University of North Carolina Press, 1948), pp. 170–71

DOROTHY WEST   He hated Negro society, and since dark skins were never the fashion among Negro upper classes, the feeling was occasionally mutual. In his book, *The Blacker the Berry*, whose dedication reads, "To Beulah [his mother], the goose who laid the not so golden egg," his dark-skinned heroine suffered many of the small humiliations he would not have admitted suffering himself. For he was never humble or apologetic, and he laughed very hard when things hurt him most.

Negro society was taking itself very seriously in those days. Carl Van Vechten had revealed its inner workings in the pages of his *Nigger Heaven*, and Harlem had become a mecca for the smart set thrill-seekers. Downtowners sought any means to gain *entrée* to uptown parties. Van Vechten could hardly lead the throng, for his unfortunate choice of title for his book, the exotic types he had chosen as typifying Negro society, the whole exposé, had made him outcast to all but the close friends from whom he had drawn his chief characters.

Harlem, however, had had the taste of white patronage and found it sweet to the palate. There was no party which did not have its quota of white guests who were distinguishable from the fairest Negroes only by their northern accents, the majority of fair-skinned Negroes having southern accents. The artists were the liaison group. They were not exactly an exemplary lot, but they knew the downtowners, and a carefully worded note instructing them to bring a friend, any friend, was read between the lines. The young artist showed up slightly drunk, having been paid in the preferred coin of alcohol by a grateful white, and proceeded to lap up his hostess' liquor as further payment for providing her the privilege of sending another important name to the society columns of the Negro papers.

It was Thurman's delight to take a whole entourage of whites, some of them sleazy, to these parties. He earned the enmity of many hostesses by his companions' silly behavior and his own inability not to pass out and be carried bodily from a party. The conservative group disinherited him. Though he despised them for their insularity and their aping of privileged whites, still he allowed himself to grow extremely sensitive following their changed attitude and to believe that it was his black skin that had made him *déclassé*. He mocked their manners and their bastard beginnings, and divorced himself completely from a conventional way of life.

> Dorothy West, "Elephant's Dance: A Memoir of Wallace Thurman," *Black World* 20, No. 1 (November 1970): 79–80

MAE GWENDOLYN HENDERSON   Comparing the literature of the Renaissance with the works of great writers made Thurman a severe critic, particularly of his own works. He puzzled over the reasons for what he considered to be the lack of productivity and creativity among the Renaissance artists. In his novel ⟨*Infants of the Spring*⟩, he asked whether the failure was the result of "some deep-rooted complex [racial]" or an "indication of a lack of talent." In most instances Thurman thought the black artist was hindered by a preoccupation with his racial identity. Thurman had grappled with this problem when writing his earlier novel, *The Blacker the Berry*. Earlier, in his *Notes of a Stepchild*, he had written of himself: "He tried hard not to let the fact that he had pigmented skin influence his literary or mental development."

There were two ways in which he felt the major black writers dealt with the fact of race identity in their works. In *Infants of the Spring*, Raymond [Thurman] rejects on the one hand those writers "who had nothing to say, and who only wrote because they were literate and felt they should apprise white humanity of the better classes among Negroes." Most of the early writers of the period fell under this condemnation. Those were the writers whom Thurman called the "propagandists" and whose contribution to the Renaissance he had earlier described as "sociological rather than literary." Another group of black writers was composed of those who wanted to escape their racial identity through a denial of everything black. Again speaking as Raymond, Thurman wrote: "He had no sympathy whatsoever with Negroes . . . who contended that should their art be Negroid, they, the artist, must be considered inferior." Such artists "did not realize by adhering to such a belief" they were, in effect, "subscribing to the theory of Nordic superiority." ⟨. . .⟩

The weakness of the Renaissance was that all traits of individuality had been destroyed by the canker of a destructive race complex. That Thurman was only vaguely aware of his own preoccupation with race is indicated by his constant disavowals of such influences and his deliberate efforts to transcend the self-imposed limitations of race consciousness. He discovered the resolution through a philosophy of individuality. Raymond, the hero of his second novel, comments:

> Negroes are a slave race and a slave race they'll remain until
> assimilated. Individuals will arise and escape on the
> ascending ladder of their individuality.

Such a statement, however, reveals the degree to which Thurman is a victim of his own self-hatred arising from his racial identity. In *The Blacker the Berry* he resolved this dilemma of race consciousness and individuality through an acceptance of oneself and racial identity. In this, his second novel, the answer seems to be a rejection of one's racial identity through a doctrine of what he once described as Nietzschean individuality.

Mae Gwendolyn Henderson, "Portrait of Wallace Thurman," *The Harlem Renaissance Remembered*, ed. Arna Bontemps (New York: Dodd, Mead, 1972), pp. 165–67

DANIEL WALDEN   Thurman undeniably was a writer of power and talent. An insider in the Harlem literary circles, he was even referred to as one of the central pivots of the Harlem Renaissance. Yet when Thurman is weighed as a writer, it is certain that he will be found wanting. Unable to control the rich literary material with which he worked, he consistently imposed a morbid look on his characters and developed stories and novels so atomized that he ultimately wound up at cross purposes with himself. His irony was well placed, whether in "Cordelia the Crude" in *Fire*, 1

(November 1926), or in *Harlem* (1929). In the latter work, a simple Southern mother seeing her family torn apart by the vagaries of Harlem, by the "sweetback" of the "hot-stuff man," by lotteries and vice, by the necessity of having rent parties, is helpless to intervene; religion and family are her refuge of last resort. Cordelia, caught up in the wild life of the city, is almost destroyed by poverty and the city. It was a startlingly realistic drama. It was also a very successful, overly dramatic play about the harshness of life and black disillusionment. In Edith Isaacs's opinion, "Violent and undisciplined as the play was, it left a sense of photographic reality."

In the same way, Thurman's talent burst out in *The Blacker the Berry* and *Infants of the Spring*. In debunking the "Negro Renaissance," in parading his pessimism, Thurman exemplified how strongly he felt about the enduring quality of the literature of the Harlem writers. He believed, as one of his characters phrased it in *Infants of the Spring*, "Being a Negro writer in these days is a racket, and I'm going to make the most of it while it lasts." No wonder Langston Hughes described him as having a prodigious capacity for gin, though he detested it; no wonder Hughes wrote that Thurman liked being a Negro but thought it a great handicap. Most significantly, as a very dark-skinned black man who met discrimination everywhere, he set out to record honestly and realistically black life in Harlem, but wound up compromising his principles. As Margaret Perry says, "he usually settled for capitalizing on its exotic-erotic elements in order to succeed." Unhappy when forced to be with blacks, rejected so often when with whites, he wrote "I was fighting hard to refrain from regarding myself as martyr and an outcast." Yet it was both the martyr and outcast that dominated the content and the style of his writing. In the end he exhausted himself trying to please the public while at the same time trying to write with a New Negro honesty. It is entirely appropriate that *Infants*, a neurotic novel in which he brooded introspectively on the "failure" of the Harlem Renaissance, derives its title and theme from Laertes' advice to Ophelia:

> The canker galls the infants of the spring
> Too oft before their buttons be disclosed.
> And in the morn the liquid dew of youth
> Contagious blastments are most imminent.

Thurman's pessimism dominates his satire. The cancer that gnawed at his vitals, the cancer of Bohemianism, was a combination of color, caste and dilettantism. If he had the talent, his heavy-handedness, mixed with equal parts of disillusion and despair, of himself and the alleged achievements of the 1920s, overcame his native ability. "The most self-conscious of the New Negroes," writes Robert Bone, "he ultimately turned his critical insight against himself and the wider movement with which he identified." Wanting to be a very great writer, he seems to have known he was merely a journalist. Melancholy, suicide-prone, he tried to say but ended up shouting that phoniness in the Harlem Renaissance was rampant even as he insisted, with Emersonian firmness, that capitulation to badges and names, to large societies, and dead institutions must give way to the free and individual spirit. Where he meant to write fiction, he wrote criticism; he wrote didactically. He failed, but he failed magnificently.

> Daniel Walden, " 'The Canker Galls . . .,' or, The Short Promising Life of Wallace Thurman," *The Harlem Renaissance Re-examined*, ed. Victor A. Kramer (New York: AMS Press, 1987), pp. 208–9

Bibliography

Negro Life in New York's Harlem: A Lively Picture of a Popular and Interesting
    Section. 1928.
The Blacker the Berry: A Novel of Negro Life. 1929.
Infants of the Spring. 1932.
The Interne (with Abraham L. Furman). 1932.

◈ ◈ ◈

Jean Toomer
1894–1967

JEAN TOOMER was born Nathan Pinchback Toomer in Washington, D.C., on December 26, 1894, the son of Nathan and Nina Pinchback Toomer. At his grandfather's insistence he was called Eugene Toomer, and later he adopted the first name Jean because he thought it had a more literary connotation. Nathan Toomer abandoned the family soon after Jean was born, and Nina Toomer, after living with her parents for some years, moved in 1906 to New Rochelle, New York, where she lived with her white husband. She died in 1909, and Jean returned to Washington to live with his grandparents.

Toomer attended several universities between 1914 and 1919, including the University of Wisconsin and the City College of New York, but finally abandoned academic life to pursue literature, writing poetry and fiction for such magazines as the *Little Review*, *Secession*, and *Broom*. Toomer disliked the use of race labels, insisting he was neither white nor black but "simply an American." He held the belief that race was not a fundamental constituent in one's self-definition, and was accordingly criticized for the lack of a black focus in his later works.

Toomer is best remembered for his first book, *Cane* (1923), a miscellany of stories, verse, and a drama concerned with the lives of black Americans in the United States. Much of the source material for this work was derived from a trip to Georgia he took in the fall of 1921. *Cane* is now regarded as one of the most remarkable novels of its time because of its prose-poetic language, its amalgamation of literary genres, and its rich evocation of the lives of both northern and southern black Americans.

Toomer's other works are *Balo*, a play included in Alain Locke and Montgomery Gregory's *Plays of Negro Life* (1927); "York Beach," a novella included in the anthology *The New American Caravan* (1929); *Essentials* (1931), a collection of aphorisms; and other stories, essays, and poems. All these works, as well as a selection from his autobiographical writings, have

134

been gathered in *The Wayward and the Seeking: A Collection of Writings by Jean Toomer* (1980), edited by Darwin Turner.

In the mid-1920s Toomer became interested in the work of the mystic Georges Ivanovitch Gurdjieff. Gurdjieff's philosophy stressed the union of physical, mental, and psychological functions to achieve inner harmony, and Toomer taught the Gurdjieff method between 1925 and 1933. In 1931 he resided in a communal arrangement with eight unmarried male and female friends in Portage, Wisconsin; later he married one of the participants, Margery Latimer, who later died while giving birth to their only child. Alternative spiritual disciplines obsessed Toomer, who later in life devoted himself to L. Ron Hubbard's Scientology. It is frequently asserted that Toomer's devotion to Gurdjieff, Scientology, and other pseudoscientific religions ruined him as a writer, as it made his later work dogmatic and excessively didactic.

In 1934 Toomer married again, this time to Marjorie Content, whose father gave the couple a farm in Bucks County, Pennsylvania, where Toomer lived until his death on March 30, 1967.

▣ *Critical Extracts*

GORHAM B. MUNSON   There can be no question of Jean Toomer's skill as a literary craftsman. A writer who can combine vowels and liquids to form a cadence like "she was as innocently lovely as a November cotton flower" has a subtle command of word-music. And a writer who can break the boundaries of the sentences, interrupt the placement of a fact with a lyrical cry, and yet hold both his fact and his exclamation to a single welded meaning as in the expression: "A single room held down to earth . . . O fly away to Jesus . . . by a leaning chimney . . .", is assuredly at home in the language and therefore is assuredly free to experiment and invent. Toomer has found his own speech, now swift and clipped for violent narrative action, now languorous and dragging for specific characterizing purposes, and now lean and sinuous for the exposition of ideas, but always cadenced to accord with an unusually sensitive ear.

It is interesting to know that Toomer, before he began to write, thought of becoming a composer. One might have guessed it from the fact that the early sketches in *Cane* (1923) depend fully as much upon a musical unity as upon a literary unity. "Karintha," for example, opens with a song, presents a theme, breaks into song, develops the theme, sings again, drops back into prose, and dies away in a song. But in it certain narrative functions—one might mention that lying back of the bald statement, "This interest of the male, who wishes to ripen a growing thing too soon, could mean no good to her"—are left undeveloped. Were it not for the songs, the piece could scarcely exist.

But electing to write, Toomer was too canny to try to carry literature further into music than this. *Cane* is, from one point of view, the record of his search for suitable literary forms. We can see him seeking guidance and in several of the stories, notably "Fern" and "Avey," it is the hand of Sherwood Anderson that he takes hold. But Anderson leads toward formlessness and Toomer shakes him off for Waldo Frank in such pieces as "Theatre" where the design becomes clear and the parts are held in a vital esthetic union. Finally, he breaks through in a free dramatic form of his own, the play *Kabnis* which still awaits production by an American theatre that cries for good native drama and yet lacks the wit to perceive the talent of Toomer. ⟨. . .⟩

He is a dynamic symbol of what all artists of our time should be doing, if they are to command our trust. He has mastered his craft. Now he seeks a purpose that will convince him that his craft is nobly employed. Obviously, to his search there is no end, but in his search there is bound to occur a fusion of his experience, and it is this fused experience that will give profundity to his later work. His way is not the way of the minor art master, but the way of the major master of art. And that is why his potential literary significance outweighs the actualized literary significance of so many of his contemporaries.

Gorham B. Munson, "The Significance of Jean Toomer," *Opportunity* 3, No. 3 (September 1925): 262–63

JEAN TOOMER   In my writing I was working, at various times, on all the main forms. Essays, articles, poems, short stories, reviews, and a long piece somewhere between a novel and a play. Before I had even so much as glimpsed the possibility of writing *Cane*, I had written a trunk full of manuscripts. The phrase "trunk full" is often used loosely. I mean it literally and exactly. But what difficulties I had! I had in me so much experience so twisted up that not a thing would come out until by sheer force I had dragged it forth. Only now and again did I experience spontaneous writing. Most of it was will and sweat. And nothing satisfied me. Not a thing had

I done which I thought merited publication—or even sending to a magazine. I wrote and wrote and put each thing aside, regarding it as simply one of the exercises of my apprenticeship. Often I would be depressed and almost despair over the written thing. But, on the other hand, I became more and more convinced that I had the real stuff in me. And slowly but surely I began getting the "feeling" of my medium, a sense of form, of words, of sentences, rhythms, cadences, and rhythmic patterns. And then, after several years work, suddenly, it was as if a door opened and I knew without doubt that I was *inside. I knew literature!* And what was my joy!

But many things happened before that time came! ⟨. . .⟩

I came in contact with an entirely new body of ideas. Buddhist philosophy, the Eastern teachings, occultism, theosophy. Much of the writing itself seemed to me to be poorly done; and I was certain that the majority of the authors of these books had only third or fourth-rate minds, or less. But I extracted the ideas from their settings, and they seemed to me among the most extraordinary I had ever heard. It is natural to me to put my whole heart into anything that really interests me—as long as I am interested. For the time being, only that thing exists in the world. These ideas challenged and stimulated me. Despite my literary purpose, I was compelled to know something more about them. So, for a time, I turned my back on literature and plunged into this kind of reading. I read far and wide, for more than eight months. Then, I became dissatisfied with just reading. I wanted to do some of the things they suggested. I wanted to see some of the things with my own eyes. I myself wanted a personal all-around experience of the world these books seemed to open. I tried several of the exercises; but then, abruptly stopped them. I concluded they were not for me. In general, I concluded that all of that was not for me. I was in this physical, tangible, earthly world, and I knew little enough of it. It was the part of wisdom to learn more and to be able to do more in this, before I began exploring and adventuring into other worlds. So I came back to earth and to literature. But I had profited in many ways by my excursion. The Eastern World, the ancient scriptures had been brought to my notice. Also, our own Christian Bible. I had read it as if it were a new book. Just simply as a work of literature I was convinced that we had nothing to equal it. Not even Shakespeare— my old God—wrote language of such grand perfection. And my religious nature, given a cruel blow by Clarence Darrow and naturalism and atheism, but not, as I found, destroyed by them—my religious nature which had been sleeping was vigorously aroused. ⟨. . .⟩

Once during this period I read many books on the matter of race and the race problem in America. Rarely had I encountered the nonsense contained in most of these books. It was evident to me, who had seen both the white and the colored worlds, and both from the inside, that the authors of these writings had little or no experience of the matters they were dealing with. Their pages showed very little more than strings of words expressive of personal prejudices and preferences. I felt that I should write on this matter. I did write several fragments of essays. And I did a lot of thinking. Among other things, I again worked over my own position, and formulated it with more fullness and exactitude. I wrote a poem called, "The First American," the idea of which is, that here in America we are in the process of forming a new race, that I was one of the first conscious members of this race.

Jean Toomer, "The Cane Years" (c. 1932), *The Wayward and the Seeking: A Collection of Writings by Jean Toomer*, ed. Darwin T. Turner (Washington, DC: Howard University Press, 1980), pp. 117–21

STERLING BROWN   Deriving in part from Anderson and Waldo Frank, Jean Toomer's *Cane* (1923) has much greater intimacy with Negro life, dealing equally well with the black belt of Georgia and bourgeois Washington. Toomer is master of fluid, evocative prose; some of his stories are prose-poems.

> The sun is hammered to a band of gold. Pine-needles, like mazda, are brilliantly aglow. No rain has come to take the rustle from the falling sweet-gum leaves. Over in the forest, across the swamp, a sawmill blows its closing whistle. Smoke curls up. . . . Curls up and spreads itself pine-high above the branch, a single silver band along the eastern valley. A black boy . . . you are the most sleepiest man I ever seed, Sleeping Beauty . . . cradled on a gray mule, guided by the hollow sound of cowbells, heads for them through a rusty cotton field.

His faithfully portrayed Georgia landscape Toomer has peopled with faithfully drawn characters, such as Fern, the shiftless, ignorant beauty of the Georgia Pike, and Becky, a white outcast, who bears two Negro children. "Blood Burning Moon" tells of the rivalry between a Negro and a white man for a Negro girl, that ends in a murder and a lynching. Not propaganda in the manner of the apologists, it is tragic realism at its best.

Neither debunking Negro society nor glorifying it, Toomer pictures Washington with the thoughtfulness of one who knew it from the inside. The futile, and in the story of "Avey," the drably tragic revolt against the smugness of a rising middle-class, are brilliantly set before us. Toomer was sharply criticized by Negroes for his "betrayal"; his insight and tenderness seemed to escape them. "Kabnis" is a long, occasionally obscure story of a northern Negro teaching school in Georgia. No one has done so well as Toomer the hypocritical school principal, a petty, puritanical tyrant who truckles to the whites. Laymon, a preacher-teacher who "knows more than would be good for anyone other than a silent man"; Halsey, a self-assured, courageous artisan; and Kabnis, a weakling idealist driven to cynicism and dissipation until he discovers, mystically, the strength of his people, are similarly well drawn. Toomer reveals in "Kabnis" an insight that makes his failure to write a novel about Negro life one of the undoubted losses of contemporary literature.

Sterling Brown, *The Negro in American Fiction* (Washington, DC: Associates in Negro Folk Education, 1937), pp. 153–54

ROBERT BONE   In spite of his wide and perhaps primary association with white intellectuals, as an artist Toomer never underestimated the importance of his Negro identity. He attained a universal vision not by ignoring race as a local truth, but by coming face to face with his particular tradition. His pilgrimage to Georgia was a conscious attempt to make contact with his hereditary roots in the Southland. Of Georgia, Toomer wrote: "There one finds soil in the sense that the Russians know it—the soil every art and literature that is to live must be embedded in." This scene of soil is central to *Cane* and to Toomer's artistic vision. "When one is on the soil of one's ancestors," his narrator remarks, "most anything can come to one."

What comes to Toomer, in the first section of *Cane*, is a vision of the parting soul of slavery:

> . . . for though the sun is setting on
> A song-lit race of slaves, it has not set;
> Though late, O soil, it is not too late yet
> To catch thy plaintive soul, leaving, soon gone.

The soul of slavery persists in the "supper-getting-ready songs" of the black women who live on the Dixie Pike—a road which "has grown from a goat path in Africa." It persists in "the soft, listless cadence of Georgia's South," in the hovering spirit of a comforting Jesus, and in the sudden violence of the Georgia moon. It persists above all in the people, white and black, who have become Andersonian "grotesques" by virtue of their slave inheritance. Part I of *Cane* is in fact a kind of Southern *Winesburg, Ohio*. It consists of the portraits of six women—all primitives—in which an Andersonian narrator mediates between the reader and the author's vision of life on the Dixie Pike.

Robert Bone, *The Negro Novel in America* (New Haven: Yale University Press, 1958), pp. 81–82

DARWIN T. TURNER   The actual beginning of Jean Toomer, writer, probably can be dated from ⟨. . .⟩ the spring of 1920. While chasing many gleams, he had read extensively in atheism, naturalism, socialism, sociology, psychology, and the dramas of Shaw. To these scientific, philosophical, and social writings, he had added *Wilhelm Meister* of Goethe, the romances of Victor Hugo, and the verse of Walt Whitman. After his abortive crusade in the shipyard, he had reaccepted capitalism as a necessary evil. Dismayed because his atheism had shocked a Quaker girl, he had reaffirmed his faith in God and in religion, even though he refused to believe in orthodox creeds and churches. Introduced now to a literary world of such people as Lola Ridge, Edwin Arlington Robinson, and Waldo Frank, he was dazzled with the prospect of retiring from arid philosophies into a cultural aristocracy.

Looking back from a diary written in 1930, he saw the Toomer of the early twenties as a vanity-burdened poseur who adopted the manners of a poet, a poet's appearance, and a French-sounding name—Jean. A more objective observer sees a seriously confused young man of twenty-five, who was not content to be average, but who had discovered nothing at which to be great; who wanted to guide, to instruct, to lead, to dominate, but who would withdraw completely if he could not; and who habitually discontinued studies with startling abruptness, not because he had mastered them, but because he had lost interest or, as with music, had decided that he could not become a master. This, however, was the tortured soul hidden by the ever present mask of intellect, confidence, and charm which caused Waldo Frank to write, "You are one of those men one must see but once to know the timbre and the truth of."

Darwin T. Turner, "Jean Toomer: Exile," *In a Minor Chord: Three Afro-American Writers and Their Search for Identity* (Carbondale: Southern Illinois University Press, 1971), pp. 10–11

CHARLES W. SCRUGGS　　　⟨A⟩ fuller understanding of *Cane* comes from Toomer's letter to Waldo Frank upon completion of the novel. Critics may be skeptical about finding any structure in the work, and certainly *Cane* may be appreciated without one, but Toomer himself apparently had a plan. "My brother!" he says to Frank on December 12, 1922:

> Cane is on its way to you! For two weeks I have worked steadily
> at it. The book is done. From three angles, Cane's design is a circle.
> Aesthetically, from simple forms to complex ones, and back to
> simple forms. Regionally, from the South up into the North,
> and back into the South again. Or from the North down into
> the South and then a return North. From the point of view
> of the spiritual entity behind the work, the curve really starts
> with Bona and Paul (awakening), plunges into Kabnis,
> emerges in Karintha etc. swings upward into Theatre and Box
> Seat, and ends (pauses) in Harvest Song. . . . Between each
> of the three sections, a curve. These, to vaguely indicate the
> design.

Toomer's outline both puzzles and informs. It puzzles because, although the novel moves from South to North to South, it does not parallel the spiritual pattern he employs. The published work begins with the Karintha section and ends with "Kabnis." The curves drawn on separate pages between the sections hint at a circular design, but the reader tends to associate them only with the South-North-South structural scheme.

The key, I think, lies in the word "pauses" (". . . and ends (pauses) in Harvest Song"). Toomer is describing *Cane* in organic terms, and therefore it never really ends. It is simply a matter of beginning all over again with "Bona and Paul," the story that follows "Harvest Song."

Organic form interests Toomer as he reacts to the industrialization of his age. In a letter to Gorham Munson (March 19, 1923) he compares his aesthetic form to a tree, with the sap as the sustenance and the arrangement of leaves as the meaning. "A machine," he says, "is all form, it has no leaves. Its very abstraction is . . . the death of it." Even earlier, in a letter to Waldo Frank (July 19, 1922), he mentions plans for a collection entitled *Cane* with the sections "Cane stalks and choruses" ("Kabnis" and "K.C.A."—probably "Karintha," "Carma," and "Avey"); "leaves and syrup songs" (the poems), and "Leaf Traceries in Washington" (the vignettes).

Charles W. Scruggs, "The Mark of Cain and the Redemption of Art: A Study of Theme and Structure of Jean Toomer's *Cane*," *American Literature* 44, No. 2 (May 1972): 279–80

WALDO FRANK   The year *Holiday* was published (1923) Jean
Toomer gathered his verse and prose into a volume, *Cane*, which Liveright
brought out with an introduction by Waldo Frank. It said:

> A poet has arisen among our American Youth who has known
> how to turn the essences and materials of his southland into
> the essences and materials of literature . . . who writes, not as a
> southerner, not as a rebel against southerners, not as a Negro,
> not as apologist or priest or critic: who writes as a *poet*. . . . For
> Toomer, the Southland is not a problem to be solved; it is
> a field of loveliness to be sung: the Georgia Negro is not a
> downtrodden soul to be uplifted; he is material for gorgeous
> painting; the segregated, self-conscious, brown belt of
> Washington is not a subject to be discussed and exposed; it
> is a subject of beauty and drama. . . .

I was right about Toomer's lush genius; I was wrong about Toomer's
ability to write not primarily as a Negro but as a human being. The foreword
continued:

> The gifted Negro has been too often thwarted from becoming
> a poet because his world was forever forcing him to recollect
> that he was a Negro. . . . The English poet is not forever
> protesting and recalling that he is English. It is so natural
> and easy for him to be English that he can sing as a man. . . .

Toomer's trauma was deeper than the others'. In his need to forget he
was Negro, he joined the transcendental pseudo-Hindu cult of Gurdjieff,
whose psychological techniques aimed at obliterating in the catachumen
the condition of being a man. *Cane*, a chaotic beginning, became Toomer's
only publication. As a poet, and as a natural leader of his folk, he vanished.

Waldo Frank, "From *Our America* to *City Block* and *Holiday*," *Memoirs of Waldo
Frank*, ed. Alan Trachtenberg (Amherst: University of Massachusetts Press, 1973),
p. 107

SUSAN L. BLAKE   Between Jean Toomer and ⟨*Cane's*⟩ characters
is a creative persona—represented sometimes by a narrator, sometimes simply
by the narrative voice—who shares his characters' goals and whose story
unifies the book. Like Kabnis, like any artist, he wants to give form to
experience, and *Cane* is the record of his attempt. Gorham B. Munson has
called this persona the "spectatorial artist," a term which suggests the artistic

process outlined in the book: the persona progresses from a spectator in the first stories to an artist in "Kabnis." His progress is measured by his distance from his characters. Both the spectator and the artist are detached from their material, but the understanding that distinguishes the detached creator of the final story from the detached observer of the first comes from a transitional stage of involvement.

The central conflict in *Cane* is the struggle of the spectatorial artist to involve himself in his material. The characters in the individual stories are engaged in the same conflict. Their "material" is life; involvement for them means acceptance of its chaos. The protagonists in the first stories are unaware of the conflict; the men who try to buy Karintha do not know what they are missing, "do not know that the soul of her was a growing thing ripened too soon." Kabnis knows; and the sight of "hills and valleys, heaving with folk-songs, so close to me that I cannot reach them" drives him mad. For the spectatorial artist, involvement in his material means identification with his characters and recognition that the dilemma he is portraying in them is also his dilemma. Their characters become more complex as they become more aware of their experience; they become more aware as their creator, becoming more involved with them, put his own awareness into them. Thus characters and creative voice develop in parallel in *Cane*, and the book resembles neither a novel nor a collection of short stories as much as it does a sketchbook—a record of artistic development.

Susan L. Blake, "The Spectatorial Artist and the Structure of *Cane*," *CLA Journal* 17, No. 4 (June 1974): 516–17

NELLIE Y. McKAY   Like all of Toomer's work of this late-1920s period, "Easter" embraces a universal vision. It is a surrealistic piece, with images that are absurd, grotesque, and influenced by Eastern thought. The title of the story is ironic. In place of the serious thoughtfulness associated with the time and events immediately preceding the Christian Easter, Toomer presents a background of bedlam against which he superimposes images that are bizarre, absurd, and even repulsive. No triumphant redeemer appears at the end, only a creature that causes such consternation that the faithful watchers flee in alarm. "Easter" is the satiric portrayal of the failure of Western thought and religion to effect the spiritual regeneration that the modern world desperately needs and for which it seeks. ⟨. . .⟩

"Easter" is interesting because of its language and because of what it tells us about Jean Toomer's thinking at this time in his life. In this story, he calls on a variety of conventional literary forms—ambiguity, puns, and satire among them—and also uses surrealistic techniques to great advantage with the absurd and grotesque elements of the story. He shows great skill in combining these various forms and succeeds in producing another verbal portrait, almost as powerful in its own way as *Cane*. Here is an image of the disharmonious nature of the world and the helplessness of the traditional spiritual resources. Thematically, the work shows him moving away from the concerns that are peculiar to any one group of people by attempting to illuminate a world situation. As he began to explore the possibilities of cosmic consciousness, ordinary consciousness and its spiritual components took on new meanings for him, and it is these new meanings that begin to bear on his writings and which first show up in "Easter."

> Nellie Y. McKay, *Jean Toomer, Artist: A Study of His Literary Life and Work, 1894–1936* (Chapel Hill: University of North Carolina Press, 1984), pp. 202–3, 205–6

CYNTHIA EARL KERMAN and RICHARD ELDRIDGE

⟨Toomer⟩ was not seeking a shift in a category attached to his own name, such as from black to white; he wished to be neither white nor black. The vision of the universal man was the benchmark of his identity, and perhaps he accurately perceived himself as the embodiment of the greater American soul, a concept that Waldo Frank and others continued to encourage. Toomer's appearance, he noted, caused people on separate occasions to think that he was of eleven different nationalities. As for biological forebears, he could not be sure but was probably somewhere between one-eighth and one-sixteenth black. And he had lived among blacks, among whites, among Jews, and in groups organized without racial labels around a shared interest such as literature or psychology, moving freely from any one of these groups to any other. One mark of membership in the "colored" group, he said, was acceptance of the "color line" with its attendant expectations; neither his family nor he had ever been so bound. To be in the white group would also imply the exclusion of the other.

> What then am I?
> I am at once no one of the races and I am all of them.
> I belong to no one of them and I belong to all.
> I am, in a strict racial sense, a member of a new race.

This new race of mixed people, now forming all over the world but especially in America, "may be the turning point for the return of mankind, now divided into hostile races, to one unified race, namely, to the human race."

It was a new race, but also the oldest. The different racial and national groups could still contribute their distinctive richness: "I say to the colored group that, as a human being, I am one of them. . . . I say to the white group that, as a human being, I am one of them. As a white man, I am not one of them. . . . I am an American. As such, I invite them [both], not as [colored or] white people, but *as Americans*, to participate in whatever creative work I may be able to do."

Thus Toomer propounded the rather unpopular view that the racial issue in America would be resolved only when white America could accept the fact that its racial "purity" was a myth, that indeed its racial isolation produced blandness and lack of character. On the other hand, racial purity among blacks was just as much a myth and only encourages defensiveness and unconscious imitation, like that of an adolescent who defines his revolt against his parents by the very values he is trying to renounce. Race, he said, was a fictional construct, of no use for understanding people: "Human blood is human blood. Human beings are human beings. . . . No racial or social factors can adequately account for the uniqueness of each—or for the individual differences which people display concurrently with basic commonality."

Cynthia Earl Kerman and Richard Eldridge, *The Lives of Jean Toomer: A Hunger for Legibility* (Baton Rouge: Louisiana State University Press, 1987), pp. 341–42

RUDOLPH P. BYRD   By 1925 the perceptive, androgynous philosopher-poet of *Cane* was fading quickly from view. The poet who wrote forcefully and lyrically of the women of Sparta, Georgia, the poet who provided us with one of the first views of the interior life of African-American women, the poet who extended and improved upon Gertrude Stein's efforts to explore black female sexuality and personhood in "Melanctha," would continue, even after these successes, his search for the "intelligible scheme" that would give his life definition and meaning. Moreover, the poet who refused to romanticize American race relations; the poet, like Charles Chesnutt in such works as *The Marrow of Tradition*, who wrote in opposition to the plantation school of American letters; the poet, like James Weldon Johnson in *The Autobiography of an Ex-Coloured Man*, who clarified further the pressures and compromises endured by African-Americans, would seek solutions to the problems of race in extraliterary constructs. Finally, the poet, like W. E. B. Du Bois in *The Souls of Black Folk*, who celebrated and mourned the passing of an African-American folk culture, the poet who employed the distinctive language of the group to suggest more clearly something of the history and experience of the group, the poet who experimented with the application of musical forms to literature, would abandon these values and interests after 1923 when the "intelligible scheme" assumed a recognizable, tangible form in the person of George I. Gurdjieff.

Within one year of his fateful visit to Fontainebleau, the poet of *Cane* had largely disappeared and in his place appeared the determined, confident social critic and spiritual reformer whose voice dominates "The Gallonwerps" and "Transatlantic." When he wrote these novels, the search for the "intelligible scheme" was behind Toomer. With the enthusiasm and unshakable optimism of a Gurdjieffian evangelist, Toomer attempted to describe in these novels the emptiness and aimlessness of modern life. ⟨. . .⟩

While we may be impatient with Toomer's undisguised enthusiasm for Gurdjieff's theories and disappointed by the awkward, fumbling manner in which they are integrated into his narrative, nonetheless we must admire his faith in the possibilities of human development. Although the differences between *Cane* and "The Gallonwerps" and "Transatlantic" are great, although we mourn particularly the disappearance of an African-American presence and a racial consciousness, the vital link that joins these three works is theme. Toomer's great theme of human development places these works in the same dynamic current of creative expression. Each work marks Toomer's struggle as an artist to achieve the sense of wholeness that he imparted to many of the men and women who inhabit his fictional universe.

Rudolph P. Byrd, Jean Toomer's Years with Gurdjieff: Portrait of an Artist 1923–1926
(Athens: University of Georgia Press, 1990), pp. 176–79

▦ *Bibliography*

Cane. 1923.

Essentials. 1931.

The Flavor of Man. 1949.

The Wayward and the Seeking: A Collection of Writings. Ed. Darwin T. Turner. 1980.

Collected Poems. Ed. Robert B. Jones and Margery Toomer Latimer. 1988.

❖ ❖ ❖

Walter White
1893–1955

WALTER FRANCIS WHITE, civil rights activist and writer, was born on July 1, 1893, in Atlanta, Georgia. His parents, George and Madeline White, were a relatively well-educated and prosperous couple who managed despite economic and racial barriers to send all seven of their children to college. White attended Atlanta University and worked briefly for an insurance agency, first as a clerk and then as a cashier. He quickly became involved with the National Association for the Advancement of Colored People (NAACP), establishing an Atlanta chapter. In 1918 he became assistant secretary for the organization, which at that time had only three paid officials. White moved to Harlem that year and began the first of the forty-one lynching investigations that marked his career with the NAACP. Relying on his ability to pass for white, White would enter a community in which a lynching had taken place, investigate the crime, and publish his findings when he returned to New York.

In 1922 White married fellow NAACP staffer Leah Gladys Powell, with whom he had a daughter, Jane, and a son, Walter, Jr. White produced his first novel, *The Fire in the Flint*, in 1924. The novel, an antilynching tale, created a storm of controversy in the South that resulted in large sales. Buoyed by the financial success of this novel, White published his second—and last—piece of fiction, the novel *Flight*, in 1926. Although *Flight* never achieved the popularity of *The Fire in the Flint*, it brought White to the attention of the Guggenheim Foundation, which awarded him a fellowship in 1926. Accepting the fellowship in 1927, White took his family to France to live for a year while he worked on what became *Rope and Faggot: A Biography of Judge Lynch* (1929), a study of the causes and history of lynching in the United States. Around this time he also wrote two pamphlets for the Little Blue Books series published by the Haldeman-Julius Company, *The American Negro and His Problems* (c. 1927) and *The Negro's Contribution to American Culture* (1928).

White continued his civil rights work in the United States, becoming acting secretary of the NAACP in 1929 and secretary in 1931. He received the prestigious Spingarn Medal in 1937 for his efforts to eradicate lynching. With Thurgood Marshall he wrote an analysis of the Detroit race riots (1943) and published *A Rising Wind: A Report of the Negro Soldier in the European Theater of War* in 1945 after visiting American troops and observing racial discrimination in the military in Europe and the Pacific during World War II. He summed up his views on this matter in a brief lecture, *Race Problems and World Peace* (1947).

In 1947 White and Leah Gladys Powell were amicably divorced and White suffered his first heart attack. In 1948 he published his memoirs, *A Man Called White*, and while working on the book met white South African writer Poppy Cannon, whom he married in 1949. Following his marriage his power as secretary of the NAACP was severely restricted; nonetheless, he remained with the organization until his death. Walter White died of a heart attack on March 28, 1955. His last work was an evaluation of America's progress on civil rights entitled *How Far the Promised Land?*, published posthumously late in 1955.

◈ *Critical Extracts*

W. E. B. DU BOIS   Walter White has written in *The Fire in the Flint* a good, stirring story and a strong bit of propaganda against the white Klansman and the black pussyfoot. White knows his Georgia from A to Z. There is not a single incident or a single character in the book which has not its prototype in real life today. All Mr. White's white people are not villains nor are all his Negroes saints, but one gets a thrilling sense of the devilish tangle that involves good and evil in the southern South.

Perhaps most significant however is the fact that a book like this can at last be printed. For years a flood of filth about the Negro has poured out of the South while no northern firm would consider a book telling even temperately the well-known and widely proven facts concerning the Negro. Subtly and slowly the change has come and Mr. White has been among the first to sense it and to persist courageously and doggedly in having his say.

Of course one can criticise any book and particularly a first one. Perhaps on the economic side Mr. White succumbs too easily to the common mistake of piling the blame of southern wickedness on the "poor whites" and absolving the aristocrats and former slave holders. This is, of course, based on the propaganda which the sons and daughters of slave-barons have spread, but it is far from true. On the human and artistic side, with the possible exception of the younger brother, Mr. White's characters do not live and breathe and compel our sympathy. They are more like labeled figures on a chess board. But despite all this, the story goes and the reader goes with it and that is the first business of a story.

     W. E. B. Du Bois, "Fall Books," *Crisis* 29, No. 1 (November 1924): 25

CARL VAN VECHTEN   It is a pleasure to be able to state that Mr. White's second novel ⟨*Flight*⟩ is much better than his first. It is written with a calm detachment of which *The Fire in the Flint* contains no hint. Furthermore, in Mimi Daquin, a Negro Creole girl with ivory skin and hair of reddish gold, the author has drawn a character entirely new to Afro-American fiction. Instead of the persecuted figure with which books on this general subject have made us so familiar, we are presented with a heroine who is mistress of her own fate, a woman whose ultimate acts are governed by her will. Mimi does not long permit herself to be hampered by the restrictions of Negro life and she is equally independent in her relations with the two men who play important parts in her career. She refuses to marry the father of her child; later, she leaves her white husband to return to the heart of her own race. ⟨. . .⟩

    Mr. White approaches the subject ⟨of passing for white⟩ from a new and sufficiently sensational point of view. Mimi Daquin does not leave the colored world because she has been insulted or humiliated by white people; she leaves it because of her momentary dissatisfaction with Negroes. In the end ⟨. . .⟩ realizing that both races have their peculiar faults and virtues, she decides for purely logical reasons that she is happier with her colored brethren and she deserts her white husband to return to Harlem.

    This, then, is the distinguishing merit of this novel, that it focuses attention upon a Negro character who is not materially hindered in her career by white prejudice. It is the simple chronicle of a beautiful, intelligent, dignified, self-supporting Negro girl. There is, indeed, a curious resemblance between Mimi and the self-reliant heroines of Miss Ellen Glasgow.

    The story takes the reader from the Creole quarter in New Orleans through the race riots of Atlanta (1906), in which Mimi as a child acquires her race-consciousness, through a brief episode in Philadelphia where her child is born, on to Harlem, and finally into white Manhattan. The incidental Negro characters are in nowise depicted as paragons of propriety and good taste. In fact, occasionally the author deals with them even a little cruelly. The petty gossip, the small meannesses, the color snobbery of Negro society (Mimi's father, Jean, says of the group in Atlanta: "Colored people here are always talking about prejudice, and they're just about as full of prejudice against Catholics, Jews and black Negroes as white people themselves") are fully described, but Mr. White makes it plain that in these respects there is little to choose between the two worlds.

> Carl Van Vechten, "A Triumphant Negro Heroine," *New York Herald Tribune Books*, 11 April 1926, p. 3

SINCLAIR LEWIS   Before I had ever met ⟨White⟩ or learned anything whatsoever about him personally, I had read his *Fire in the Flint* and found that although there was too much propaganda in it, there was also an authentic and important literary quality, a fidelity to life combined with a sense of beauty, which I was very glad to praise publicly. ⟨. . .⟩

He has the integrity combined with beauty of which I spoke: he has a sense of drama; he is not afflicted by the triviality which makes so many of our clever young writers insignificant, but rather a feeling of dignity and importance in his work; he has sharp observation and an admirable sense of words.

> Sinclair Lewis, Letter to the Guggenheim Foundation (c. 1926), cited in Edward E. Waldron, *Walter White and the Harlem Renaissance* (Port Washington, NY: Kennikat Press, 1978), p. 11

JAMES WELDON JOHNSON   ⟨White's⟩ book, *Rope and Faggot*, is, up to this time, the most complete and authoritative treatise on lynching. He discusses the subject from historical, economic, psychological, sex, religious, and political viewpoints, and with regard to the various theories of race superiority and inferiority.

Mr. White's book on lynching supersedes all other publications on this topic and makes it unnecessary for any other book on the subject to be written for many years to come.

> James Weldon Johnson, Letter to George E. Haynes (1929), cited in Edward E. Waldron, *Walter White and the Harlem Renaissance* (Port Washington, NY: Kennikat Press, 1978), p. 12

CLARENCE DARROW ⟨*Rope and Faggot*⟩ is written with care and discusses every phase of lynching and burning from its inception around the year 1830 to the present time. The facts are not taken from biased reports, but from statistics and newspaper accounts published in the vicinity of the operations. Some of the book is gruesome in the extreme, and it is impossible to understand how any people, savage or civilized, could be guilty of the atrocities depicted. The number of lynchings and burnings are taken from official figures and "credited" to the various states where they occurred. It is perfectly obvious that most of the Negroes who are the victims of those outrages were lynched and burned because they were Negroes. ⟨. . .⟩

Mr. White shows that in the most religious communities, where lynchings are highest, practically no minister ever raises his voice against them. Recent outbreaks he attributes to the growth of the absurd doctrine of Nordic supremacy, and to the new Ku Klux Klan, which was organized by a Methodist preacher, while many of its sub-organizers were Protestant clergymen formerly connected with the Anti-Saloon League.

Many suggestions are made as to what to do, all useful and enlightening. Mr. White seems to favor the Federal anti-lynching law. I am not so sanguine; I have seen too much of extending Federal powers to want to see any more of it, especially in a good cause. He overestimates the effect of punishment, as most people are wont to overestimate it. The truth is that even those who commit crimes often consider the penalty very little, and mobs notoriously give it no heed. ⟨. . .⟩

To any one who cares to know about the question of race, the alleged differences between the whites and colored—if there happens to be any one of this kind—I would especially commend Mr. White's chapter on Science, Nordicism and Lynching. I am convinced that he has been a good student of anthropology and knows what he is talking about. This book should be read by every citizen of the United States. It might possibly do them some good.

Clarence Darrow, "The Shame of America," *New York Herald Tribune Books*, 21 April 1929, p. 3

CLAUDE McKAY Walter White, the present secretary of the National Association for the Advancement of Colored People, possessed a charming personality, ingratiating as a Y.M.C.A. secretary. One felt a strange, even comic, feeling at the sound of his name and the sight of his extremely white complexion while hearing him described as a Negro.

The White stories of passing among the crackers were delightful. To me the most delectable was one illustrating the finger-nail theory of telling a near-white from a pure-white. White was traveling on a train on his way to investigate a lynching in the South. The cracker said, "There are many yaller niggers who look white, but I can tell them every time."

"Can you really?" Walter White asked.

"Oh sure, just by looking at their finger nails." And taking White's hand, he said, "Now if you had nigger blood, it would show here on your half-moons."

That story excited me by its paradox as much as had the name and complexion of Walter White. It seemed altogether fantastic that whites in the South should call him a "nigger" and whites in the North, a Negro. It violates my feeling of words as pictures conveying color and meaning. For whenever I am in Walter White's company my eyes compose him and my emotions respond exactly as they do in the case of any friendly so-called "white" man. When a white person speaks of Walter White as a Negro, as if that made him a being physically different from a white, I get a weird and impish feeling of the unreality of phenomena. And when a colored person refers to Walter White as colored, in a tone that implies him to be physically different from and inferior to the "pure" white person, I feel that life is sublimely funny. For to me a type like Walter White is Negroid simply because he closely identifies himself with the Negro group—just as a Teuton becomes a Moslem if he embraces Islam. White is whiter than many Europeans—even biologically. I cannot see the difference in the way that most of the whites and most of the blacks seem to see it. Perhaps what is reality for them is fantasy for me.

> Claude McKay, *A Long Way from Home* (1937; rpt. New York: Harcourt, Brace & World, 1970), pp. 110–11

GEORGE STREATOR   As time moves on, the educated Negro tends increasingly to revolt against the "Bourbon" South and lately against Northern apologists for this backward area. If there is a definite trend of Negroes to direct action and revolt, would it point to alliance with the Northern proletariat? The South fears another carpet-bag era, and conservative Negroes tend to share with them this fear.

Mr. White does not indicates this trend ⟨in *A Rising Wind*⟩. He visualizes on an international scale a rising tide of color: "World War II has given to the Negro a sense of kinship with other colored—and also oppressed—peoples of the world."

And also, "The Negro soldier is convinced that as time proceeds that identification of interests will spread even among some brown and yellow peoples who today refuse to see the connection between their exploitation by white nations and discrimination against the Negro in the United States."

Is this the road to the solution of world race problems, or is the unity of the colored races as fantastic as the unity of the white races? Is the problem of race basically economic, as the communists argue, or is it a consequence of the breakdown of Europe's spiritual power which, some Catholics argue, came with the Renaissance?

The "rising tide of color" was the menace pictured by Europe and America following the consciousness of the spiritual if not economic decline of the Western world beginning with World War I. Mr. White has reversed the banner. Using Wendell Willkie as a prophet, he sees a rise of colonial peoples demanding social justice in Asia and Africa and the United States.

Where will the races meet after this war, in madness or in a spirit of mutual responsibility? Walter White has toyed with and enlarged for the popular reader the Pan-Africa dream of W. E. B. Du Bois, which followed the last war. Will we blend this with Oswald Spengler, and drum out civilization? Is this the decline of the West? Will we spend the next century killing off colored people until the last gallon of high-octane gas is gone?

Now, where is the Christian power? Does it not seem that the militant Negro in America has lost his faith in the Cross? Will it be the Colored Commune? Do we still allow the white man's pride of race to drive large segments of the colored world to racism? After Japan, will it be America, then Africa? This, in the main, is Walter White's challenge.

George Streator, [Review of A Rising Wind], Commonweal, 13 April 1945, p. 652

WALTER FRANCIS WHITE   Shortly after meeting ⟨H. L.⟩ Mencken I received one of his characteristically terse and salty notes asking what I thought of Birthright, a novel about the Negro by T. S. Stribling of Tennessee. Flattered, I wrote a lengthy and painfully erudite criticism of the book pointing out that the novel had courage in depicting Negroes as human beings instead of as menials or buffoons, but that it obviously was written from the outside looking in. I said that Stribling's depiction of Negro servants was not too bad, but that he fell down badly in his portrayal of what educated Negroes feel and think. Mencken replied, "Why don't you do the right kind of novel? You could do it, and it would create a sensation."

Such an idea was at first preposterous. I had never even thought of attempting to write fiction. Mencken, Jim ⟨James Weldon Johnson⟩, and I talked over the notion as they both tried to convince me that the variety of experiences which my appearance made possible by permitting me to talk with white people as a white man and with my own people as a Negro gave me a unique vantage point. Mary White Ovington generously joined the conspiracy by offering Gladys and me the use of her cottage "Riverbank" at Great Barrington, Massachusetts. We took the train with typewriter, paper, pencils, and little other equipment—and certainly no clearly thought out plot for a novel. I had a rather misty notion of using as my central character a Negro doctor, trained in a first-class Northern medical school and returned to his native Georgia small town, but what would happen to him was not thought out at all.

I started to write and found that many of the characters seemed to rise up begging to be described, and creating their own story. I wrote feverishly and incessantly for twelve days and parts of twelve nights, stopping only when complete fatigue made it physically and mentally impossible to write another word. On the twelfth day the novel was finished and I dropped on a near-by couch and slept for hours.

Back in New York I ran into John Farrar, now a publisher but at that time editor of *The Bookman*, a scholarly monthly of the arts published by George H. Doran and Company. In answer to his friendly query as to how I had spent the summer I hesitantly confessed I had written a novel. John asked to see it ⟨. . .⟩

Not long afterward I received from Mr. Doran the most exciting—the most deliriously exciting—letter I had ever received in my life. We like your novel, he wrote, and will publish it after a few changes have been made which we wish to discuss with you. ⟨. . .⟩

We talked for an hour or more, and it became increasingly clear that someone had convinced Mr. Doran that even though there were Negro college graduates who talked correct English instead of dialect, the number of such Negroes was too small to justify their being written of as educated and normal human beings. I learned some time later that Mr. Doran had submitted my novel to Irvin S. Cobb, the Kentucky humorist, who had been so shocked by its outspokenness that he had advised against its publication, fearing that it would cause race riots in the South.

Walter Francis White, *A Man Called White: The Autobiography of Walter White* (New York: Viking Press, 1948), pp. 65–67

ANNE L. GOODMAN   Primarily, ⟨A Man Called White⟩ is the story of the NAACP's continuing fight against lynchings, disfranchisement and the lack of education facilities for the Negro in the South, against job and housing discrimination and sometimes violence in the North, and against segregation and prejudice in the armed forces. White relates his experiences in an easy and readable manner, but his facts, not his writing, give the book its force. However familiar the details of American race prejudice during the last thirty years may be, this factual, personal recapitulation of them comes with a new shock. That the struggle White describes is one of the most important parts of the most important struggle in America today— the struggle to realize as well as to preserve the democracy we boast of— seems self-evident. Discussing the Scottsboro case, which he investigated, he writes:

> ... The tragedy of a Scottsboro lies, not only in the bitterly
> cruel injustice it works upon its immediate victims, but also,
> and perhaps even more, in the cynical use of human misery by
> Communists in propagandizing for communism, and in the
> complacency with which a democratic government views the
> basic evils from which such a case arises. A majority of
> Americans still ignore ... the plain implications in similar
> tragedies.

Anne L. Goodman, "Blockade Runner," *New Republic*, 18 October 1948, pp. 23–24

GERALD W. JOHNSON   ⟨How Far the Promised Land?'s⟩ thesis is that whereas our enemies, especially the Communists, harp constantly on the fact that after nearly a hundred years the American Negro is still not quite free, the really remarkable thing is that in less than a hundred years former chattels have climbed almost to the rank of first-class citizens, as far as the law is concerned.

This feat is without historical parallel. So White regards the fact that the American Negro's complete success is now plainly in sight as vindication of the theory of democratic government.

The book nowhere suggests it, but the fact is that much of the credit for the feat belongs to the author. Walter White was a Negro leader not by act of God, but by his own deliberate choice. I remember my own astonishment when I first encountered him a quarter of a century ago. His eyes were blue and his skin and hair definitely lighter than my own. At any time, by moving his residence perhaps twenty miles and changing his name to Black he might have acquired all the rights and privileges appertaining to a representative of the Anglo-Saxon race. H. L. Mencken once asked him why on earth he did not do so, and his answer was that as a Negro he could accomplish five times more than as a white man.

Nevertheless, White must have been aware that, although he scorned to go through it, there was always behind him an open door of escape. This raises a question as to what extent he was truly representative, psychologically, of black men for whom there is no escape. It probably accounts for the fact that among darker-skinned Negroes White's leadership, while admittedly valuable, was always regarded as a little doctrinaire, a trifle bookish. To them he stood somewhat as Woodrow Wilson stood in relation to most Democratic politicians—great, certainly, but a little apart, a shade aloof.

It is possible that his last book may be regarded in that same light by the bulk of the Negro population. Ralph Bunche, it is true, takes no such attitude in the very moving foreword he contributes to the volume, but Dr. Bunche can hardly be accepted as typical of the common man. It would be imprudent, to put it mildly, for a white reviewer to call the book representative of Negro opinion. On the other hand, it is definitely not representative of any widespread white opinion. It is, rather, an in-between opinion, and by that same token it may be closer to the objective truth than the dominant habit of thought in either race.

Gerald W. Johnson, "An American Testament," New York Times Book Review, 6 November 1955, p. 46

ROBERT BONE   At the present time it is no longer required of a Negro author that he enter political life, nor of a Negro political leader that he write novels. There was a time, however, before the present age of specialization, when a Negro intellectual of national stature was expected to double in brass. Only a few men of rare versatility such as James Weldon Johnson were equal to the challenge. Others, like Walter White and W. E. B. Du Bois, were sometimes tempted into waters beyond their depth. Able political leaders and competent writers of expository prose, these men lacked the creative imagination which is the *sine qua non* of good fiction.

Walter White's first novel, *The Fire in the Flint* (1924), is an antilynching tract of melodramatic proportions. It was written in twelve days, according to White, and the novel itself provides no grounds for doubting his word. It is essentially a series of essays, strung on an unconvincing plot, involving the misfortunes of a colored doctor and his family in a small Southern town. White's second novel, *Flight* (1926), is an undistinguished treatment of passing, perhaps more susceptible to the influence of the Harlem School than most novels of the Rear Guard. Taken together, Walter White's novels comprise an object lesson in what Blyden Jackson has called "Faith without Works in Negro Literature."

> Robert Bone, *The Negro Novel in America* (New Haven: Yale University Press, 1958), pp. 99–100

EDWARD E. WALDRON   The real strength of *The Fire in the Flint* lies, finally, in what it says, not in how well it says it. There are flaws in the story and, as Bone points out, there is too much exposition for narrative fiction. White's treatment of the love story involving Kenneth Harper and Jane Phillips is incredibly naive and more fitting a sentimental novel than a novel of protest. And the characters, with a few exceptions, are flatly drawn types. The Reverend Mr. Wilson is given some depth, but only after a rather stereotyped caricature of him as a "pompous, bulbous-eyed" and vain man, "exceedingly fond of long words, especially of Latin derivation." It is almost as if White changed his mind about the good Reverend in the process of writing the story. The treatment of white characters in *Fire* is even more sparse; there are few admirable white representatives in it. Judge Stevenson is one exception, and Roy Ewing is another, although Ewing at first wants nothing to do with the "nigger doctor" who operates on his daughter. Sheriff Parker and the rest of the white townspeople are presented as ignorant, bovine creatures who mull over murder as other men debate the necessity of removing crabgrass.

But we must keep in mind that this is 1924, a time when people were still being lynched with some regularity and when most white Americans' concept of Negroes was based upon the caricatures of the minstrel shows and the beasts haunting the pages of Thomas Dixon and his compatriots. *Fire* not only presented a sympathetic examination of the trials confronting an educated black man in a society geared to grind him into submission or a grave, it also presented a look at some of the foibles of that society as seen from a black perspective. For example, at the beginning of the novel Roy Ewing comes to Kenneth Harper for treatment of a "social disease" contracted during a night of abandon in Macon. As White says: "That was Kenneth's introduction to one part of the work of a colored physician in the South. Many phases of life that he as a youth had never known about

... he now had brought to his attention." Harper was also appalled by the whorehouses thriving in Central City, especially the ones in "Darktown": "Here were coloured women who seemed never to have to work. Here was seldom seen a coloured man. And the children around these houses were usually lighter in colour than in other parts of 'Darktown.' " White makes good use of his naive hero in these passages. A seasoned cynic would hardly remark the obvious discrepancies of what the whites preached about segregation and what they practiced; he would simply accept it as a matter of course. Through the eyes of the innocent Kenneth Harper, though, White can let his white reader see a world through eyes that are just as unused to the light as his own. Judging from the reactions of people who wrote White after reading the novel, this is exactly the effect the book had, at least in some quarters.

> Edward E. Waldron, *Walter White and the Harlem Renaissance* (Port Washington, NY: Kennikat Press, 1978), pp. 46–47

▨ *Bibliography*

The Fire in the Flint. 1924.

Flight. 1926.

The American Negro and His Problems: A Comprehensive Picture of a Serious and Pressing Situation. c. 1927.

The Negro's Contribution to American Culture: The Sudden Flowering of a Genius-Laden Artistic Movement. 1928.

Rope and Faggot: A Biography of Judge Lynch. 1929.

What Caused the Detroit Riot? An Analysis (with Thurgood Marshall). 1943.

A Rising Wind: A Report of the Negro Soldier in the European Theater of War. 1945.

Race Problems and World Peace. 1947.

A Man Called White: The Autobiography of Walter White. 1948.

How Far the Promised Land? 1955.

◈ ◈ ◈

Richard Wright
1908–1960

RICHARD NATHANIEL WRIGHT was born on September 4, 1908, near Natchez, Mississippi, to a schoolteacher mother and an illiterate sharecropper father. His father abandoned the family when Wright was very young, and he was raised by his maternal grandmother. After ninth grade, he dropped out of school and moved to Memphis, then to Chicago and New York. He educated himself, and was particularly interested in literature, sociology, and psychology. In 1932 he joined the Communist party, and his literary career was encouraged by the Communist-affiliated John Reed Club. Much of his early writing appeared in leftist publications. He worked for the Federal Negro Theatre Project and the Federal Writers' Project; while associated with these organizations he published *12 Million Black Voices* (1941), a Marxist analysis of the American class struggle. He was Harlem editor for the *Daily Worker* in New York. In 1938 he married Rose Dhima Meadman; they were later divorced, and Wright married Ellen Poplar, with whom he had two children. From 1947 until his death he lived in Paris.

Wright first came to the attention of the American reading public with the publication of *Uncle Tom's Children: Four Novellas* in 1938; the stories concern the struggles to maturity of oppressed black women and men. An augmented edition including the novelette "Bright and Morning Star" appeared in 1940. Wright's second book, *Native Son* (1940), was his major critical and popular breakthrough, and remains one of the most influential American novels of the twentieth century. It concerns the life and destruction of Bigger Thomas, a poor black youth from the slums of Chicago. Wright's evocative portrayal of a life of fear and enslavement struck a powerful chord with his readership, despite some critics' complaints that the latter third of the book is expository and slow-moving.

Though none of Wright's subsequent books had the immediate impact of *Native Son*, he was admired as a solid stylist and spokesman for the poor and oppressed. His later novels are *The Outsider* (1953), *Savage Holiday* (1954), *The Long Dream* (1958), and *Lawd Today* (1963). *Eight Men*, a collection of stories, was published posthumously in 1961. His autobiography, *Black Boy: A Record of Childhood and Youth* (1945), and his sociological studies, including *Black Power: A Record of Reactions in a Land of Pathos* (1954), *The Color Curtain: A Report on the Bandung Conference* (1956; originally published in French in 1955), *Pagan Spain* (1956), and *White Man, Listen!* (1957), were also widely read and admired. Wright died on November 28, 1960. Another autobiography, *American Hunger*, was published in 1977; *Richard Wright Reader*, edited by Ellen Wright and Michel Fabre, was published in 1978.

Critical Extracts

ZORA NEALE HURSTON   This ⟨*Uncle Tom's Children*⟩ is a book about hatreds. Mr. Wright serves notice by his title that he speaks of people in revolt, and his stories are so grim that the Dismal Swamp of race hatred must be where they live. Not one act of understanding and sympathy comes to pass in the entire work.

But some bright new lines to remember come flashing from the author's pen. Some of his sentences have the shocking-power of a forty-four. That means that he knows his way around among words. With his facility, one wonders what he would have done had he dealt with plots that touched the broader and more fundamental phases of Negro life instead of confining himself to the spectacular. For, though he has handled himself well, numerous Negro writers, published and unpublished, have written of this same kind of incident. It is the favorite Negro theme just as how the stenographer or some other poor girl won the boss or the boss's son is the favorite white theme. What is new in the four novelettes included in Mr. Wright's book is the wish-fulfillment theme. In each story the hero suffers but he gets his man. ⟨. . .⟩

Since the author himself is a Negro his dialect is a puzzling thing. One wonders how he arrived at it. Certainly he does not write by ear unless he is tone-deaf. But aside from the broken speech of his characters, the book contains some beautiful writing. One hopes that Mr. Wright will find in Negro life a vehicle for his talents.

Zora Neale Hurston, "Stories of Conflict," *Saturday Review*, 2 April 1938, p. 32

RICHARD WRIGHT   It was not until I went to live in Chicago that I first thought seriously of writing of Bigger Thomas. Two items of my experience combined to make me aware of Bigger as a meaningful and prophetic symbol. First, being free of the daily pressure of the Dixie environment, I was able to come into possession of my own feelings. Second, my contact with the labor movement and its ideology made me see Bigger clearly and feel what he meant.

I made the discovery that Bigger Thomas was not black all the time; he was white, too, and there were literally millions of him, everywhere. The extension of my sense of the personality of Bigger was the pivot of my life; it altered the complexion of my existence. I became conscious, at first dimly, and then later on with increasing clarity and conviction, of the vast, muddied pool of human life in America. It was as though I had put on a pair of spectacles whose power was that of an x-ray enabling me to see deeper into the lives of men. Whenever I picked up a newspaper, I'd no longer feel that I was reading of the doings of whites alone (Negroes are rarely mentioned in the press unless they've committed some crime!), but of a complex struggle for life going on in my country, a struggle in which I was involved. I sensed, too, that the Southern scheme of oppression was but an appendage of a far vaster and in many respects more ruthless and impersonal commodity-profit machine. ⟨. . .⟩

The more I thought of it the more I became convinced that if I did not write of Bigger as I saw and felt him, if I did not try to make him a living personality and at the same time a symbol of all the larger things I felt and saw in him, I'd be reacting as Bigger himself reacted: that is, I'd be acting out of *fear* if I let what I thought whites would say constrict and paralyze me.

As I contemplated Bigger and what he meant, I said to myself: "I must write this novel, not only for others to read, but to free *myself* of this sense of shame and fear." In fact, the novel, as time passed, grew upon me to the extent that it became a necessity to write it; the writing of it turned into a way of living for me.

Richard Wright, "How 'Bigger' Was Born" (1940), *Native Son* (1940; rpt. New York: Harper & Row, 1989), pp. xiv–xv, xxi–xxii

---

MARGARET MARSHALL   Mr. Wright's style often reminds one of a stream "riled" by a heavy storm. Its element of Biblical rhetoric is not out of place since it is part of the colloquial heritage of the Negro in

America, but there is in addition a bookish quality, often encountered in the self-educated writer, which should be weeded out. Mr. Wright's boldness in choosing to develop his theme through the story of a "bad nigger" is all to the good, but his flair for the melodramatic could bear curbing.

These defects cannot be described as minor, but they are extenuated by the wealth of evidence in *Native Son* that they can be overcome by a writer whose talent and seriousness are apparent on every page, who displays a maturity of thought and feeling beside which the eloquence of *The Grapes of Wrath* grows pale. And Mr. Wright's youth demonstrates once more that maturity is not necessarily a matter of years.

Margaret Marshall, "Black Native Son," Nation, 16 March 1940, pp. 367–68

RICHARD WRIGHT   I ran across many words whose meanings I did not know, and I either looked them up in a dictionary or, before I had a chance to do that, encountered the word in a context that made its meaning clear. But what strange world was this? I concluded the book with the conviction that I had somehow overlooked something terribly important in life. I had once tried to write, had once reveled in the feeling, had let my crude imagination roam, but the impulse to dream had been slowly beaten out of me by experience. Now it surged up again and I hungered for books, new ways of looking and seeing. It was not a matter of believing or disbelieving what I read, but of feeling something new, of being affected by something that made the look of the world different.

As dawn broke I ate my pork and beans, feeling dopey, sleepy. I went to work, but the mood of the book would not die; it lingered, coloring everything I saw, heard, did. I now felt that I knew what the white men were feeling. Merely because I had read a book that had spoken of how they lived and thought, I identified myself with that book. I felt vaguely guilty. Would I, filled with bookish notions, act in a manner that would make the whites dislike me? ⟨. . .⟩

I knew of no Negroes who read the books I liked and I wondered if any Negroes ever thought of them. I knew that there were Negro doctors, lawyers, newspapermen, but I never saw any of them. When I read a Negro newspaper I never caught the faintest echo of my preoccupation in its pages. I felt trapped and occasionally, for a few days, I would stop reading. But a vague hunger would come over me for books, books that opened up new avenues of feeling and seeing, and again I would forge another note to the white librarian. Again I would read and wonder, feeling that I carried a secret, criminal burden about with me each day.

Richard Wright, *Black Boy* (1945), *Richard Wright Reader*, ed. Ellen Wright and Michel Fabre (New York: Harper & Row, 1978), pp. 18, 21

RALPH ELLISON   As a writer, Richard Wright has outlined for himself a dual role: to discover and depict the meaning of the Negro experience; and to reveal to both Negroes and whites those problems of a psychological and emotional nature which arise between them when they strive for mutual understanding.

Now, in *Black Boy*, he has used his own life to probe what qualities of will, imagination and intellect are required of a Southern Negro in order to possess the meaning of his life in the United States. Wright is an important writer, perhaps the most articulate Negro American, and what he has to say is highly perceptive. Imagine Bigger Thomas projecting his own life in lucid prose, guided, say, by the insights of Marx and Freud, and you have an idea of this autobiography.

Published at a time when any sharply critical approach to Negro life has been dropped as a wartime expendable, it should do much to redefine the problem of the Negro and American Democracy. Its power can be observed in the shrill manner with which some professional "friends of the Negro people" have attempted to strangle the work in a noose of newsprint.

What in the tradition of literary autobiography is it like, this work described as a "great American autobiography"? As a non-white intellectual's statement of his relationship to Western culture, *Black Boy* recalls the conflicting pattern of identification and rejection found in Nehru's *Toward Freedom*. In its use of fictional techniques, its concern with criminality (sin) and the artistic sensibility, and in its author's judgement and rejection of the narrow world of his origin, it recalls Joyce's rejection of Dublin in *A Portrait of the Artist*. And as a psychological document of life under oppressive conditions, it recalls *The House of the Dead*, Dostoievsky's profound study of the humanity of Russian criminals.

Such works were perhaps Wright's literary guides, aiding him to endow his life's incidents with communicable significance; providing him with ways of seeing, feeling and describing his environment. These influences, however, were encountered only after these first years of Wright's life were past and were not part of the immediate folk culture into which he was born. In that culture the specific folk-art form which helped shape the writer's attitude toward his life and which embodied the impulse that contributes much to the quality and tone of his autobiography was the Negro blues. This would bear a word of explanation:

The blues is an impulse to keep the painful details and episodes of a brutal experience alive in one's aching consciousness, to finger its jagged grain, and to transcend it, not by the consolation of philosophy but by squeezing from it a near-tragic, near-comic lyricism. As a form, the blues is an autobiographical chronicle of personal catastrophe expressed lyrically. And certainly Wright's early childhood was crammed with catastrophic incidents. In a few short years his father deserted his mother, he knew intense hunger, he became a drunkard begging for drinks from black stevedores in Memphis saloons; he had to flee Arkansas, where an uncle was lynched; he was forced to live with a fanatically religious grandmother in an atmosphere of constant bickering; he was lodged in an orphan asylum; he observed the suffering of his mother, who became a permanent invalid, while fighting off the blows of the poverty-stricken relatives with whom he had to live; he was cheated, beaten and kicked off jobs by white employees who disliked his eagerness to learn a trade; and to these objective circumstances must be added the subjective fact that Wright, with his sensitivity, extreme shyness and intelligence, was a problem child who rejected his family and was by them rejected.

Thus along with the themes, equivalent descriptions of milieu and the perspectives to be found in Joyce, Nehru, Dostoievsky, George Moore and Rousseau, *Black Boy* is filled with blues-tempered echoes of railroad trains, the names of Southern towns and cities, estrangements, fights and flights, deaths and disappointments, charged with physical and spiritual hungers and pain. And like a blues sung by such an artist as Bessie Smith, its lyrical prose evokes the paradoxical, almost surreal image of a black boy singing lustily as he probes his own grievous wound.

> Ralph Ellison, "Richard Wright's Blues" (1945), *Shadow and Act* (New York: Random House, 1964), pp. 77–79

JAMES BALDWIN   Now the most powerful and celebrated statement we have yet had of what it means to be a Negro in America is unquestionably Richard Wright's *Native Son*. The feeling which prevailed at the time of its publication was that such a novel, bitter, uncompromising, shocking, gave proof, by its very existence, of what strides might be taken in a free democracy; and its indisputable success, proof that Americans were now able to look full in the face without flinching the dreadful facts. Americans, unhappily, have the most remarkable ability to alchemize all bitter truths into an innocuous but piquant confection and to transform their moral contradictions, or public discussions of such contradictions, into a proud decoration, such as are given for heroism on the field of battle. Such a book, we felt with pride, could never have been written before— which was true. Nor could it be written today. It bears already the aspect of a landmark; for Bigger and his brothers have undergone yet another metamorphosis; they have been accepted in baseball leagues and by colleges hitherto exclusive; and they have made a most favorable appearance on the national screen. We have yet to encounter, nevertheless, a report so indisputably authentic, or one that can begin to challenge this most significant novel. ⟨. . .⟩

Negroes are Americans and their destiny is the country's destiny. They have no other experience besides their experience on this continent and it is an experience which cannot be rejected, which yet remains to be embraced. If, as I believe, no American Negro exists who does not have his private Bigger Thomas living in the skull, then what most significantly fails to be illuminated here is the paradoxical adjustment which is perpetually made, the Negro being compelled to accept the fact that this dark and dangerous and unloved stranger is part of himself forever. Only this recognition sets him in any wise free and it is this, the necessary ability to contain and even, in the most honorable sense of the word, to *exploit* the "nigger," which lends to Negro life its high element of the ironic and which causes the most well-meaning of their American critics to make such exhilarating errors when attempting to understand them. To present Bigger as a warning is simply to reinforce the American guilt and fear concerning him, it is most forcefully to limit him to that previously mentioned social arena in which he has no human validity, it is simply to condemn him to death. For he has always been a warning, he represents the evil, the sin and suffering which we are compelled to reject. It is useless to say to the courtroom in which this heathen sits on trial that he is their responsibility, their creation, and his crimes are theirs; and that they ought, therefore, to allow him to live, to make articulate to himself behind the walls of prison the meaning of his existence. The meaning of his existence has already been most adequately expressed, nor does he wish, particularly not in the name of democracy, to think of it any more; as for the possibility of articulation, it is this possibility which above all others we most dread. Moreover, the courtroom, judge, jury, witnesses and spectators, recognize immediately that Bigger is their creation and they recognize this not only with hatred and fear and guilt and the resulting fury of self-righteousness but also with that morbid fullness of pride mixed with horror with which one regards the extent and power of one's wickedness. They know that death is his portion, that he runs to death; coming from darkness and dwelling in darkness, he must be, as often as he rises, banished, lest the entire planet be engulfed. And they know, finally, that they do not wish to forgive him and that he does not wish to be forgiven; that he dies, hating them, scorning that appeal which they cannot make to that irrecoverable humanity of his which cannot hear it; and that he *wants* to die because he glories in his hatred and prefers, like Lucifer, rather to rule in hell than serve in heaven.

James Baldwin, "Many Thousands Gone" (1951), *Notes of a Native Son* (Boston: Beacon Press, 1955), pp. 23–24, 33–35

EDWARD MARGOLIES   When Richard Wright planned *The Long Dream* he evidently foresaw it as the first in a series of books dwelling on the life and career of Fishbelly Tucker, a Mississippi Negro boy who goes to live in France. The autobiographical resemblances between the author and his protagonist are not however confined to mere geography. In many respects the psychic lives of the two appear to be very close—not to mention the fact that they both seem to have shared almost identical traumatic experiences. A reading of *Black Boy* alongside *The Long Dream* is instructive in this regard. Both Wright and Fishbelly, for example, at the age of six discover that their fathers are having illicit relations with women. Both boys have dreadful fears of being abandoned by their mothers; indeed Fishbelly has a dream not unlike the nightmares the four-year-old Wright suffered in the opening pages of *Black Boy*. Both boys do not come into any real contact with the brutality of the white world until their adolescent years, a fact which may account for their singular independence of spirit and defiance of caste ordinances. As a result both Fishbelly and Wright come to the conclusion that they are unable to accept the traditions and values of either white world or black, and must therefore seek the meaning of their lives in a different environment. In *The Long Dream* and *Black Boy* critical moments are described relating to the lynching and mutilation of a Negro bellhop who had been having an affair with a white prostitute. For both Fishbelly and Wright the death of the bellhop provides central insights into the connection between sex and caste. The Negro, they discover, who submits to white oppression is as much castrated psychologically as the bellhop is physically. Thus, for them the lynchings become symbolic of the roles they are expected to play in life. Finally, one is almost tempted to say that both Wright and Fishbelly share certain bourgeois backgrounds. Although Fishbelly is relatively affluent and Wright frequently destitute, both are reared in a middle-class milieu. (Wright's mother, aunts, and uncles, it will be remembered, were school teachers—and his grandparents owned property in Jackson.) Whatever else may be said of *The Long Dream* it would be difficult to deny that Wright was once again reliving deeply embedded memories as a primary source for his new novel.

> Edward Margolies, *The Art of Richard Wright* (Carbondale: Southern Illinois University Press, 1969), pp. 129–30

RUSSELL CARL BRIGNANO   In *The Outsider*, Cross Damon, a Negro, is isolated and alienated from other men *because* he is a man. The novel is one of the few examples in American fiction of an author's conscious attempt to shape existential themes. The work also offers an unflattering commentary on the Communist Party. In many respects, and especially in its treatment of the Party, *The Outsider* may be compared to Ralph Ellison's *Invisible Man* (1952), published only a few months before Wright's novel. One striking parallel between Ellison's unnamed central narrator and Cross Damon is their search for identity beyond the context of racial conflict. In both works it is the Party that feels it can provide a basis for identity, and in both works it is the Party that exploits the fact of the main figure's color, for political and propagandistic gain. In terms of the Marxist content in *The Outsider* ⟨. . .⟩, the Party's treatment of Cross Damon clearly echoes words set down by Wright in a 1945 publication, only months before his formal break with the Party, but years before he wrote *The Outsider:* "Both the political Left and the political Right try to change the Negro problem into something that they can control, thereby denying the humanity of the Negro, excluding his unique and historic position in American life." This attitude is essentially the basis for Wright's attack on the Party in *The Outsider*. It reflects the position that he had taken earlier in his essay in *The God That Failed*.

> Russell Carl Brignano, *Richard Wright: An Introduction to the Man and His Works* (Pittsburgh: University of Pittsburgh Press, 1970), pp. 82–83

JEAN-FRANÇOIS GOUNARD   Obviously, the controversial reaction to *Black Boy* was typical of the attitudes of American society to black achievements—while Wright gained recognition for his work as a writer, he continued to encounter many bitter and demeaning personal experiences all caused by the color of his skin. In New York where he and his white Jewish wife lived, the painfulness of these experiences was undoubtedly intensified by the fact that he had received acceptance as a writer.

Recognition of Wright's literary achievements even came from abroad, and the French government extended an official invitation for the black author and his family to come to France. Given the frustrating circumstances he encountered in the United States, it is not surprising that Wright readily accepted this considerable honor, and from May to December 1946, he and his family lived in Paris. Here they were treated as privileged guests by many French admirers, and Wright could not help but be impressed by the respect for human dignity and relative lack of racial prejudice in France. After retasting the bitter realities of life in New York for only six months, Wright and his family returned to France to live permanently in July 1947. ⟨. . .⟩

Why did Wright choose to address his audience from the viewpoint of an exile? Oddly enough, some critics state quite adamantly that the reason why Richard Wright chose exile was that he hated black people and, consequently, loathed himself. Talking about this much-debated point, Robert Bone tells us: "Wright suffers, no doubt, from rootlessness, but the source of that rootlessness is self-hatred." Such a statement is rather serious and most damaging to make. Obviously, Robert Bone does not seem to consider, or remember, that many projects and ideas Richard Wright had in mind when he once wrote a childhood friend: "There is a great novel yet to be written about the Negro in the South; just a simple, straight, easy, great novel, telling how they feel each day; what they do in the winter, spring, summer and fall. Just a novel telling of the quiet ritual of their lives. Such a book is really needed."

Richard Wright did hate conditions in the Southern United States, but it seems totally unfair to maintain that he disliked black people on the grounds that they had absolutely nothing to offer. He was painfully aware that any fault in the matter lay with the white man, not the black. In "Big Boy Leaves Home" and "Long Black Song," for instance, Big Boy and Sarah lead a happy and carefree life in the Garden of Eden we know to be Richard Wright's South. Unfortunately, the beautiful dream is brutally destroyed by the fatal intrusion of the white man; Big Boy has to escape hurriedly to the North, and Sarah helplessly witnesses her husband's violent but courageous death.

There was a certain type of Negro that Richard Wright did hate—the apathetic and humble black man who accepted his tragic and inhuman plight in complete surrender. For Richard Wright, such a Negro was as guilty as his white torturers because he was an accomplice in his own humiliation and sufferings. Tom, in "The Man Who Saw The Flood," represents quite well that type of dull Negro who is totally submitted to the powerful will of the white world. Richard Wright was very fond of his own people and was also deeply attached to his native South. In other words, when Wright left the United States, he was simply fleeing the inhuman atmosphere created by the whites. His activities abroad indicate that his own heart always kept a secret, special and affectionate place for his colored brothers.

Jean-François Gounard, "Richard Wright as a Black American Writer in Exile," CLA
Journal 17, No. 3 (March 1974): 308, 312–13

MICHEL FABRE   The depiction of the black struggle under adverse social and racial conditions often explicitly constitutes the subject of Wright's writing, but because of his sometimes conflicting attitudes towards black life in the United States the coherence of his purpose is not always apparent. It does not appear, either, that his major purpose was to demonstrate the universality of the black struggle as a reflection and example of the condition of modern man (although certainly much can be made, as will be seen, of Wright's contention that "the Negro is America's metaphor"). Wright's enduring concern was in fact, more personal and more basic: it amounted to nothing less than the interchange and conflict between the individual and society.

Rooted as it is in an existential sense of freedom, Wright's blossoming into print should be constructed as an act of defiance, an assertion of the equation between literature and rebellion, an avatar of the myth of Prometheus who stole fire and knowledge from the Gods for the benefit of all men. In Wright's case, the gap between life and literature is so narrow that the awakening and development of his avocation closely follow the expanding circles of his self-awareness and his intellectual growth.

Michel Fabre, "Introduction," *Richard Wright Reader*, ed. Ellen Wright and Michel
Fabre (New York: Harper & Row, 1978), p. ix

PAUL NEWLIN   Although Wright set out to compose a novel so hard that it would deny tears over the fate of the victims, he claims consciously to have then worked in a guilt theme after completing the first draft. By implication, he acknowledges that guilt was hinted at in the first draft, and it seems impossible to me that it was not there from the establishment of Bigger's character-destiny in the scene with the rat. Wright doesn't elaborate on *who* is guilty for *what* in "How 'Bigger' Was Born," but guilt is part of "the heritage of us all" and need not be spelled out except when it plays a dramatic purpose, as it does with Jan's and Mary's pathetic attempts at expiation in their uneasy gestures at brotherhood. Guilt is everywhere— from Mrs. Thomas' cruel questioning of why she brought Bigger into this world, Mrs. Dalton's collective guilt as a symbolic representation of a blind, self-praising, affluent white society, and Bigger's own irascible bullying of his street pals in an effort to assuage his fears, to Max's appalled recognition of what Wright called the moral of the novel: "the horror of Negro life in the United States." ⟨. . .⟩

The horror of which Richard Wright wrote in 1940 still infuses *Native Son* today. In telling us how Bigger was born, Wright has also told us why Bigger lives on. One can make a strong case that "the horror of Negro life in the United States" has diminished since Bigger was born in 1940. Yet black youngsters still wake up to battle rats or worse in ever-enlarging black urban ghettoes, and though Bigger and Gus currently could sit undisturbed in the orchestra of Chicago's movie houses, one need look no further than the June 1986 *FBI Law Enforcement Bulletin* to know how Bigger's presence in Mary Dalton's bedroom would be interpreted in Chicago today. Bigger Thomas' position in the literary canon of twentieth-century American literature is secure precisely because rape remains "the representative symbol of the Negro's uncertain position in America." Passage of time modifies heritage but slowly, and the fear, the guilt, the horror of Wright's *Native Son* infuses each generation of readers with its moral: "the horror of Negro life in the United States." Is there any wonder my students are affected by *Native Son* as by no other book I teach?

> Paul Newlin, "Why 'Bigger' Lives On: Student Reaction to *Native Son*," *Richard Wright: Myths and Realities*, ed. C. James Trotman (New York: Garland, 1988), pp. 143–45.

MARGARET WALKER   Although these eight stories ⟨in *Eight Men*⟩ are uneven in quality, they uphold Wright's literary reputation as being at his best in the short story form. Tautness of plot, organization, excellent characterization, lively dialogue, heightened suspense, Freudian psychology, and general thematic structure, as well as melodramatic tone, are evident in these pieces. Perhaps the critics are biased when they generally agree that the four earlier stories, written before Wright's exile, are better in that they are less contrived, more artfully formed, and show greater skill in craftsmanship. There may be, however, some natural differences of opinion here. Neither "Slit" nor the newly named "The Man Who Saw the Flood" is as fine a piece as "Down by the Riverside." Why? For a number of reasons: the frenetic or even daemonic quality of "Down by the Riverside" reveals not only the freshness of Wright's imagery and the southern welter of black folklore and feeling out of which it comes, but like all the stories in *Uncle Tom's Children*, it also shows Wright's early obsession with revision, writing, and rewriting until he could be satisfied with a sharpened effect. The tensions in the work are poignant, the suspense heightened, the emotional effects of the words have stunning impact. Wright's genius is never more daemonic or frenetic than in those four novellas which comprise *Uncle Tom's Children.*

Dialogue is another well-crafted element in the first stories of *Eight Men* which is not nearly as effective as in the last four. The latter stories are perhaps most innovative in subject matter and theme, for there is almost as much variety as there are tales. I have already explored the mythic nature of "The Man Who Lived Underground," its surrealism and existentialism. "The Man Who Killed a Shadow" is also surreal, but instead of existentialism there is an element of Freudianism. Both "Big Black Good Man" and "Man, God Ain't Like That" deal with a folk belief or primitive religious concern, including ethical constructs in African and Afro-American religious and superstitious beliefs. "Man of All Works" deals cynically with economic determinism and satirizes Communists or the lumpenproletariat as victims. Two pieces are patently autobiographical, "The Man Who Was Almost a Man" and "The Man Who Went to Chicago." There is no doubt in my mind, however, that all of the stories have autobiographical elements in them because as demonstrated again and again, Wright was writing and rewriting *one* story, the story of himself. *Eight Men* or ten men, they were all one man. The subject was universal man, the specific man was everyman.

Margaret Walker, *Richard Wright, Daemonic Genius* (New York: Warner, 1988), pp. 330–31

JOHN M. REILLY   ⟨. . .⟩ it is Wright's decision to use a narrative point of view closely identified with Bigger's, though not identical to it, that accounts for readers' taking his side. Closely associated with Bigger's thought and expository of his feelings, the presiding narrative voice blurs the color lines and gives readers—white and black—the sensations and perspective of an underclass character. The subtle narrative reports Bigger's thought and preconscious feeling in the language of third-person story-telling; but while maintaining the third-person reference, the narrative also suggests a simulation of the character's own mental discourse. That technique, known as "free indirect discourse," is not in itself unusual. When employed in the service of a character like Bigger, however, it becomes a remarkable innovation in American realistic fiction, rarely matched before 1940 except by Mark Twain's giving the frontier ruffian Huck Finn the right to tell his own story, or by Theodore Dreiser's investment of subjectivity in working women like Carrie Meeber. In the line of realism, from the frontier sketches through the fiction of William Dean Howells and Stephen Crane, when outsiders or bottom dogs such as frontier settlers, immigrants, and ethnic characters appear, they are presented in a frame story or through the mediation of narrative voice firmly middle-class in its language, taste, and orientation. Thus the frontier humor of the Old Southwest is often reported by a narrator who comes from a metropolitan center, introducing an exotic country person who is allowed to tell a story in dialect before the reporter reestablishes his presence in standard English. Even the city of New York can appear to be full of aliens in such a novel as Howell's *A Hazard of New Fortunes*, which presents the industrial working class as beyond the ken of the editor Basil March, who is the focal point of the narrative, or Crane's *Maggie*, in which the narrative voice reductively presents its Irish-American subjects with hardly any indication that they even possess consciousness. Each of these representative texts in the tradition of American realism illustrates the habit of enforcing the perception shared by a dominant class. By distancing the narrative from socially subordinate groups distinguished by strong differences in dialect or appearance, by withholding explanation of their behavior, and above all by establishing a narrative viewpoint readily identifiable as old stock, formally educated, and more learned than frontier settlers, workers, and ethnics, these normative texts create an identification between readers and authors that expresses the monopoly of discourse by a ruling caste or class. That monopoly is exactly what Richard Wright aims to subvert in *Native Son* by use of a narrative point of view that draws readers beneath the externals of surface realism, so that as they are led into empathy with Bigger, they will be denied the conventional attitudes of American racial discourse.

John M. Reilly, "Giving Bigger a Voice: The Politics of Narrative in *Native Son*," *New Essays on* Native Son, ed. Keneth Kinnamon (New York: Cambridge University Press, 1990), pp. 45–46

ALFRED KAZIN   At a time when white supremacy was especially cruel and hysterical among poor whites in the rural South, and the young boy could be knocked down for forgetting to say "sir" immediately to any cretin who seemed to live for violence to blacks, Richard Wright was stripped naked by his mother and beaten with a barrel stave until he became feverish because he had fought back against white boys. His grandmother, a fanatical Seventh-day Adventist, slapped him around for listening to a story—"Devil stuff in my house"—and after he had finally retaliated with an obscene remark, beat him so horribly that he was sure she would kill him if he did not get out of her reach.

"I used to mull over the strange absence of real kindness in Negroes," Wright wrote in *Black Boy*, that extraordinary personal history of almost unrelieved opression in and out of the black community that becomes a great literary accomplishment through Wright's superb sense of momentum—of how to build up a narrative so that the reader duplicates his own intensity. As he was not afraid to admit, he had more than a touch of cruelty himself. When his terrible father ordered his sons to get rid of a kitten, Richard and his brother hanged it from a tree as a way of triumphing over their father.

Killing is as routine in Wright's work as in Dostoyevsky's great crime novels. Dostoyevsky used the act of murder to highlight everything hidden in the human soul. The race question in Wright is certainly not hidden. As for all black writers, it is the atmosphere they breathe, it is America itself. What makes Wright so remarkable an artist of this extreme situation is that the rage at the center of his work becomes a wholly individual drama without ceasing to be an accusation of our society in general. You can quarrel with the belief that the "Negro," as Wright still put it, was a tabula rasa given his character entirely by slavery. Whether he believed this or not in his erratic political career as a sometime Marxist (and he often contradicted himself in his search for a position), Wright was always more convincing describing characters in terms of action, pulse, deed on deed, than in ascribing reasons for their actions.

Alfred Kazin, "Too Honest for His Own Time," *New York Times Book Review*, 29 December 1991, p. 3

Bibliography

Uncle Tom's Children: Four Novellas. 1938, 1940 (as *Uncle Tom's Children: Five Long Stories*).

Bright and Morning Star. 1938.

Native Son. 1940.

How "Bigger" Was Born: The Story of Native Son, *One of the Most Significant Novels of Our Time, and How It Came to Be Written.* 1940.

Native Son (The Biography of a Young American) (drama; with Paul Green). 1941.

The Negro and Parkway Community House. 1941.

12 Million Black Voices: A Folk History of the Negro in the United States. 1941.

Black Boy: A Record of Childhood and Youth. 1945.

A Hitherto Unpublished Manuscript by Richard Wright: Being a Continuation of Black Boy. c. 1946.

The F B Eye Blues. 1949.

The Outsider. 1953.

Savage Holiday. 1954.

Black Power: A Record of Reactions in a Land of Pathos. 1954.

The Color Curtain: A Report on the Bandung Conference. 1956.

Pagan Spain. 1956.

White Man, Listen! 1957.

The Long Dream. 1958.

Eight Men. 1961.

Lawd Today. 1963.

Letters to Joe C. Brown. Ed. Thomas Knipp. 1968.

The Man Who Lived Underground. Ed. Michael Fabre, tr. Claude Emonde Magny. 1971.

American Hunger. 1977.

Richard Wright Reader. Ed. Ellen Wright and Michel Fabre. 1978.

⟨*Works.*⟩ 1991. 2 vols.